GOING
GLOBAL

GOING GLOBAL

GLOBAL

Transforming Relief and Development NGOs

MARC LINDENBERG
and
CORALIE BRYANT

Kumarian
Press, Inc.

Going Global: Transforming Relief and Development NGOs

Published 2001 in the United States of America by Kumarian Press, Inc.
1294 Blue Hills Avenue, Bloomfield, CT 06002 USA.

Copyedited by Nicholas Kosar
Index and proofreading by Bob Land

Production and design by ediType, Yorktown Heights, N.Y.

The text of this book is set in 10/12 Adobe Sabon.

Printed in the USA on acid-free paper by Thomson-Shore, Inc.
Text printed with vegetable oil–based ink.

∞ The paper used in this publication meets the minimum requirements of the American National Standard for Information Sciences—Permanence of Paper for Printed Library Materials, ANSI Z39.48-1984.

Library of Congress Cataloging-in-Publication Data

Lindenberg, Marc
    Going global : transforming relief and development NGOs / Marc Lindenberg and Coralie Bryant.
      p. cm.
    Includes index.
    ISBN 1-56549-135-1 (pbk.: alk. paper) – ISBN 1-56549-136-X (cloth: alk. paper)
    1. International relief. 2. Non-governmental organizations. 3. Globalization.
I. Bryant, Coralie. II. Title.

HV544.5 .L56 2001
361.2'6 – dc21

                          2001029974

---

10 09 08 07 06 05 04   10 9 8 7 6 5 4 3   First Printing 2001

Contents

Illustrations

Figures

Tables

Preface

THIS BOOK IS ABOUT the implications of globalization for the goals, programs, processes, and staff of international relief and development NGOs. Societies everywhere are increasingly turning to nongovernmental organizations (NGOs) for leadership and assistance on issues once addressed, or yet to be addressed, by governments. Globalization, and with it the changing role of the state, pulls NGOs into new roles and their staff in ever more dangerous and complex circumstances as they respond to war, natural disasters, and intractable problems of poverty and suffering. Globalization has changed both the roles that states and NGOs play and the context within which they do their work. These changes are ongoing. As a result, the shifting terrain between state and NGO roles is nowhere resolved—in Europe, or Africa, or elsewhere on the globe.

The idea that we should convey some sense of what is happening for the international relief and development NGOs began in Bellagio in September 1998 at a retreat with the senior leadership of several well established NGOs—CARE, Oxfam, Médecins Sans Frontières, PLAN International, World Vision International, and Save the Children. The meeting was graciously funded by a grant from the Rockefeller Foundation and the special support of its vice president, Lincoln Chen. That meeting led to another in Seattle carried out with the support of the Bill and Melinda Gates Foundation due to the special interest of William H. Gates Sr. Yet another meeting took place with many of the same participants in Oxford, July 2001. Why these meetings? Why this book?

The meetings came about because senior NGO leaders wanted new opportunities to talk with one another given the common problems and pressures they face. One of us knew many of these pressures firsthand: as CARE USA's Senior Vice President for Programs between 1992 and 1997, Marc worked closely with Lincoln Chen and Peter Bell, CARE USA's president, to form the Bellagio Group. Then both of us worked to turn the idea of an annual Relief and Development NGO Presidents' Retreat into a reality. We believed that senior leaders have too little time for reflection and even fewer opportunities to share and compare experience with their counterparts. The challenges they confront in the rapidly changing global context come with no road map; their possible ways forward are often devised with few opportunities to consult with others facing comparable problems. That initial idea has proved its worth. By the end of the first conference at Bellagio, the leaders were already discussing both the location and agenda of a second meeting.

In October of 1999, we convened an Advisory Committee at the Brookings Institution in Washington to help us think through our earliest outlines and key themes for the chapters. This group included L. David Brown from Harvard's Hauser Center, Peter Hall from the Yale University Program on Non-Profit Organizations Center at Yale Seminary, Ray Horten from Columbia Business School's Nonprofit Management Program, Virginia Hogkinson from Georgetown University's Center for the Study of Voluntary Organizations, Crispin Gregoire from the National Center for Nonprofit Boards in Washington, and Julie Fisher from the Kettering Foundation. Their suggestions and comments helped us shape the work in progress. Steven R. Smith, the editor of *Nonprofit and Voluntary Sector Quarterly* (NVSQ) and his editorial board graciously agreed to publish a special journal issue with articles from the Bellagio meeting.

In March 2000 we began to augment the material gathered in group discussions with extensive interviews of senior team members at Médecins Sans Frontières, Save the Children UK, and Oxfam GB in order to fill in gaps of our understanding of the other, European-based, national members of these global networks. Meetings with David Lewis and Helmut Anheier at the London School of Economics, with John Healey, Tony Killick, and Lucia Hamner at the Overseas Development Institute, and Rosemary McGee at the Institute for Development Studies, University of Sussex, helped us to update material for Chapter 4 on reducing poverty and changing programming approaches. Meanwhile, with the help of a Bill and Melinda Gates Foundation grant, we conducted additional in depth interviews and used more structured questionnaires to gather even more information, particularly about the problems of relief and development programming. We could not have done this without the dedicated assistance of San Cornelia Ng and Christina Kappaz, our research assistants, who worked tirelessly on these efforts. San's efforts were particularly helpful in the chapter that focused on the problems of global humanitarian response (Chapter 3). Among other things San braved a forced landing on a runway in Kosovo during her field research. (The same plane crashed the next week, killing all passengers.) Christina worked tirelessly on the chapter on advocacy (Chapter 7) and is its major author.

In May 2000 we held our second conference in Seattle and broadened the group to include the presidents of the International Rescue Committee, Mercy Corps International, the International Medical Corps, and World Concern. The agenda was full. One of the highlights was discussing in-depth the issues of humanitarianism with Francis Deng, UN

Secretary General Kofi Annan's Special Deputy for Internally Displaced People. There was also a session on accountability led by Professors Mark Moore and L. David Brown from the Hauser Center at Harvard's Kennedy School of Government. We hosted a session on future relations between globalizing Southern and Northern NGO networks with special participation of the President of the Grameen Foundation, Alex Counts; the President of CIVICUS, Kumi Naidoo; the Executive Secretary of the Asociación Latino Americano de Organizaciones de Promoción (ALOP), Manuel Chiriboga; and the Executive Director of Community Organizers Multiversity located in the Philippines, Corazon "Dinky" Juliano-Soliman. They provided their views on the alliances among Southern NGOs and their work on advocacy. At another session, theologian William McKinney, President of the Pacific School of Religion at Berkeley, Kennedy School Professor Ronnie Heifitz, and Sousan Abadian discussed ways to keep meaning and ethics central in order to keep the meaning of this work in place. Dave Olsen, Starbucks Senior Vice President for Corporate Social Responsibility, joined Peter Blomquist, Director of a microcredit foundation called Global Partnerships, in a live case study on new corporate and nonprofit partnerships. Harvard Business School Professor James Austin led the case discussion and provided additional insights on private and nonprofit partnerships. A lively session on the potential of the Internet was led by Eileen V. Quigley of Real Impact as she focused on ways that NGOs are getting their messages out to larger audiences. Over lunch, the Bill and Melinda Gates Foundation helped NGO leaders meet the new leaders from Pacific Northwest foundations. The foundation hosted a special reception for the group. William H. Gates Sr., Jack Faris, and Terry Meersman of the Gates Foundation attended the sessions and offered their insights.

As our discussions continued an important gap in current research appeared evident to us. While much is written about what NGOs are doing, little is written about how they are doing what they do, and how process affects product. Students of nonprofit management often find the literature to be incomplete, although it is growing. The ways that globalization has impacted on the work of international relief and development NGOs is not as well covered as it might be. While aspects of the NGO stories are documented, few books or articles look at the intersection of management processes with the substance of their work.

The core of our material focuses on CARE, Oxfam, PLAN International, Médecins Sans Frontières, World Vision, and Save the Children. Their leaders were regular participants at these meetings. By focusing on stories from these organizations, we are not claiming that these are the most important NGOs, nor that the stories of other NGOs are not equally compelling. Indeed, representatives from other NGOs (such as International Rescue Committee, Mercy Corps International,

International Medical Corps, and World Concern) were included as the meetings continued. We would have enjoyed the opportunity for more time and resources to widen our reach.

We try to accomplish three objectives in this book. First, we bring the reader into the discussions at the Bellagio and Seattle meetings (as well as in between them in follow-up interviews) on the new challenges of globalization and how NGOs are adjusting their missions, programs, and systems to respond. This material is largely found in Chapters 1, 2, 5, 6, and 8. Second, we turn to look in more detail at the substance of their work in reducing poverty, meeting the needs brought about by internal wars and natural disasters, and in advocacy work. This material comes in Chapters 3, 4, and 7. Reader will feel the change to different voices as they get into these chapters—and that is because much of our detailed backup interviews focused on these topics. Third, we look at these issues through a different lens from the socially critical one customarily worn by social scientists. We look through the lens of the actors themselves in the drama rather than through the lens of the social critic. The logic is that students of nonprofit management have much to learn from seeing the view from the "driver's seat," rather than from the "sidewalk": from the perspective of the senior teams on a new journey in uncharted territory with no road maps. The last thing we try to do grows out of this last issue; since often we are conveying what our interlocutors shared with us, we have tried to step back and reflect on what might not have been said, and what elements might be missing. For this reason, readers will find within each chapter a section on ethnology in which we speak more directly in our own voice. By ethnology we mean the study of the history, development, similarities, and differences in comparative (organizational) cultures. The conclusion to the book is also written in our own voice.

For both of us, this book has been an odyssey—opening us to new perspectives on problems and views that both illuminate and complicate assumptions we might have had about nonprofit management. We also came away with tremendous respect for the creativity, capacity, energy, and motivation of those who work in this sector—often under dangerous and difficult conditions. Moreover, working on different coasts, with editors in other sites, completing this book has brought home the advantages of the new technology—electronic file transfers made the whole thing possible. Meanwhile, both of us have incorporated a great deal more material from this process and ancillary research on NGOs into curriculum at the Daniel J. Evans School of Public Policy, University of Washington, and at the School of International and Public Affairs, Columbia University.

We have had, as you can already tell, more help from more people than most authors receive. The veritable host of those who have contributed cannot all be listed without making this book so long that it would become unwieldy. We have, however, appended a list of those interviewed and those who attended or presented at the meetings and want to thank those who gave so generously of their time to answer our questions when their work is already overly demanding. Upon occasion in various chapters we have also listed those who contributed to our thinking. Yet we must express our deepest debt of gratitude to the NGO presidents: Peter Bell, David Bryer, Ray Offenheiser, John Greensmith, Philippe Biberson, Jean Herve-Bradol, Richard Stearns, and Charles MacCormack. Their graciousness throughout made this work possible. We have surely learned more from them than we can capture or express in spoken or written words. Along with them we have deep debts of gratitude to Ernst Ligteringen, Burkhard Gnaerig, James Orbinski, and Guy Tousignant, who helped us to understand some of the challenges of leading the international offices of these NGOs. There was also help above and beyond the call of duty from Reynold Levy, Neal Keny-Guyer, Nancy Aossey, Nancy Lindborg, Ken Casey, Justin Forsyth, Chris Roche, Susan Holcombe, Joel McClellan, Kevin Henry, Michael Edwards, Françoise Saulnier, Susanna Smith, Joelle Tanguy, Subhadra Belbase, Karen Foreman, Stephen Commins, Alex Counts, Carolyn Miller, Bill Bell, Angela Penrose, Serge Duss, and Andy Pugh. Academic colleagues provided us with more help than one can reasonably ask for from friends. With chagrin at their thoughtfulness, we want to thank Jim Austin, Mark Moore, L. David Brown, Julie Fisher, Patrick Dobel, Steven R. Smith, Shubham Chaudhuri, Fida Adely, Ray Horton, Michael Lipton, and David Lewis. Steven R. Smith and Patrick Dobel also attended our retreats and helped coordinate sessions.

As often happens, the talented next generation of leaders in the development field are frequently asked to do more than is fair. This surely happened in this project as in others, and thus we admit that we asked more from our research assistants, San Cornelia Ng, Christina Kappaz, and Janet Salm, than was fair. Their patience with our demands and their constant ability to deliver warrants a special thank you. Janet was responsible for the overall coordination of the first Bellagio meeting and for helping edit the first journal publication from that meeting. She prepared a fascinating article on globalization and NGOs for the first special journal issue of *NVSQ*. Christina emerged from this process as the author of Chapter 7, and as a co-author with Corky on the forthcoming book *Reducing Poverty: Increasing Choice*. Deborah Bryant and Natasha Walker helped with figures. San organized and coordinated the Seattle Presidents' Retreat with the help of graduate students from the Evans School (Wendy Prosser, Jennifer Petree, Brian Bushley, and Alexandra Tres). She spearheaded the research on the problems in global humanitarian response which appears in Chapter 3 as well as co-authored with Marc the Gates Foundation Study on that topic and a forthcoming journal article as well. We knew we needed an editor, and hence want to thank Valerie Kallab for that role. Above all, this book would not have even emerged without the amazing patience and enduring talent for detail of Brittany Faulkner.

As readers, you will encounter errors either of fact, or interpretation, or omission. These are ours to own and none of those named above should be implicated in any manner.

– 1 –

Responding to Globalization

SINCE THE 1970s, a profound shift has taken place in the roles of the public, private, and nonprofit sectors. In the wake of fiscal crisis, the Cold War, ideological attacks, and privatization, the scope and capacity of national governments has declined. The expansion of the private sector has continued, and a new, more global nonprofit sector has emerged. This sector of nonprofit, nongovernmental organizations (NGOs) has begun to fill in the vacuum left by nation-states in international relief and development activities.

Along with the changes in state capacities, the magnitude of challenges to NGOs (and states) has grown. Failed states, the end of the Cold War, and the rise of ethnic identity movements have spawned civil wars and human disasters. In both the developing and the developed world, global economic changes have generated new economic disparities as well as changes in the form and depth of poverty. Competitive pressures and regional commitments (for example, the European Union) further limit the ability of governments to respond to all of the social and economic demands made by citizens. These profound changes raise new issues concerning the role and future of voluntarism in a world where state resources for human services have eroded and where solutions to global poverty and war continue to elude us.

Our book is about the globalization of the Northern, nonprofit relief and development sector.[1] Leaders of these NGOs, their staff, and their supporters are deeply committed to work that focuses on reducing poverty and human suffering. They view a broad concept of development as being about increasing human capability and freedom.[2] Doing so means saving the lives of people at risk because of war or natural disasters, working with people so they may improve their access to assets and income-generating work, improved health and education, and participation in key decisions affecting their rights and welfare.

What we present here is the story of the international NGOs' recent response to globalization and the challenges of the new millennium from their own perspective, using the results of in-depth interviews, detailed questionnaires, and document reviews. As in any effort in ethnology, we will at times step back from our attempt to accurately present their

1

story through their eyes in order to ask what their perspective reveals as well as what it may conceal about the world they face.

We focus principally on several of the largest and best-established international relief and development organizations. Many of them—Oxfam, Save the Children, PLAN International, Médecins Sans Frontières (also known as MSF and Doctors Without Borders in English), World Vision International, and CARE—have names that are widely familiar in Europe, Canada, Japan, and the United States. Their combined revenue accounts for approximately 20 percent of the entire Northern NGO sector. These agencies operate in most developing countries, in the newly independent states that emerged from the former Soviet Union, and in their own home countries. Their programs run the spectrum of emergency relief, rehabilitation, and long-term development as well as service delivery, advocacy, and development education.

Substantial attention has been paid to the development of the Southern NGO movement, but the changes in Northern relief and development organizations have not been studied in much detail. The leaders of Northern NGOs find themselves so involved in the day-to-day pressures of emergency response in places like Bosnia, Kosovo, Chechnya, and Rwanda that they have had little time to discuss common problems and responses with colleagues whose headquarters are often almost next door. Furthermore, the cultural and structural differences among NGOs based in continental Europe, the United Kingdom, Canada, and the United States make cooperation problematic. Still greater difficulties inhibit broader exchanges with organizations from all parts of the globe.

In writing this book, we wish to:

1. Identify the challenges that Northern relief and development NGO leaders and senior team members believe they face as a result of the changing global environment;

2. Review how these leaders believe they are adapting organizational goals and programs of their agencies in response to these challenges;

3. Discuss the ways in which international NGO organizational structures and programs are evolving in response to calls for broader participation with larger numbers of affiliates, cost pressures, competition, and other changes;

4. Consider ways in which international NGOs might cooperate more closely in activities like global advocacy, fundraising, and poverty alleviation; and

5. Present the Northern NGO story as seen by the teams that lead the major Northern organizations—as well as at times step back

to comment on what their "insider" perspective both shows and may conceal about the world in which they operate.

This chapter documents the growth of the sector, identifies underlying causes of growth, and provides a brief overview of the organizations that collaborated in this study, and their leadership teams' perceptions of the major challenges they face as they enter the new millennium.

Accelerating Growth of the International Nonprofit Sector

The 1960s began a new era in the rapid development of the multinational corporation. The new giants experimented with a multitude of forms of global organization. Some corporations developed fully multinational boards and staff. They engaged in production as well as in support functions on a worldwide basis. Other corporations maintained clear ownership and control, producing goods and services in Northern countries and exporting to the developing world. A few observers of this expansion feared intense conflicts between globally organized corporations and nationally organized states. They were convinced that national sovereignty would clash with multinational imperatives.[3] Others saw multinationals as a force for efficient, cooperative, global organization.[4]

A second transformation began more quietly in the late 1960s. Almost totally obscured by the intense attention given to the tidal shift in corporate-state relations, a global nonprofit sector began to emerge. This sector began to fill the vacuum in human services left in international relief and development work by both corporations and nation-states. The international nonprofit sector's growth took off in the 1970s and accelerated in the 1980s and 1990s. The changes have been profound.

While figures on NGO growth vary widely, most sources agree that since 1970 the international humanitarian and development nonprofit sector has grown substantially. Table 1.1 on the following page shows that in the United States alone the number of internationally active NGOs formally registered with U.S. Agency for International Development (USAID) and their revenues grew much faster than both U.S. total giving to charities and the U.S. gross domestic product (GDP). By 1994, the annual revenues of U.S. international NGOs had increased to $6.8 billion.

Similar trends are evident in the twenty-five OECD Northern industrial countries (see Table 1.2).[5] The Organization for Economic Cooperation and Development (OECD) estimates that the number of Northern NGOs with international programs grew from 1,600 in 1980 to more than 2,500 in 1990.[6] This includes organizations like Oxfam,

Table 1.1. Changes in U.S. International NGO Sector, 1970–94
($$ in U.S. Billions)

Year	NGOs[a]	Revenues[a]	U.S. Giving[b]	US GDP[c]
1970	52	$.614	$23.4	$1,010.0
1994	419	$6.839	$129.8	$6,379.4
Growth since 1970	8.05 times	11.3 times	5.6 times	6.3 times

a. USAID, *Annual Reports on US Voluntary Foreign Aid Programs*, Washington, D.C., 1995.
b. American Association of Fund-Raising Counsel and the AAFRC Trust for Philanthropy.
c. "Giving USA 1994," *Annual Report of Philanthropy*, 1994, 13.

Table 1.2. Growth in Revenue of Northern NGOs
Involved in International Relief and Development[a]

Flow of Funds from NGOs to Developing Countries
by Source ($$ in U.S. Billions)

Year	Private	Public	Total[d]	U.S. Share[e]
1970[b]	$800	$200	$1,000	50%
1997[c]	$4,600	$2,600	$7,200	38%

a. From DAC Table 13. Public revenue includes both ODA contributions *to* NGOs (Table 1) and ODA Grants *through* NGOs (Table 18).
b. UNDP, *Human Development Report 1993* (New York: Oxford University Press, 1993), 88.
c. OECD, *Development Cooperation Report 1998* (Paris: OECD, 1999). Private revenue figure.
d. From DAC Table 13. Public revenue includes both ODA contributions *to* NGOs (Table 1) and ODA Grants *through* NGOs (Table 18).
e. U.S. share represents an average of private and public contributions. Private revenues of U.S.

Save the Children, Médecins Sans Frontières, and CARE. Although the U.S. share of the total annual revenues for Northern industrial NGOs with international activities was still at 45 percent in 1990, it is declining as the proliferation of European and Japanese NGOs continues.

Within the developing world, the number of local NGOs with a relief and development focus has also mushroomed. Although estimates of the size of the NGO sector, or the numbers of NGOs in any given country, are often unreliable, one source reports that there are more than 250,000 Southern NGOs.[7] Among these are more than 200,000 grassroots membership organizations, whose community members form or join village councils, agricultural cooperatives, and women's credit groups; and roughly 50,000 grassroots support organizations, which are

Table 1.3. Growth and Changes in the Composition of Nonprofit Sector in Ethiopia between 1980 and 1999

Organizations	1979	%	1980– 1984	%	1985– 1989	%	1990– 1994	%	1995– 1999	%
International	21	61%	28	61%	49	54%	68	43%	80	28%
National	13	39%	18	39%	41	46%	92	57%	200	72%
Total	34		46		90		160		280	
% Growth			39%		95%		77%		75%	

Source: ITC/MIS Report 1995–2001, CDPP, Ethiopia special data run May 11, 1999.

nationally based, professionally staffed, and often channel international as well as national funds to grassroots membership organizations. More conservative estimates place the number of local NGOs in developing countries in a much lower, 20,000–50,000 range.[8]

The rapid growth and changing composition of the NGO sector in recent years can also be observed within developing countries. Table 1.3, for example, provides an overview of growth and the changing sectoral dynamics of Ethiopia's nonprofit organizations. The sector has grown substantially in the last decade, and the number and proportion of national organizations has grown much more rapidly than that of international organizations. A more careful review of organizational lists shows that before 1980 both national and international organizations were primarily faith-based. Today there are more secular organizations operating in Ethiopia. Regardless of which estimates one accepts for the growth of NGOs involved in international development, the globalization of the NGO sector is now too prominent and fast-paced to be ignored. Yet the growing transnational NGO sector appears to be a seriously understudied topic.[9]

Some Basic Definitions

Before examining the causes of this dynamic growth, some basic definitions are in order. For the purposes of this book, "NGOs" are organizations that:

1. Provide useful (in some specified legal sense) goods or services, thereby serving a specified public purpose.

2. Are not allowed to distribute profits to persons in their individual capacities.

3. Are voluntary in the sense that they are created, maintained, and terminated on the basis of voluntary decisions and initiatives by members or a board of directors.

4. Exhibit values-based rationality, often with ideological components.[10]

This structural/operational definition has been used with sufficient reliability in different national settings to serve our purpose.[11]

This book is about relief and development organizations that were founded in Northern industrial countries but are becoming multinational—in that they now have simultaneous operations in more than one country. To track these NGOs' "journey" to work beyond their own borders, we will use three terms along a continuum: "national" NGOs, "multinational" NGOs, and "fully multinational" (sometimes "transnational") NGOs. These are the same terms as those initially used in the 1960s to describe the emergence of multinational corporations by Stephen Hymer, Niel Jacoby, and Ron Mueller.[12] The terminology they used was based on differences in where corporations: (1) locate their operations, (2) produce and deliver their core services and products, (3) undertake their support services like accounting or human resource services, (4) get their staff, money, and equipment, and (5) undertake their governance through national and international boards.

In our book, with its focus on Northern NGOs, national organizations do all of these things within their own borders. For example, a nonprofit organization in the United States called NPower provides technology services for other not-for-profits. It is incorporated in the United States and provides its services and raises funds there. Both its board and staff members are U.S. nationals.

We call NGOs that have begun to work beyond their own borders multinational NGOs. However, some NGOs that work beyond their own borders are more multinational than others; we will therefore talk about three stages of becoming multinational. In *stage one,* an organization has its home office in its country of origin, gets its staff and resources nationally, and has a national board—but it begins to export its services to another country. It does not, however, set up long-term offices in other countries, or hire staff from numerous countries, or multinationalize its board. Médecins Sans Frontières—founded in France—began as such an organization. It was made up primarily of French staff and incorporated in France with a largely French board, but it provided its services in relief operations in Africa. It flew its doctors and medicines to Africa without establishing permanent offices there, and it shut down its operations when the crisis was over.

In *stage two,* an NGO may do more than simply export services. It may set up overseas offices and design and deliver its programs in overseas settings through its own registered organizations or affiliate partners. It may hire local field staff more likely in technical and support capacities than in upper management—but it does not have many international staff in headquarters, and it has not multinationalized its board or its governance. An example of such an NGO is Mercy Corps International, a relief and development organization based in Portland, Oregon.

In *stage three,* the NGO takes on many, but not all, multinational features. For example, it not only has many offices that produce and provide services in other countries but also affiliates and partners in those countries. It may have regional offices in Africa, Asia, or Latin America that provide technical support and services. Its headquarters service functions—accounting, auditing, staffing, procurement—may be provided in the country where these functions can be carried out most efficiently. Local office staff are largely from those countries, but middle- and upper-level field managers increasingly are multinational. Its head-quarters staff and board members, however, are still largely from the headquarters country. CARE USA and Oxfam GB are still examples of such largely stage-three multinational NGOs. In 1996, CARE USA had thirty-six country offices. Its programs were designed and tai-lored to each country situation by its largely national (rather than expatriate) staff, but its country directors were multinational. It had regional support offices in several continents. Some of its support ser-vices—for example, accounting support for the consolidation of CARE USA financial statements—were provided from the Philippines. Its U.S. headquarters staff and board were made up largely of U.S. nationals.

The extreme end of our continuum of terms is reserved for organi-zations that have become fully multinational. In such organizations, production, sourcing, support services, staff in both headquarters and in the field as well as board members would all be multinational. Although no international relief and development NGO is as yet fully multi-national in these terms, some, like World Vision, are quite advanced in making their structure and board representation more multinational. Others—like CARE, Save the Children, PLAN International—are also in the process of transforming their global structures as well as their governance.

The relief and development NGOs that are the subject of this book still largely provide services themselves or in collaboration with part-ners. They also have their initial origins and headquarters in Europe, Canada, and the United States. We therefore refer to them as Northern multinational relief and development nonprofit service providers.

Finally, we refer to the "journey" that many of these Northern organi-zations are making—due to external forces as well as deliberately—to become more multinational as part of the process of globalization of the nonprofit sector. There is extensive debate today about the meaning and impact of "globalization"; in our book, we use the term to mean the increasing spread of NGO governance structures, resource acquisition, information sharing, staff, and service delivery across national boundaries.[13] The globalization of Northern NGO relief and development service providers often involves a transition from their export of relief and development services across national boundaries to their broader multinational governance, staff, information flows, resource acquisition, and service delivery.

Many of the larger Northern NGOs started as relief and development service exporters immediately after World War II. Today, most have Northern multi-country representation in their umbrella-like coordinating structures, and most have Northern-country member organizations that raise their funds largely in the industrial countries. While citizens from the Northern countries dominate their members' headquarters staffs and boards, increasing numbers of Southern staff manage as well as implement their field-based service delivery—largely in the developing world. Both resources and general program strategic directions often move in a North to South direction.

One can identify a smaller number of Northern NGOs with the following attributes: both Northern and Southern representation in governance structures; burgeoning, separately incorporated, licensed, or franchised Southern affiliates; and increasing Southern staff representation in headquarters as well as field operations. As yet, however, no international relief and development NGOs are fully multinational in all dimensions.

Reasons for Rapid Growth

Many different forces have fueled the worldwide expansion of international humanitarian and development NGOs over the past three decades. In the 1970s, numerous private Northern foundations and bilateral donors provided resources to stimulate community-based institutional capacity building and organizational development; they did so in reaction to the failures of the big-government approach to development and of private sector philosophies of "trickle-down" such as growth and social improvement.[14] During this period, organizational experiments—such as the U.S.-based Inter-American Foundation, with its mandate to help develop grassroots organizations in Latin America— were seen as alternatives to large public bilateral programs like those of USAID.[15] In the 1980s, a worldwide vacuum was created as public delivery of social services imploded in the wake of world recession and fiscal crisis. A host of Northern NGOs as well as Southern community-based organizations grew into this vacuum. The end of the 1980s saw the bloodless revolution in the Philippines and increased movement toward democratization in Latin America. In the 1990s, the end of the Cold War set off a chain reaction in Eastern Europe and in the former Soviet Union. Because international communications carried these changes around the globe, other countries were affected. (For example, watching this unwinding, the apartheid government of South Africa released Nelson Mandela and began negotiating constitutional changes.) These changes in turn led to political instability in former client states in the developing world. This chain reaction helped spark a wave of complex humanitarian emergencies. The international and national NGO community continued to grow as such organizations increasingly were called upon to fill the breach left by the United Nations, the multilateral institutions, and collapsed national governments.

According to our Northern senior-team informants, the growth of the Northern international NGO sector—already noticeable in the 1970s— became a torrent in the 1980s and 1990s due to six important factors (see Figure 1.1 on the following page). Two of these factors, public fiscal crisis and the collapse of the Soviet Union, created the vacuum into which Northern international NGOs were pulled. Three further factors—democratic "openings," bilateral and multilateral incentives, and private giving served as magnets to stimulate Northern NGO development. A sixth factor, improved global communications, helped the sector grow more rapidly than it could have in earlier decades.

According to our colleagues, the void created by the first two factors, global public fiscal crisis and the end of the Cold War, left many unfilled community needs. International and national NGOs moved to fill the vacuum. In the 1980s, to stave off economic collapse, stabilization and structural adjustment programs were carried out in more than thirty of ninety developing countries.[16] To reduce fiscal deficits, budgets for health, education, water, and sanitation were slashed dramatically. Experiments with the privatization of services and greater cost recovery from communities became a necessity; many national and international NGOs developed community-based water and sanitation programs as well as income-generating activities. In some countries, economic crisis led to reduction in the size of the state. Elsewhere—for example, the horn of Africa—some states collapsed totally. Thus, in Somalia, national as well as local human services broke down completely. Communities were left without municipal, state, or national government as well as without water, electricity, health, sanitation, or educational systems. Clan-based armies replaced the national military and police. People were forced to live in the midst of heightened violence and social conflict. In such settings, both Northern NGOs and small community-based organizations began to provide some solutions to community needs.

Moreover, in the wake of the collapse of the Soviet Union, the international NGO community rallied to respond to the human wreckage and refugee movements resulting from violent intrastate conflicts in Bosnia, Kosovo, Chechnya, Russia, and Armenia—in addition to those

Figure 1.1. Stimuli to NGO Sector Growth since 1980

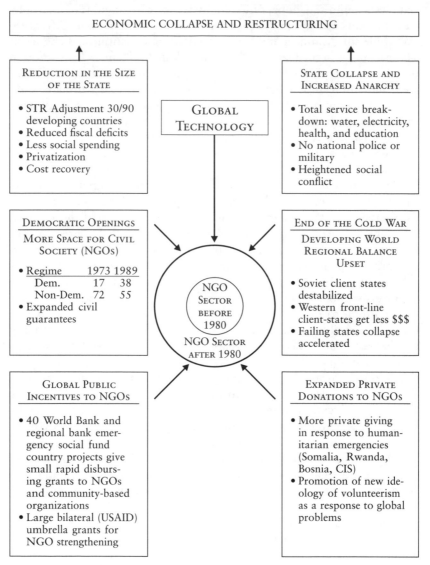

ECONOMIC COLLAPSE AND RESTRUCTURING

REDUCTION IN THE SIZE
OF THE STATE

• STR Adjustment 30/90
  developing countries
• Reduced fiscal deficits
• Less social spending
• Privatization
• Cost recovery

GLOBAL
TECHNOLOGY

STATE COLLAPSE AND
INCREASED ANARCHY

• Total service break-
  down: water, electricity,
  health, and education
• No national police or
  military
• Heightened social
  conflict

DEMOCRATIC OPENINGS
MORE SPACE FOR CIVIL
SOCIETY (NGOs)

• Regime   1973 1989
  Dem.   17   38
  Non-Dem.   72   55
• Expanded civil
  guarantees

NGO
SECTOR
BEFORE
1980

NGO SECTOR
AFTER 1980

END OF THE COLD WAR
DEVELOPING WORLD
REGIONAL BALANCE
UPSET

• Soviet client states
  destabilized
• Western front-line
  client-states get less $$$
• Failing states collapse
  accelerated

GLOBAL PUBLIC
INCENTIVES TO NGOs

• 40 World Bank and
  regional bank emer-
  gency social fund
  country projects give
  small rapid disburs-
  ing grants to NGOs
  and community-based
  organizations
• Large bilateral (USAID)
  umbrella grants for
  NGO strengthening

EXPANDED PRIVATE
DONATIONS TO NGOs

• More private giving
  in response to human-
  itarian emergencies
  (Somalia, Rwanda,
  Bosnia, CIS)
• Promotion of new ide-
  ology of volunteerism
  as a response to global
  problems

in Rwanda, Somalia, and Sierra Leone. For example, in 1997 a patch-work of national and international NGOs provisioned more than one million refugees in Tanzania, Burundi, and Zaire who fled the Rwanda crisis at the request of UN agencies like UNHCR, the World Food Programme, as well as private citizens and governments.

The end of the Cold War has in fact resulted in the removal of important constraints on international NGO humanitarian interventions.[17]

These interventions could not take place as long as two competing Cold War ideologies kept such NGOs frozen out of large parts of the world's geography. Since the collapse of the Soviet Union, the UN Security Council has legitimized cross-border interventions for humanitarian purposes, usually by Northern NGOs, in the interest of furthering "regional peace and security" as permitted under the UN Charter. Furthermore, many governments unable to clarify their own policy responses have strongly encouraged Northern NGOs to respond instead—as a substitute to direct action by themselves.

While the fiscal crisis of the state and the end of the Cold War created a void in civil space into which the Northern NGO community was drawn, three other important factors served as magnets to stimulate growth of both the Northern and Southern NGOs. The first of these has been the worldwide movement for democratic openings. Between 1973 and 1989, the number of regimes classified as democratic (open elections with no major accusations of fraud) has increased from 17 to 38 in the developing world of a total of 90 developing-country regimes.[18] These new regimes provided expanded civil guarantees that permitted local NGOs to register and to organize without great fear of reprisal, and allowed Northern NGOs to enter countries where they previously could not work. A second magnet has been an increasing use of public bilateral and multilateral resources to stimulate the development of both Northern and local NGOs and community-based organizations. For example, more than forty World Bank or regional development bank-funded social investment funds have sprung up whose role it is to provide small, rapid-disbursing grants to NGOs and community-based organizations for building roads, bridges, small water systems, and other projects. Some of the bilateral donors (for example, USAID) provide umbrella grants to international NGOs (for example, CARE in Somalia) that are then used to fund capacity-building and infrastructure projects designed and implemented by local NGOs. Similarly, Northern NGOs are the most important implementors of the refugee relief and feeding programs, respectively, of the Office of the UN High Commissioner for Refugees (UNHCR) and the World Food Programme (WFP).

Private citizens have provided yet another magnet, through their substantial donations to the international NGOs, to help them respond to the complex humanitarian emergencies in Somalia, Rwanda, and Bosnia, as well as to increase resources for development programs like micro-enterprise lending, education for girls, and reproductive health. While overall private giving in the United States as a proportion of GDP has remained stable since the 1960s, in the past seven years, the portion of total giving designated for international purposes has doubled from 1 percent to 2 percent. This has been accompanied by the rise of a new ideology in which both politicians and many private citizens see voluntarism as part of the solution to global problems. It is now considered regular practice for large national newspapers to carry long lists of NGOs and their addresses to encourage citizen contributions during times of civil violence or natural disasters.

Finally, inexpensive global communications technologies such as faxing, e-mail, and the Internet have made it easier for members of the emerging NGO sector to communicate.[19] In the days of the rise of the multinational corporation, this communication would have been prohibitively expensive. Today, it is a critical factor enabling low-cost global NGO networks to develop more rapidly than in the past. Many Northern NGOs like CARE, CRS, and World Vision are now connected to their far-flung country-level operations by e-mail, fax, and the Internet. Today, for example, some CARE staff members in otherwise inaccessible rural Ethiopia receive and send e-mail directly from their jeeps.

Profiles of Some Northern
Relief and Development NGOs

While the organizations that comprise the Northern relief and development NGO community number in the hundreds, it is useful to take a closer look at the profiles of a sample of typical small, medium-size, and large organizations. Here we provide a snapshot of the twelve organizations whose senior teams recently participated in the Rockefeller Foundation–funded Bellagio Conference on Globalization and Northern NGOs in September 1998: ACORD, CARE International, CARE USA, World Vision International, Save the Children US, Save the Children International, Oxfam GB, Oxfam America, MSF International, Habitat for Humanity, InterAction, and the Steering Committee for Humanitarian Response.[20] The combined budget of these twelve NGOs in FY1998 totaled $3 billion. Of these organizations, three (CARE International, World Vision, and PLAN International) were large (with budgets of over $300 million per year), three (MSF, Oxfam GB, and Save the Children US) were medium-size ($50 to $300 million per year), and five (Oxfam America, ACORD, InterAction, Save the Children International, and the Steering Committee for Humanitarian Response) were small (less than $50 million per year).[21] In 1999 the combined resources of the six global organizational families whose more detailed stories are the subject of this book totaled US$2.5 billion (PLAN, SAVE, CARE, MSF, Oxfam, and World Vision).

The majority of these organizations delivered operational programs, although three provided umbrella coordination and standards for a broader group of international NGOs. Most managed networks of relatively autonomous local affiliates. The combined annual relief and development expenditures of this Northern group were equal to almost one half of the annual U.S. government foreign assistance budget development activities in 1998.

They share a profound commitment to combat poverty, hunger, and social injustice (see Figure 1.2 on the following page for a summary of mission statements). Most carry out both relief and development activities, although Habitat for Humanity focuses primarily on shelter and MSF delivered largely in humanitarian relief programs. All organizations with the exception of World Vision and Habitat for Humanity consider themselves to be secular in their ethos. All have different histories and origins that continue to impact on their current organizational culture and choices. For this reason it is worth detailing at least a summary of these histories. In this book we will focus most comprehensively on the multipurpose relief and development organizations: CARE, Save, Oxfam, World Vision, PLAN International, and MSF.

History and Evolving Missions

Save the Children, one of the oldest Northern NGOs, was founded in the United Kingdom in 1919 by two sisters, Eglantyne Jebb and Dorothy Buxton, in response to the aftermath of World War I and the Russian Revolution. The founders were determined to secure international recognition for the rights of children. They also wanted to respond to the immediate needs of children orphaned by World War I. Save the Children's early mission was to promote worldwide safeguards for children and the formal international recognition of the rights of children. PLAN International was founded in 1937 as Foster Parents Plan for Children in Spain to help children whose lives were disrupted by the Spanish Civil War. With the outbreak of World War II, PLAN extended its work to include displaced children within war-torn Europe. Oxfam began during World War II, as a response of Oxford academics and Quakers to famine in Nazi-occupied Greece. CARE, established in 1945 as the Cooperative for American Remittances to Europe, began by delivering the famous "CARE packages" to Germany and other countries in Europe. World Vision, an international Christian, nonprofit, relief, and development organization started its work in 1950 to help children orphaned by war, widows, the poor, and the starving and to care for the sick. Médecins Sans Frontières grew out of the student solidarity movement in Paris. The youngest organization, it was formally organized in 1971 as a response to the human impact of the Biafra War. During that conflict, a group of French doctors joined together to provide medical assistance in places where the International Red Cross could not intervene in the absence of governmental approval. The doctors of MSF felt duty-bound to provide medical and humanitarian services in a more rapid and less legally constrained manner.

The founding purposes and operating missions of these organizations

Figure 1.2. Examples of International NGO Mission Statements

ACORD
Reduce poverty and vulnerability, help people win their basic rights, cope with conflict, and build peace.

CARE USA
Affirm the dignity and worth of individuals and families in some of the poorest countries of the world. We seek to relieve suffering, provide economic opportunity, build capacity for self-help, and affirm the ties among human beings everywhere.

MÉDECINS SANS FRONTIÈRES (MSF)
We offer assistance to populations in distress, victims of natural or man-made disasters, and victims of armed conflict irrespective of race, creed, and political affiliation. We believe in neutrality, respect of our professional code, independence, and non-compensation of staff other than what MSF can afford to provide.

OXFAM GB
Relieve poverty, distress, and suffering in any part of the world, and educate the public concerning the nature, causes, and effects of poverty.

OXFAM AMERICA
Create lasting solutions to hunger, poverty, and social injustice through partnerships with poor communities around the world.

PLAN INTERNATIONAL
PLAN's vision is of a world in which children realize their full potential in societies with respect for people's rights and dignity.

SAVE THE CHILDREN USA
Save the children by mobilizing citizens everywhere through the world—we envision a world in which every child has the right to survival, protection, development, and participation as set forth in the UN convention of the rights of the child.

WORLD VISION
Is a partnership of Christians whose mission is to follow our Lord and Savior Jesus Christ in working for the poor and oppressed to promote human transformation, seek justice, and bear witness to the good news of the Kingdom of God.

reflect their subsequent histories. Like people, they bear the imprints of their early years. For example, Oxfam GB in its early days walked a skillful line as Nazi Germany occupied Greece and there was a British law outlawing food gifts to people under occupation. Oxfam's founders—pragmatic academics, including the famous Greek scholar Charles Murray, negotiated with the War Office for ways in which exceptions could and should be made for Greece. Today, Oxfam GB engages in national-level advocacy when it is deemed essential (as we discuss in Chapter 7). Oxfam America, which is younger, has a different history as well as national setting; for example, unlike Oxfam GB, it does not accept any government funding, but does relatively little advocacy on U.S. national domestic issues. It does, however, lobby Congress on international issues.

Some of the organizations discussed here are secular, and some are faith-based. CARE and World Vision are both broad-spectrum relief and development organizations. CARE, a secular organization, seeks "to relieve human suffering, to provide economic opportunity, to build sustained capacity for self-help, and to affirm the ties of human beings everywhere."[22] World Vision's mission is based on principles of Christian charity, "to follow our Lord and Savior Jesus Christ in working with the poor and oppressed to promote human transformation, seek justice and bear witness to the good news of the Kingdom of God."[23]

Within ten years of their founding, many NGOs had expanded into a multinational entity, and the nature of their services has changed and evolved over time in response to changing world humanitarian needs. Save the Children organizations based in Australia and Canada started up soon after Jebb and Buxton's original U.K.-based Save the Children organization. CARE's transition from a U.S.-based to an international NGO began in the late 1970s, and there are now CARE International member organizations in ten countries. MSF France was soon joined by Swiss, Belgian, and American MSF organizations. Within ten years, the "CARE package" was transformed into large-scale supplementary feeding programs in Asia and Africa. Many of the original child-sponsorship programs turned to village-wide instead of individual-child programs.

Today, one important way NGOs are changing to cope with the demands of a globalizing world is to become more global themselves. While some still do direct-service delivery with no coordinating body, the national chapters of an organization increasingly are bonding together more closely to deliver services and to coordinate aid. The Steering Committee for Humanitarian Response (SCHR) and Inter-Action do no development programming; both are coordination and advocacy organizations. The percentage of worldwide multi-member funds controlled by a particular organization ranges from 4 percent (Oxfam US) to 70 percent (CARE US). Four organizations (ACORD,

CARE, MSF, PLAN International) work primarily in service delivery with their own staff; the remainder (InterAction, Oxfam GB, Oxfam America, SCHR) work with and through NGO partner organizations or as advocacy organizations.

Programs and Staffing

Approximately three-quarters of the combined expenditures of the NGOs that participated in the Bellagio Conference go overseas (72 percent), and domestic programming takes up 4 percent. As a percentage of total headquarters staff, program staff ranges from 23 percent to 52 percent, with the average being 34 percent. Among organizations that do direct service delivery, the percentage of funds and staff going directly to programs is even higher. Twenty percent of expenditures are for fundraising and administrative costs—a figure well within the 25 percent limit prescribed by the U.S. nonprofit standards of the Financial and Accounting Standards Board (FASB). Of all activities performed by an organization, service delivery, development education, and network building are ranked as the top three priorities. In addition, most organizations also do advocacy.

While these organizations respond rapidly and effectively to humanitarian emergency needs, they are devoted to longer-term rehabilitation and development programming. Within the budgets of these organizations, the largest share (72 percent) of revenue goes to development activities, 17 percent to rehabilitation, and 12 percent to relief. The organizations' average existence in operation age is 45 years—ranging from start-ups in 1919 (Save the Children) to 1971 (Médecins Sans Frontières).

Of the twelve organizations participating in the Bellagio Conference, six also conduct programs in their home countries. For some organizations, such domestic programs are a natural outgrowth of their missions. For example, Oxfam's mission is to educate the people of the world about poverty and human suffering in order to awaken them to the needs of the world. This naturally lends itself to domestic, local hunger-awareness programs. MSF believes in the right of all people to health care, and does not turn a blind eye to populations at home, such as drug users and the homeless, who are denied health care. Other organizations may choose not to do domestic programming due to their organizational missions, either because they are solely advocacy groups (with no service delivery activities), or because they have been conceived to deliver specific types of activities, such as PLAN International's child sponsorship programs.

Examples of domestic programming fall into two major categories: development education and building capacity in marginalized communities. Public development education programs are vital to energizing donors to respond to poverty and suffering; they also bear some relationship to eventual advocacy work, as we will see in Chapter 6. Oxfam's programs are emblematic, for example, inviting groups to experience the average Third-World diet while donating that day's food budget—thus making a clear connection between what "they" have and what "we" have. Public education is a key ingredient in influencing political attitudes toward poverty as well, pressuring governments to pay their United Nations dues or support foreign assistance budgets. Public education programs introduce an international perspective into the analysis of domestic poverty, addressing the links between race, poverty, and exclusion. Domestic programs run by MSF and Oxfam GB work to build capacity in marginalized domestic communities—including advocacy of health care access for the homeless, illegal immigrants, children, and drug addicts; building confidence and skills; creating cooperative income-producing enterprises; and providing entrepreneurial training. By organizing members of poor and marginalized communities, they seek to enhance these communities' voice in public policy forums to pressure governments for better policies, both domestically and internationally.

Worldwide, these organizations employed over 27,000 staff. In headquarters operations, the percentage of citizens from the headquarters country ranges from 77 percent to 100 percent, with the average being 90 percent. In the field, the presence of headquarters-country citizens ranges from 0 to 75 percent, averaging 18 percent. MSF is highest at 75 percent, which is not surprising, given that the majority of its field staff are doctors and health professionals volunteering abroad. The gender breakdown of headquarters staff is 64 percent female to 36 percent male, whereas in the field this proportion is reversed (61 percent male to 39 percent female).

Globalization, Challenges, and NGO Responses

The Bellagio Conference participants could not agree upon a single, clear definition of globalization. It is interesting, therefore, to compare their definitions with the more general definition provided earlier in this chapter. The participants did indicate that they felt globalization's pressures and believed they were working on a different scale than in the past. Three different aspects of the process proved useful in framing the major issues:

1. "Globalization refers to the emergence and spread of a supraterritorial dimension of social relations. In institutional terms, the process has unfolded through the proliferation and growth of so-called transnational corporations, popular associations and

regulatory agencies (sometimes called, respectively, global companies, global civil society, and global regimes.)"[24]

2. "Globalization is the internationalization of major financial markets, technology, and of important sectors of manufacturing and services.... The world economy (becomes)... dominated by uncontrollable global market forces and has as its principal actors and major agents of change truly transnational corporations which [that] owe allegiance to no nation state and locate wherever on the globe market advantage dictates."[25]

3. "Globalization is a process that has been going on for the past 5000 years but has significantly accelerated since the demise of the Soviet Union in 1991. Elements of globalization include transborder capital, labor, management, news, images, and data flows. ... From a humanist perspective, globalization entails both positive and negative consequences: it is both narrowing and widening the income gaps among and within nations, [both] intensifying and diminishing political domination, and [both] homogenizing and pluralizing cultural identities."[26]

The group reported having experienced the impact of globalization in its supraterritorial aspects, which included transnational capital, labor, management, news, images, data flows, and technology. These impacted not just the magnitude of their task, but also the way they organize, raise money, create identity, and hire staff. Three viewpoints emerged about the effects of globalization. Some viewed globalization as an evil [substitute: as destructive], with strong negative effects on worldwide poverty. Others considered it to have both positive and negative features. Still others treated globalization as simply a fact.

The Challenges of Globalization

All of the Bellagio Conference participants agreed that economic, political, social, and technological globalization had created new challenges for the Northern relief and development NGOs. They identified a large number of such challenges (see Figure 1.3), emphasizing seven as particularly important.

The first two challenges relate to keeping people alive in times of complex humanitarian crisis and to helping families and communities improve their lives.

1. New Waves of Complex Emergencies

The end of the Cold War, the collapse of the Soviet Union, and the weakness of many new states fostered heightened intrastate conflicts. These conflicts have resulted in major new global refugee flows that overwhelmed global institutional-response capacity and heightened risks to

Figure 1.3. Globalization and New Challenges for the NGO Community

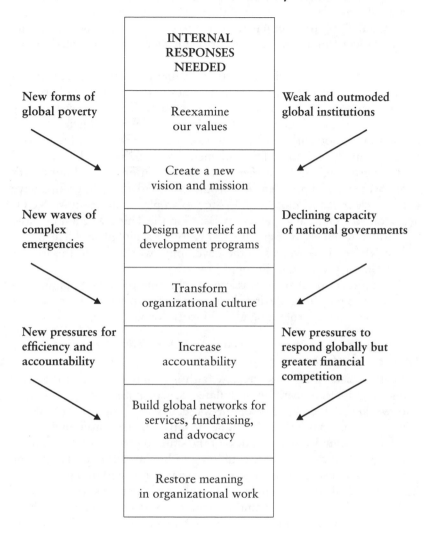

New forms of
global poverty

New waves of
complex
emergencies

New pressures for
efficiency and
accountability

**INTERNAL
RESPONSES
NEEDED**

Reexamine
our values

Create a new
vision and mission

Design new relief and
development programs

Transform
organizational culture

Increase
accountability

Build global networks for
services, fundraising,
and advocacy

Restore meaning
in organizational work

Weak and outmoded
global institutions

Declining capacity
of national governments

New pressures to
respond globally but
greater financial
competition

refugees, internally displaced people, and relief workers. A key change has been that, since the mid-1990s, due to increased intrastate conflict, the annual number of newly internally displaced people has exceeded that of new refugees. These new trends have resulted in a host of new ethical, operational, and structural dilemmas for the relief and development NGOs.

2. New Forms of Global Poverty

Although economic globalization resulted in the creation of new wealth and employment in many parts of the world, new forms of poverty have accompanied it. For example, the drive to create market systems in the former Soviet Union and Eastern Europe has been accompanied by the collapse of social safety nets that have left the unemployed and the elderly without basic social protection. In many developing countries—for example, Indonesia and Thailand—new urban wage workers tied to enterprises in the expanding global economy have discovered they are subject to global economic shocks. Without access to land to grow food, and without urban social services, such workers are highly vulnerable. Finally, although unemployment has been low in the industrial north, increasingly large segments of the population are without health care coverage. The problems of chronically disadvantaged groups have become clearer and more visible—for example, homelessness. NGOs accustomed to focusing on poverty issues in the Third World must now reconsider whether to respond to poverty as a global problem in the industrial North as well as in the developing world and in the former Soviet Union and Eastern Europe.

A second set of challenges relates to the role the NGO community may want to play in catalyzing changes in public, private, and nonprofit sector roles and in promoting global institutional reform.

3. Declining Capacity of National Governments and Changing Private and NGO Roles

Increasing distrust of the state, new faith in free markets, and the pressures of global competition stimulated severe public sector cutbacks and weakened the capacity of the state. As the global economy integrated, more national and ethnic groups sought autonomy, which further compounded the weakness of the state to provide social services, and aggravated the intrastate conflicts and humanitarian disasters. The redistributive mechanisms to produce social goods within nation-states have been weakened and there are few clear mechanisms for producing global social goods as a counterweight to expanding economic globalization.[27] The challenges to the NGO community include deciding whether to function as a substitute for declining state services or to pressure the state to play a stronger role again; and deciding whether to form new partnerships for poverty alleviation with the private sector or to engage in strong advocacy efforts to press the private sector for more "socially responsible" enterprise activity.

4. Weak and Outmoded Global Institutions

The existing global institutions such as the International Monetary Fund, the World Bank, and the United Nations system—all created in the post–World War II era—are ill-equipped to deal with new dimensions of global poverty, massive refugee flows, intrastate conflicts, or events like the Asian financial crisis. These developments have been accompanied by calls for redesign of the global financial architecture. As the number of internally displaced people has increased with the growth of intrastate conflict, some organizations—like the Office of the United Nations High Commissioner for Refugees (UNHCR), traditionally responsible for the protection of refugees, not internally displaced persons—have been forced to reexamine their mandates. The World Trade Organization, recently formed in 1994, appears ill equipped to deal with the relationship between trade issues and the environment, or child labor. It is viewed by some as secretive in its decision-making, as the protests at the Seattle WTO round in 1999 demonstrated.[28] An important question for the NGO community is whether to concentrate on direct service provision or whether to help define and advocate for the redesign of global institutions through participating in global civil society movements.

The third set of challenges has to do with improved internal performance, organizational learning, and appropriate structures for effective global action.

5. New Pressures for Accountability and Efficiency

As resources become tighter, NGOs face new pressures for greater accountability for program impact and quality. Private donors want to know whether their dollars really improve peoples' lives. Public donors, more subject to scrutiny by their parliaments and congresses, want to know if their resources were used effectively. NGO staff members have a strong sense of mission and want to know more than ever before about whether their programs matter. As a result, NGO senior teams must decide how to evaluate and document program impact and how to reengineer their internal processes to become more efficient users of scarce donor funds. They face the deeper problem of how to create organizations that learn from their experiences and engage in continuous improvement.

6. New Pressures to Respond Globally

As economic globalization continues, the unmet needs for global poverty and environmental policy response become clearer. NGOs must decide whether to engage in global advocacy and worldwide social movements such as the International Campaign to Ban Landmines or Jubilee 2000 Third World debt forgiveness campaign. They also must consider which forms of global organizational structures make the most sense for their own multi-organizational efforts in relief and development programs and for global fundraising. Finally, they must reconsider whether their role as Northern organizations must change, for example, from direct service delivery to advocacy and resource mobilization.

The final important challenge perceived by the senior teams of the Northern relief and development NGOs is a philosophical one:

7. Recreating Purpose and "Mystique"

In light of the frequency and magnitude of humanitarian emergencies and the decline of public capacity to address poverty and relief, many NGO staff expressed a sense of malaise about their ability to make a difference in society. Their own increasing professionalization and bureaucratization as they grew to address the global problems contributed to this worry about their ability to sustain commitment and mission. All say they face challenges of connecting with and mobilizing younger generations in middle-aged organizations that began their efforts with enthusiasm in the World War I–World War II period. Of our small sample, only MSF, formed in 1971, does not believe it shares this problem of "mid-life crisis."

Emerging Organizational Imperatives

As the challenges set out above imply, the structural changes in the world will continue to generate poverty, conflict, and dislocation. The magnitude of these problems will not let up for the foreseeable future. The decline of public capacity and perceived lack of trust in governments also will not be easily reversed. These realities will continue to place immense pressure upon the NGO sector to engage in efforts to try to alleviate some of these problems, and they can hope to accomplish this only with the scale and scope of global bodies. Yet the very imperatives of size and resources will also unleash organizational dynamics that can undermine the purposes of the new global agencies. The greatly expanded scale and resources also will make it difficult to coordinate or maintain the legitimacy that they have gained as other public-oriented bodies have declined.

Most of the NGO leaders interviewed believe that they should reexamine their missions and values and create compelling new visions to motivate staff and donors. They must transform their increasingly large, bureaucratic organizations into dynamic, live organizations with strong "learning" cultures. They want to capitalize on the opportunity to build global networks to respond to world problems—especially to create linkages across the North-South divide. They want to employ new cybertechnology in their work. They are also struggling to find ways of coping with the new pressures for accountability, transparency, and efficiency.

In response to questions about their aspirations for their own organizations in the next decade, the group expressed no clear consensus, but the following perceptions of management tasks were widely shared:

Reexamine Values and Create a New Vision and Mission

Organizations must search anew for a deep, motivating sense of meaning and mission that will attract both the young and citizen involvement. They must find a work style and culture that balances passion and commitment with professionalism. This new work style must identify themes that will capture the imagination of future generations.

Redesign Relief and Development Programs

The sector must develop a more effective approach to humanitarian responses that focuses first of all on conflict prevention; that places a premium on quick and comprehensive emergency response and on more fluid inter-organizational cooperation; and that responds to the ethical, operational, and structural problems of the current global system. NGOs must also struggle to understand the new aspects of global poverty and develop even more effective global responses to poverty.

Transform Organizational Culture and Increase Accountability

NGOs must increasingly develop learning cultures in which evaluation is not thought of as cause for punishment but rather as a process of partnership among all interested parties for organizational learning and improvement.

Build Global Networks for Services, Fundraising, and Advocacy Institutions

The international relief and development NGOs must develop more responsive and inclusive global NGO structures to have an even greater impact on global poverty. They will need to harness the potential for greater inter-organizational cooperation especially in the areas of global advocacy and development education. The sector should take the lead in building a global civil society and a new social contract—with more clearly delineated rights and responsibilities—among the public, private, and nonprofit sectors.

Ethnology and Beyond

Part of the purpose of our book is to provide an accurate description—an ethnology—of what the senior leaders of Northern NGOs whom we interviewed think shapes their world. By ethnology we mean a description of the history, development, and similarities and differences in comparative (organizational) cultures. So far we have reported leaders' and senior teams' views on the causes of NGO growth in the last four decades, on the new challenges they believe their organizations face as a result of globalization, and on their own organizational responses. But it is also our intent to move beyond a description of these views—to speculate about both what this worldview reveals and what it may hide. Some of the questions we will address at the end of every chapter are: What part of the Northern senior team viewpoint can be supported with empirical data? What motivations for action may not have been explicitly discussed by our informants? What nuances and details may have been known but not explicitly commented on? What emerging trends may not have been fully explored?

Empirical Support

Most of our informants' perspectives about the causes of Northern NGO relief and development sectoral growth, new challenges, and organizational responses can be supported empirically.[29] For example, our tables in this chapter (and many other sources besides those we cite) demonstrate increased public and private resource flows to the sector and the increase in the number of registered relief and development NGOs in both the United States and Europe.[30] The combination of democratic openings and new laws permitting NGOs to register and function legally does coincide with the growth in the number of new NGOs formed and registered. We have already illustrated this with the case of Ethiopia and can document it elsewhere as well.[31] NGO budgets have grown, and the proportion of private fundraising for relief as well as of program expenses on relief have coincided with the increase in complex humanitarian emergencies and the larger numbers of internally displaced people in the 1990s. For example, a look at "organizational climate" surveys in the mid-1990s reveals deterioration in staff morale and commitment—part of the "mid-life" malaise.[32] It is more difficult to provide empirical support for some of our informants' ideas of causality. For example, our respondents believe that cutbacks in public funding for health, education, and social services in the developing world stimulated expansion of nonprofit organizations in those sectors. Since the emergence of social service NGOs in certain developing country regions often accompanies or follows public service cutbacks, it is hard to determine the causality that they suggest.

Additional Sources of Motivation for Growth and Change

Any group of informants may have difficulty accurately identifying and reporting their own deeper motivations for action. In some cases, they may not understand them well enough to report them; in other cases, they may understand them quite well but choose not to report them to others for any number of reasons. One can at best speculate about deeper motivations.

It is possible that many of these organizations began with a conception of charity that was prevalent in the post–World War II period. Perhaps Northern NGO leaders realized that they needed to redefine their role and services as well as to globalize to keep from becoming obsolete in the eyes of their own publics in Europe, Canada, and the United States. Perhaps there is a growing recognition that poverty alleviation in the new millennium may be more about partnerships and joint problem-solving than post–World War II Northern largesse. Perhaps the motivations for organizational change also spring at least partly from the desire to maintain and expand the Northern NGO role in developing countries in the face of new competition from a growing Southern NGO sector. While it is not possible to ascertain the existence of such additional motivations for NGO transformation, the possibility of their presence must be acknowledged.

Another area of ambiguity is how deeply Northern senior team members feel that the challenges their organizations face require a radical transformation of their perspectives, values, and programs or simply restructuring to achieve greater efficiency and effectiveness. There is at least initial indication from in-depth interviews that some leaders feel less strongly than others that globalization has had great impact and that radical transformation is necessary.[33]

Areas for Further Exploration

As in any discussion at a conference there may be areas of detail that our Bellagio Conference colleagues did not comment on because of lack of time, lack of knowledge or first-hand experience with the subject, or due to poorly focused questions by researchers, that the area is not important enough to make it a priority for discussion. Answers to open-ended interview questions are often very revealing because they help show what respondents spontaneously do not list as priorities as well as what they do mention. Missing details are important to acknowledge if they have the potential to result in narrow viewpoints or alternatives foreclosed.

In their discussion of causes of NGO growth and globalization both at the conference and in interviews our informants did not spontaneously speculate about possible differences in the pace of both Northern and Southern NGO growth in different regions. It is possible that many of the senior team members interviewed did not have sufficient multi-regional experience to be aware of differences among regions in their organizations' globalization. There probably are interesting differences in the development of NGO sectors by region, but few empirical studies examine this topic.[34] Greater knowledge of regional differences could have been quite useful in developing more focused strategies for NGO growth and for capacity building by region.

Nor did our informants speak spontaneously or in detail about factors that may have stimulated Southern NGO growth in recent decades. A more complete sharing of perspectives on the causes of both Northern and Southern NGO growth would be useful to the senior teams of both Northern and Southern organizations. To broaden the perspectives provided in this book, some of the factors commonly mentioned as catalyzing Southern NGO growth are: (1) the growth of a few large Southern NGOs like the Grameen Bank and the Bangladesh Rural Action Committee (BRAC) in Bangladesh which provided models for other Southern organizations; (2) the motivation of a group of Southern professionals in the 1960s to form social movements based on currents of liberation theology and a renewed consciousness of social problems; (3) the growth of secondary education in developing countries, which produced cadres of Southern professionals with new views, skills, and perspectives; and (4) increased public and private funding to create and build capacity of Southern as well as Eastern European NGOs as part of a movement to build global civil society.

The Full Implications of Emerging Trends

At times our informants did not explore the full implications of emerging trends that they identified. For example, many indicated that they believe globalization is accompanied by three new interrelated forms of poverty emerging in the former Soviet Union and Eastern Europe, in the developing world, and in the industrial North. Neither our sample of informants nor recent studies have documented such new forms of poverty, or their potential interrelationships—and no detailed understanding has been developed of their implications for Northern relief and development NGOs. More solid thinking is needed on this subject.

Yet another underexplored area relates to the broadest implications of new, complex emergencies for the roles of NGO emergency-response organizations. NGO leaders might see more efficient NGO response as a solution, while others might argue that recent experience shows that the UN system and military organizations like the North Atlantic Treaty Organization (NATO) are faster and more efficient. If this were the case, one might need to question the future role of NGOs in global humanitarian action.

A final example of the need to think even more broadly about the implications of new trends relates to private and nonprofit partnerships. Our NGO informants provided only initial speculation about the implications of new corporate interest in overseas social giving to relief and development NGOs. How will corporate involvement of their employees in social projects with NGOs affect programs? Our informants also did not consider the implications of philanthropy from newly accumulated technology-sector wealth, such as the Bill and Melinda Gates Foundation, the Glaser Family Foundation, Social Venture Partners, or Microsoft corporate giving.

An Overview of the Discussion

This introductory chapter has provided a context for our discussion of the globalization of the Northern nonprofit international relief and development sector. The chapters that follow closely mirror the themes our informants identified as the emerging imperatives—created by globalization—to which their organizations must respond. Chapter 2 examines how NGOs have begun to redefine their values, missions, and programs to adjust to globalization. The chapter explores the strategic change process that some of them have already introduced in their organizations, and their struggle to communicate and implement change within their far-flung global operations. Chapter 3 examines in detail the new world of complex emergencies—and the strategic, operational, and ethical dilemmas that such emergencies present for the Northern NGO community. Chapter 4 discusses emerging perceptions of new forms of poverty associated with globalization and reviews how development programs are being redesigned to respond to them. Chapter 5 traces the new global organizational structures that are emerging within Northern NGO families as they attempt to form creative relationships with local affiliates and to add members. Chapter 6 discusses emerging experiments with innovative private and public partnerships that extend beyond the immediate NGO family. Chapter 7 reviews experiments with global advocacy networks and the opportunities as well as problems of advocacy encountered in service-delivery organizations. In Chapter 8, we explore new issues relating to accountability and to impact and effectiveness measurement. Chapter 9 sums up our conclusions and looks to the future. It should be said at the start that we make no claim in this book that our informants or their organizations have the new or comprehensive answers for saving lives and improving well-being in the new millennium. Our purpose is to describe and reflect upon efforts they are making toward these goals.

This chapter could not have been completed without the helpful assistance of Janet Salm, who summarized the Bellagio Conference NGO informational questionnaire, and of Patrick Dobel, who provided help on the summary of the Bellagio participants' views of the challenges of globalization.

Notes

1. For interesting recent books on aspects of this same topic see: *Beyond the Magic Bullet: NGO Performance and Accountability in the Post–Cold War,* ed. Michael Edwards and David Hulme (West Hartford, Conn.: Kumarian Press, 1996), Alan Fowler, *Striking a Balance* (London: Earthscan Publications, 1998), also Michael Edwards, *Future Positive* (London: Earthscan Publications, 1999). See also *Nonprofit and Voluntary Sector Quarterly* (supplement 1999).

2. Amartya Sen, *Development as Freedom* (New York: Alfred A. Knopf, 1999).

3. Stephen Hymer, "The Multinational Corporation and the Law of Uneven Development," in *Economics and World Order,* ed. J. N. Bhagwati (New York: World Law Fund, 1970).

4. Neil Jacoby, "The Multinational Corporation: A World Power to Unite People," *The Center Magazine III,* no. 3 (May 1970): 37–56.

5. United Nations Development Programme (UNDP), *Human Development Report 1993* (New York: Oxford University Press, 1993), 84–91.

6. UNDP, *Human Development Report 1993,* 84–91.

7. Alliance for a Global Community, "The NGO Explosion," *Communications* 1, no. 7 (April 1995): 1. See also Julie Fisher, *Nongovernments* (West Hartford, Conn.: Kumarian Press, 1998), 4–12, and Thomas Carroll, *Intermediary NGOs* (West Hartford, Conn.: Kumarian Press, 1992), 9–15.

8. UNDP, *Human Development Report 1993,* 86.

9. See, for example, David Horton Smith, "Some Understudied Research Topics: The 1994 ISTR Conference and Beyond," *Voluntas* 5, no. 3 (1999): 349–58, and Brian H. Smith, "Non-governmental Organizations in International Development: Trends in Research and Future Research Priorities," *Voluntas* 4, no. 3 (1999) 326–44. For example, the number of articles about international NGOs declined from 8 percent of the topics covered in two major NGO journals in the 1970s to 4 percent in the 1980s and 1990s as is noted in Jeffrey L. Brudney and Teresa Kluesner Durden, "Twenty Years of the Journal of Voluntary Action Research/Nonprofit and Voluntary Sector Quarterly," *Nonprofit and Voluntary Sector Quarterly* 22, no. 3 (Fall 1993): 215.

10. Bryant A. Hudson and Wolfgang Bielefeld, "Structures of Multinational Nonprofit Organizations," *Nonprofit Management and Leadership* 8, no. 1 (Fall 1997): 32.

11. See Lester M. Salamon and Helmut K. Anheier, "In Search of the Non-Profit Sector: The Question of Definitions" (Baltimore: The Johns Hopkins Comparative Non Profit Sector Project, Working Paper no. 2, 1992).

12. See Hymer, "The Multinational Corporation and the Law of Uneven Development," Jacoby, "The Multinational Corporation: A World Power to Unite People," and Richard Barnet and Ronald Mueller, *Global Reach: The Power of Multinational Corporations* (New York: Simon & Schuster, 1974).

13. For a good discussion of globalization and its implications see David Korten, *When Corporations Rule the World* (West Hartford, Conn.: Kumarian Press, 1996), and *The Post-Corporate World* (West Hartford, Conn.: Kumarian Press, 1999).

14. Edgar Owens and Robert Shaw, *Development Reconsidered* (Lexington, Mass: Lexington Books, 1972).

15. Patrick Breslin, *Development and Dignity: The First Fifteen Years of the Inter-American Foundation* (Rosslyn, Va.: The Inter-American Foundation, 1987).

16. Richard Faini, Jaime de Melo, Abdel Senhadji-Semlali, and Julie Stanton, "Macro Performance under Adjustment Lending," *Policy, Planning, and Research Working Paper 190* (Washington, D.C.: World Bank, 1980).

17. I am particularly indebted to Lincoln Chen, the vice president of the Rockefeller Foundation and former director of Harvard's Population Center, for these insights about NGOs and humanitarian interventions.

18. Marc Lindenberg, *The Human Development Race* (San Francisco, Calif.: ICS Press and ICEG Publications, 1993), 150.

19. Lester Salamon has interesting insights on the role of global communications in his article "The Rise of the Nonprofit Sector," *Foreign Affairs* 73, no. 4 (1994): 117–18.

20. For articles from the conference, see *Nonprofit and Voluntary Sector Quarterly* (September 1999).

21. When one adds the two final organizations which did not participate at the Bellagio Conference, Catholic Relief Services and the International Federation of Red Cross and Red Crescent Societies (IFRC), the total reaches more than $3 billion.

22. CARE Mission statement 1996, see Figure 1.2.

23. World Vision Mission Statement 1998, see Figure 1.2.

24. J. A. Scholte, "Beyond the Buzzword: Toward a Critical Theory of Globalization," in *Globalization: Theory and Practice*, ed. Eleonore Kofman and Gillian Youngs (London: Pinter, 1996).

25. P. Hirst and G. Thompson, *Globalization in Question* (Cambridge: Polity Press, 1996), 194.

26. M. Tehranian (1996), "Definition of globalization." from: www.toda.org/conferences/sydney/papers/tehranian.html.

27. Inge Kaul, Isabelle Grunberg, and Marc Stern, *Global Public Goods* (London: Oxford University Press, 1999).

28. See "Protesters Turn Focus to a Debate on Globalization," *International Herald Tribune*, December 4–5, 1999, 9. See also "U.S. on Defensive, Struggles for Accord in a Divided WTO," *International Herald Tribune*, December 4–5, 1999, 1, and "The Battle for Seattle," *Newsweek*, December 13, 1999, 30–40.

29. See Fisher, *Nongovernments;* Edwards, *Future Positive;* Fowler, *Striking a Balance;* Edwards and Hulme, *Beyond the Magic Bullet;* Carroll, *Intermediary NGOs;* John Clark, *Democratizing Development: The Role of Voluntary Organizations* (West Hartford, Conn.: Kumarian Press, 1991).

30. See Fisher, *Nongovernments;* Edwards, *Future Positive;* Fowler, *Striking a Balance;* Edwards and Hulme, *Beyond the Magic Bullet;* Carroll, *Intermediary NGOs;* Clark, *Democratizing Development.*

31. See Fisher, *Nongovernments;* Edwards, *Future Positive;* Fowler, *Striking a Balance;* Edwards and Hulme, *Beyond the Magic Bullet;* Carroll, *Intermediary NGOs;* Clark, *Democratizing Development.*

32. See for example the *CARE organizational climate surveys* 1997–99.

33. For example, Charles MacCormack, president of Save the Children US, sees his organization's needs for change as repositioning, while Ray Offenheiser, president of Oxfam America, believes a deeper and more radical transformation will be necessary.

34. See Fisher, *Nongovernments;* Edwards, *Future Positive;* Fowler, *Striking a Balance;* Edwards and Hulme, *Beyond the Magic Bullet;* Carroll, *Intermediary NGOs;* Clark, *Democratizing Development.*

– 2 –

Managing Transformation: Tough Choices, Far-Reaching Consequences

BUFFETED BY BOTH the opportunities and challenges that come with globalization, NGO leaders know they are being called upon to do more with less, to fill in for declining state capacities, and to be responsive to unpredictable emergencies. They also need to reposition their organizations, to achieve more results, to be more accountable to wider publics, and to decide whether to get more involved in advocacy as well as how they will relate to NGOs around the globe. The commitment to change and the enthusiasm with which their organizations approach the new challenges of globalization is well illustrated by Oxfam America's recent strategic statement, which bears at its start the quotation, "A journey of a thousand miles starts where the feet are,"[1] and continues:

> The U.S. program of Oxfam America is on a journey that calls on it to create 'a world in which all people shall one day know freedom—freedom to achieve their fullest potential and to life secure from the dangers of hunger, deprivation and oppression— through the creation of a global movement for economic and social justice'... charting a path that will enable us to achieve this vision and mission... remains our greatest challenge.[2]

Given the tension between lofty aspirations and the multiple external pressures that relief and development NGOs are experiencing, what changes are the most pivotal? Since not everything can be done at once, what should guide the sequencing of change? Mission statements? Network-wide agreement on guiding principles? Reorganizing at home? Restructuring? Mergers? Or multiple incremental changes—for example, in partnerships, in programming processes, or in organizing decision-making? While it may be tempting to say "all of the above," priorities have to be set to move forward at all. This is the challenge of managing transformation.

31

Transformation in mid-life—as is the case for many Northern NGOs— is neither rapid nor straightforward. For most, the process lumbers on rather than leaps. The NGO leaders are already dealing with multiple changes in the external environment. For governments, the process of organizational change has included stripping away responsibilities and cutting budgets. The corporate sector has resorted to mergers and acquisitions in an effort to achieve greater market share and economies of scale. The international NGOs, for their part, have been increasing their efforts to develop more partnerships and rethink relationships and coordinating structures, as well as to develop their capacity for advocacy—in part pressuring governments to do their share.

Many Northern NGOs have been revisiting and revising mission statements and engaging boards, senior leaders, and multiple stakeholders in the process. Further complicating the NGO's future, official development agencies throughout Europe and North America have moved toward either steady-state or declining levels of official development assistance. As this happens, Northern national donor agencies are increasingly turning to NGOs to implement their programs. As bilateral donors do this, they are de facto also changing the role and work of NGOs.[3] The NGO leaders are more than aware of this problem, and they are struggling to come to terms with it. Some NGOs are deciding to move toward greater financial independence. That this comes on top of increased calls for more work on relief and emergency assistance adds to the complexity.

Meanwhile—even while coming to terms with an increasingly turbulent environment—these NGOs continue, rightly, to position poverty reduction and reaching those most in need (whether due to war or natural disaster) at the heart of their missions. Changes in work and objectives need to be rolled out through a series of steps in policies, programs, and projects. That process takes motivation, commitment, problem-solving skills, and time management. To achieve cumulative impact, questions of sequencing, transaction costs, organizational culture, and incentives for change must all be addressed.[4]

This agenda is daunting. Among other things, the old organizational cultures of North-South, donor and recipient, are deeply rooted— "embedded in the structures and mindsets of NGOs."[5] It has been pointed out that, "most importantly, the 21st century will require changes in organizational behavior and ethos that are built on new attitudes and ways of working."[6] Thus, in addition to structural and organizational change, senior managers have to manage change in their organizational cultures. For these among many other reasons, managing strategic change takes longer and is harder to implement in practice than in theory.

Leveraging fundamental interventions that evoke or facilitate changes throughout an organization and affect its interactions with peers, clients, partners, and donors is at the heart of transformation. Most of the "drivers" of these changes in NGOs are external. This finding matches earlier research in the management of nonprofits that found that the greater the dependency of the nonprofits on external factors, the more likely that changes were externally driven.[7] Programs for fundamental change encounter the inertia and discomfort that board, stakeholders, line managers and staff often resist. Achieving it requires looking at the big picture, linking short-term to longer-term perspectives, using information sharing to ease coordination, and mapping or negotiating support through stakeholder assessments. An organization committed to learning can build change into its culture—which is one of its major appeals. But few large complex NGOs are purposefully becoming such "learning organizations." More frequently, leaders seek out changes that are distinguishable by their impact, that have maximum impact for lower transaction costs for valued programs and staff, and that leverage the repositioning of the organization.

Achieving change at any level is all about motivation. When ideas capture the emotions and commitment of people, all kinds of things begin to happen. Structure, incentives, and organizational culture are key variables, but achieving "ownership" of common goals and tasks is more vital than formal planning or even formalized participation.[8] These are normative organizations—the most skillful managers we interviewed were clearly able to convey deep excitement and abiding commitment to that which the organization was aspiring. Thus MSF president Philippe Biberson, for example, has said: "I did not take this job in order to run an organization, or to head a bureaucracy. I am a humanitarian and a doctor and I see what we are doing as part of a large humanitarian movement." When the heads of all of the eighteen sections got together, he said, the meetings did not focus on bureaucratic issues, but turned into long, frequently intense, discussions of guiding principles. It is no surprise then to also note that MSF has been working through all the components of transformation. Rony Brauman echoes this sentiment in his foreword to *World In Crisis*.[9] Brauman says that what changed after World War II was the actual presence of NGOs on the ground during bloodbaths. Now these NGOs are also getting dizzying amounts of media attention. Their goals are as much about ethics as about anything else—which in itself can intensify tensions. Brauman points out that: "In the case of MSF, the concept of ethical responsibility is one which has come far in the organization's 25 years of existence. Yet it has always aroused heated debate between and within the various country-based sections."[10] MSF has been working hard in several of its Assembly meetings in the past two years to proceed to change while deepening its position to meet its own ethical goals.

In the sections that follow, we begin with a current picture of some NGO family networks in order to ground our subsequent discussion of what is and is not changing. We then focus on similarities and differences among the NGOs in the change strategies employed. We continue with senior team self-assessments of where change has been easiest and where it has been hardest to make progress. Then, as in every chapter, we step back and ask: What part of the Northern senior-team "point of view" can be supported by empirical data? What possible motivations may not have been discussed? What nuances have not been explicitly commented on? What emerging trends may not have been fully explored?

Diverse NGO Family Networks and the Culture of Change

The NGOs whose challenges we present in this book are large family networks in which several national member organizations carry the same name and embrace the same broad principles, usually captured in mission statements. Because they are all large, complex, global organizations, they have many generic problems in common. Their responses to problems are often similar as well.

There is, however, great diversity within any particular large, global, multicultural family network and among the six large family networks we examine in this book. That diversity is salient when these networks operate next to one another in the same country (this does happen), when they negotiate how to not do that in another country, when they each consider what an advocacy campaign entails for their particular national member, and when they develop their strategies for organizational transformation.

Diversity within and among these multicultural global family networks affects their approaches to organizational transformation. Within MSF, discussions are often rooted deeply in philosophical traditions and lead to continued review of basic values and their implications for practice. PLAN International and World Vision, while they too are highly normative organizations and in some ways similar to MSF, also differ considerably from MSF in other respects. Both World Vision and PLAN recently recruited their presidents from the private for-profit sector and tend to draw more of their inspiration from seeing themselves as large professional organizations with the social and normative goal of child welfare and human development. World Vision managers and staff use the term "corporate" to describe their internal functions but remain fully cognizant as well as proud of their ethical mandate.

Yet PLAN and World Vision also differ from one another. PLAN International is a secular organization; World Vision is a faith-based one. The statue of Jesus gathering the children in front of World

Vision's corporate headquarters symbolizes the organization's message. Although many of World Vision's stakeholders are drawn from the ranks of Christian conservatives, the organization also attracts liberals, and it works very successfully in Muslim countries as well as in countries practicing other world faiths. World Vision is as critical of social injustice as MSF, and it is one of the most outspoken NGOs on the issues of poverty and inequality. Moreover, like MSF, it is often found working where others fear to tread (in the Beira Corridor during the war in Mozambique, or on the West Bank with Palestinian communities). World Vision's domestic program reaches to many of the poorest communities in the United States.

In his book, *Stakeholders: Government-NGO Partnerships for International Development,* Ian Smillie points out that while Save the Children, Oxfam, MSF, and CARE might be thought of as multinational NGOs, PLAN and World Vision are "transnational" NGOs (or "fully multinational" in the terminology we use in this book to describe the same stage).[11] Smillie maintains that "World Vision has taken its transnationalisation much further than the others, essentially wiping out the divide between North and South. Many of its offices in developing countries have been converted into autonomous legal entities that are full members of World Vision International, participating actively at the international board and membership level. This is very new for international development NGOs."[12]

Before continuing to discuss the variety within NGO families, it is worthwhile to review some rudimentary features of these large NGO families in Table 2.1 (pp. 36–37). While different in their origins, MSF, World Vision, and PLAN International are more financially independent than the other three NGO family networks discussed here. They rarely undertake donor contracts for project implementation, since they identify and implement their own projects and programs. That may be changing, however, as, for other reasons, World Vision is beginning to do more contract work for USAID.

The variation in the number of national members, in financial strength, and in the scale of operations is striking. It is of course a limitation of this data that it shows one point in time, when in fact all of these factors are changing rapidly—due to the transformation under way in several networks. With its twenty-six national members, Save the Children is the largest in terms of number of members. World Vision is the largest in terms of its financial weight with $600 million in total revenues for its members. World Vision is largest in financial terms, while Oxfam is largest in terms of the number of country operations.

As in all families, there are within family rivalries, disputes, past history, current feelings. Some members carry more weight than others. A confluence of these factors, especially organizational history, means that

Table 2.1.
NGO Families: National Members and Revenue Sources

Name of Organization	National Offices	Year Founded	Number of Countries with Operations
PLAN International	Total: 14 Australia, Belgium, Canada, Denmark, Finland, France, Germany, Japan, Korea, Netherlands, Norway, Sweden, U.K., U.S.	1937	43
Save the Children	Total: 26 Australia, Canada, Denmark, DR, Egypt, Faroe Islands, Finland, France, Greece, Guatemala, Honduras, Iceland, Jordan, Korea, Macedonia, Mauritius, Mexico, Netherlands, New Zealand, Norway, Romania, Spain, Sweden, U.K., U.S.	1919	121
Oxfam International	Total: 11 Australia, Belgium, Canada, Hong Kong, Ireland, Netherlands, New Zealand, Quebec, Spain, U.K., U.S.	Oxfam (now Oxfam GB) was founded in 1942; Oxfam International was incorporated in 1996.	117
CARE	Total: 10 Australia, Austria, Canada, Denmark, Germany, France, Japan, Norway, U.K., U.S.	1945	70
World Vision	Total: 65 (18 doing fundraising; others primarily doing program work)	1950	92
Médecins Sans Frontières	Total: 18 Australia, Austria, Belgium, Canada, Denmark, France, Germany, Holland, Hong Kong, Italy, Japan, Luxembourg, Norway, Singapore, Spain, Sweden, Switzerland, U.S.	1971	80
Total	Range from 10 to 65 national offices	Oldest: SAVE 1919 Youngest: MSF 1971	Range from 43 to 121 countries where they operate

Source: Christina Kappaz and Coralie Bryant. Multiple sources were used including annual reports, records, Web sites, and interviews.

Table 2.1 (continued).
NGO Families: National Members and Revenue Sources

Total Revenues for All Members (US$ million)	Revenues of Largest Members (US$ millions)	Source of Revenue
US$295.2 Source: 1999 Annual report	Netherlands: $107.3 (36%) (1999) U.S.: $32.5 (11%) (1999) U.K.: $21.2 (7.2%) (1998)	Source breakdown for combined revenue: 88% sponsors 10% grants and other contributions 2% investment income
US$368 Source: 1999 Alliance Annual Report	U.K.: $138.4 (37.6%) (1998/99) U.S.: $113.4 (30.1%) (1999)	U.K.: no sponsors. 50% private contributions 40% public grants; 10% other U.S.: 21% sponsors 21% private contributions 56% public grants; 2% other
US$504 Source: 1999 Annual Reports	GB: $198.8 (39%) Netherlands: $183.9 (36%) Spain: $31.4 (6%) Australia: $13.7 (3%)	68% private; 32% public 27% private; 73% public 59% private; 41% public 65% private; 35% public
US$525 Source: 1999 CARE U.S. Office of President	US$419.6 (79%) (1999) Canada: $79 (15%) (1999)	U.S.: 15% private donations, 57% U.S. government, 13% other Gov'ts, donors 13% other CAREs U.K.: 14% private; 74% government, 12% in-kind
US$600 (1999 estimate based on individual member revenues, with estimate for Australia)	U.S.: $407.4 (68%) (1999) Canada: $71.5 (12%) (1999) U.K.: $35.5 (6%) (1999) NZ: $14 (2%) (1999)	U.S.: 81% private; 17% public; 2% other U.K.: 73% private; 24% public; 3% other Canada: 73% private; 15% public; 12% other
US$304 Source: (1999 estimate from MSF Int'l Office, Brussels)	France: $60.2 (20%) (1998) U.S.: $8.5 (3%) (1997)	Source breakdown for combined revenue of all MSF Offices: In 1998 54% was from private (individuals, foundations, corporations); 46% public governments and international agencies. In 1999 74% was from private donations; 26% from several different public sources.
Total resources in 1999 of these six families $2.5 billion; smallest PLAN with $295 million and largest World Vision $600 million	Size of the largest member ranges from 20% MSF France to 68% CARE USA	Range of % private resources from 15% at CARE USA to 90% at PLAN

in no network are all members equal to one another. In the past, before global exchanges and information technology, this was not so salient. But global exchanges and information technology shrinks space and distance. With such globalization, however, each network member has felt space and distance shrink, and with this change, its degree of freedom in the choices to be made. Oxfam GB, CARE USA, and Save the Children UK have the relatively strongest voices within their respective families. MSF France carries the greatest weight in the MSF family.

Each family member's financial situation is different—although, as already mentioned, less so among the members of PLAN International or World Vision. Within a given NGO family, some members are more comfortable with government funding while others see it as compromising their independence. Moreover, each government in turn has a different perspective about how independent an NGO can or should be when accepting funds to run programs for the official development program. In addition, the regulatory environment differs from country to country, as does the political culture and tolerance for criticism. (We will return to this issue in Chapter 7, as the implications for NGOs that undertake advocacy campaigns is most interesting.)

Consider, for example, the position of national members of all of these NGO families in the Netherlands in contrast with national members in France or Belgium—or the Netherlands itself—on the issue of government funding. The government of the Netherlands decided early on to have 10 percent of its official development assistance flow through NGOs. Not only is this the highest rate for any official donor, but the country is also one of the most politically liberal environments generally, with strong popular support for development and for NGOs. Hence few NGOs in the Netherlands feel threatened by large amounts of government support. One might thus surmise that MSF Holland might take a different view from MSF France (which takes little public money); or that NOVIB (the Dutch Oxfam) might be even more ready to accept government funding than Oxfam GB. MSF Belgium, one of the oldest members of the MSF family, has also historically accepted a large percentage of public funding—and appears not to have found that money to carry too many strings. MSF France, on the other hand, would like to see members reduce their shares of public funding.

NGOs in the United States, for their part, have found direct mail appeals for funding a more popular, readily understood, and preferable modality than turning to USAID (the U.S. bilateral development assistance agency). As already noted, PLAN International is the most financially independent of this group of six NGO families, with World Vision very close to that position. Both of these child sponsorship organizations rely above all on direct mail appeals for their funding. MSF, by contrast, is going through a great deal of discussion about whether to strengthen its independence by having a network rule of thumb of no more than 15 percent of revenue from government sources.

Many of the within-family differences result from different histories and from the context at the time in which they were founded. For example, many of the national members of Save the Children, one of the older NGOs, were formed in the interwar period; as that was also a time of limited communications technology, individual national members set their own strategies and began their programs with considerable independence from one another. Moreover, there are agencies in numerous countries that use the name Save the Children but are not members of the Save the Children Alliance and do not necessarily honor what the Alliance tries to achieve. There was no International Alliance agreement for the organizational network's first four decades, and these autonomous national members simply carried on. To this day there is more diversity within this NGO family than within any other discussed in this book.

Finally, even though these NGO families all have Northern roots, different perspectives often emerge due to language or other cultural differences. For example, one often hears discussions of differences in perspectives among the U.S., Canadian, and U.K. organizations; or among the continental European ones; or between the French-speaking organizations and those who speak other languages. Such differences often emerge when standards are being set, or in discussions of values within national member organizations' umbrella coordinating groups.

Alternative Approaches to Change

Given these differences, it is inevitable that these relief and development NGOs vary greatly in their approaches to transformation. Some, like Médecins Sans Frontières, with deep roots in French philosophical tradition, are finding their way through intense discussions about fundamental principles and core values and their implications for their future mode of operations. Others seem more comfortable with refining their mission and basic values and are instead much more deeply focused on reorganizing and streamlining systems and structures. This is the case of PLAN International, Save the Children, and World Vision. Still others, like CARE and Oxfam, have engaged in a more comprehensive and ongoing multi-year review and integral transformation of their missions, values, strategies, structures, and systems.

Within these transformations, there is still further variation in the *processes* for mobilizing change. Each organization has made different decisions about whom to involve in discussions, and whether to guide change with the help of outside consultants, or primarily with internal staff. For example, Oxfam GB held major external stakeholder reviews that included donors and different publics in fourteen differ-

Figure 2.1. General Variables in Managing Transformation

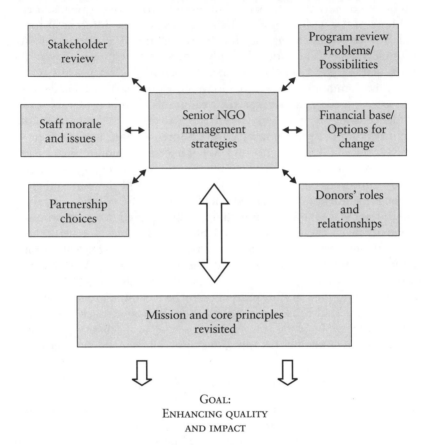

ent countries. Others—including, for example, Oxfam America—are transforming the internal culture and maximizing internal participation by striving to become a "learning organization."[13] In the private, for-profit sector, the response to globalization most frequently has been to undertake mergers. Some corporations, for example, Nokia, have done the reverse: they have developed a specific technical specialization and stripped away less profitable activities that drain strength from the enterprise. Some NGO leaders have speculated in conversation about the possibility of mergers in their future; a few of them have decided to develop a special niche with a commanding lead over others. Figure 2.1 depicts a framework and the continuum of approaches employed by the organizations whose story is the subject of this book.

The role that a national member plays in any NGO family network also affects its choices about the goals of its transformation process.

If a national member is the smallest and least financially secure of all members in a group, its options are clearly different from those of the network's heavyweights. CARE France, for example, is working very hard to build up its financial base, to make more skillful use of the Internet to connect private supporters with projects, and to increase its advocacy work. It does so precisely because it is one of the smaller members and wants to grow in order to increase its prospects within the family. The range of these choices is of course considerable; Figure 2.2 on the following page provides a place to start considering how they interact.

Finally, the role of learning transfer from one organization to another has been great. Such transfer has taken place in two important ways. First it has been accelerated when senior staff move from one of these organizations to another (as they often do). They shape their new approaches based on what worked and what could have worked better in their previous organization. For example, the president and many key staff at Mercy Corps came from Save the Children USA and brought many ideas with them.[14] The Senior Vice President of Strategic Support at World Vision US came from CARE, where he was a part of the strategic planning task force and reorganized the management information systems group. He acknowledges that his approach to reengineering key systems is based on learning and what he believes are improvements on some of CARE's approaches to systems redesign.[15] One of Habitat International's vice presidents got her initial experience in Catholic Relief Services (another of the large Northern relief and development not-for-profits but one not explicitly part of this study) and maintains that she refined her approach to partnerships based on initial experience at CRS. Further important sources of inter-organizational learning have been the workshops and retreats sponsored by InterAction, the U.S.-based umbrella organization for relief and development NGOs, and by the NGO conference at Bellagio and in Seattle.[16]

Despite their differences in approaches to transformation, the relief and development NGOs share the goal of enhancing the quality of their work and making a difference. Quality impacts on the credibility that these organizations can count on when they make a statement, start a program, or enter into any dialogue. The relief and development NGOs share the for-profit private sector's concern with quality because of what it means for brand loyalty and logo protection—but with added normative and emotional content.

Snapshots of the Change Process

CARE and Oxfam GB began their strategic reorientation in the early 1990s, much sooner than the other relief and development NGOs. At Oxfam America, World Vision US, and PLAN International, major

Figure 2.2. Strategic Change Choices from the Perspective of NGO Members in an International Family

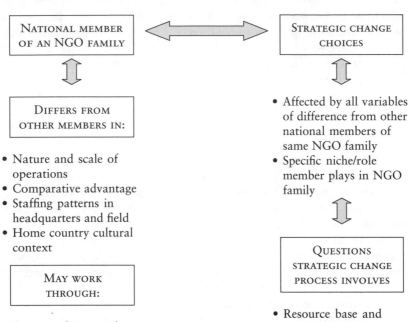

NATIONAL MEMBER OF AN NGO FAMILY

STRATEGIC CHANGE CHOICES

DIFFERS FROM OTHER MEMBERS IN:

- Nature and scale of operations
- Comparative advantage
- Staffing patterns in headquarters and field
- Home country cultural context

MAY WORK THROUGH:

- A regional approach organization
- Widely different partners
- Different sectors

- Affected by all variables of difference from other national members of same NGO family
- Specific niche/role member plays in NGO family

QUESTIONS STRATEGIC CHANGE PROCESS INVOLVES

- Resource base and options to change source of base
- Possibilities for different programming approaches
- Different criteria and indicators for effectiveness
- Different internal decision-making process
- Restructured field-headquarters relationships
- Repositioning member's role in NGO family

transformations coincided with the hiring of new CEOs in the mid- and late 1990s. By the year 2000, all had conducted exercises to redefine their missions and to identify core values but were at different stages in adjusting their systems and structures. Many involved their stakeholders (program recipients, organizational partners, donors, and others) to learn about outside perceptions of their organizational effectiveness. Most used teams of outside consultants and/or internal staff for reengineering efforts.

The change processes in which these organizations have engaged have many similarities, as the following mini "case studies" from four of the six global families help to illustrate.

CARE USA

CARE USA's transformation effort, which began in the early 1990s and spanned almost a decade, led to a redefinition of its mission, programs, global structure, and systems. The process had strong support from CARE's Chief Operating Officer Bill Novelli, President Phillip Johnson, and Board Chair Peter Bell; it accelerated when Bell became CARE's new president in 1995 and has continued into the new millennium.

The physical side of the transformation began in 1993 with a decision to reduce the cost of headquarters operations through relocation from New York City to Atlanta. The conceptual transformation started with workshops about global trends at which outside experts presented new issues in emergency response, development, partnerships, global structures, and financing to a mix of headquarters and field staff from each region. Staff were asked to develop their views on the most important challenges facing CARE and what would need to be done to respond. A "global trends" video was then sent to all thirty-five field offices. Each office held its own workshop and summarized its views. The CARE planning team developed a CARE-wide summary of organizational views and used them as key content in new workshops to revise CARE USA's mission statement. Considerable effort was taken to discuss core values, program directions, and implications for strategy and structure.

At the program level, CARE evolved a new framework for Household Livelihood Security.[17] This approach permitted staff to move beyond fragmented sectoral programs to activities that addressed more comprehensive family and community needs. The framework also stretched CARE's thinking beyond separate relief, rehabilitation, and development programs to more integrated programs to respond to family and community needs along this continuum. The key to the new programming strategy was participative, rapid field assessment of family livelihood strategies and identification of how communities could overcome the main barriers to improving their lives. In addition to program transformation, CARE staff worked with teams of outside consultants on reengineering systems and structures and in decentralizing their operations. The most recent transformation efforts include family-wide strategic planning for CARE International, global reorganization, and a new emphasis on advocacy and economic and social rights.

Oxfam Great Britain

Between 1997 and 1998, Oxfam GB undertook a strategic review. This review involved Oxfam GB's external stakeholders more extensively than the CARE process had involved its own. The Oxfam reviewer commissioned an independent report that was based on interviews with 194 stakeholders in fourteen countries. Stakeholders were chosen from six areas: two types of partner organizations (community-based groups and NGOs), civic actors, national governments, local governments, and international agencies. The countries selected were: Bangladesh, Ethiopia, Eritrea, El Salvador, Kenya, Liberia, Lebanon, Mali, Mexico, the Philippines, Senegal, Uganda, United Kingdom, and Vietnam. The review also included feedback from peer organizations. According to Oxfam staff this peer review sought to elicit the views of "colleagues whose mission like ours is to find lasting solutions to poverty, suffering, and injustice in the world."[18] The peer review included forty in-depth telephone interviews with representatives of British and other European NGOs of varying sizes, members of Oxfam International, government officials, consultants, and two World Bank officials.

The findings of the report were almost as wide-ranging as the interviews themselves. Their recommendations included statements like: "place greater importance on alliances and linkages with other organizations; reflect on the Oxfam-International family; take care not to focus on this effort to the detriment of a leadership role in the UK NGO sector; build stronger links on the ground and advocacy work; make a greater effort with partnerships in the South; pay more attention to gender; clarify values and principles."[19]

With multiple stakeholders in different national political contexts and with varying interests and needs, the challenge is to devise a process that listens to their perspectives, engages them in the dialogue, and results in a well-formulated strategy for change. For example, the review surfaced a real division of opinion about what Oxfam's future advocacy role should be. One group thought that Oxfam should try to influence governments in the South directly, although they thought this should be done jointly with local partners and with Oxfam playing a supporting role. Others felt—especially in Eritrea, Mexico, Lebanon, and the Philippines—that Oxfam should not be engaged in national-level advocacy. Moreover, among the partners interviewed, there was a divergence among those who felt that more was needed to support national-level lobbying and campaigning networks and those who felt that the crucial thing was to retain grassroots links and to strengthen grassroots organizations. Oxfam GB is in the process of thinking through the appropriate changes in programs, systems, and structures. As at CARE, the recent transformation efforts by individual affiliates have been accompanied by an effort to develop a multi-member Oxfam International plan to bring greater coherence and impact to what the Oxfam family does globally.[20]

Oxfam America

There is no single path toward strategic change. National units within all of the NGO families have shaped their approaches to conform to their local context and culture. For example, Oxfam America's transformation process began in 1997 with the naming of a new president, Ray Offenheiser, and continued in two stages. The change process is highly reflective of its small size, funding independence (no U.S. government funds for programs), unionized work force, and location in Boston—the hub of many university-based efforts to support learning organizations.

Stage one did not include a wide-ranging external review like that conducted at Oxfam GB, but a more internally reflective process of discussion with the staff, the board, and the union. The result was a review of alternative, well-vetted strategies put forward by senior-level managers. Critical attention was paid to redefinition of the mission and core values, followed by a focused commitment to four strategic directions: developing excellence in program, excellence in analysis, promoting broader policy advocacy, and building an organizational culture that supports learning. Context figured heavily into the idea of a learning culture that avoided strong labor management confrontation and took advantage of some of the thinking from Boston's Center for Organizational Learning at MIT. According to Offenheiser:

> The decision to go the Learning Org route was made in part because it was seen as compatible with the need for internal change but more importantly from the very beginning because we were asking the question: How must northern NGOs change in response to the changing realities of work with southern partners? We made a decision that key to any future success was going to be our need to operate with multiple currencies. Money would continue to be one but that we now were going to need to give equal value to other currencies like information, networking opportunities, accessing decision-makers and technical support. The learning organization seemed a much more appropriate model to this kind of northern NGO perspective than anything else we had come upon. In truth, I helped bring organizational thinking from Bangladesh where I was experimenting with pieces of it. While we have been inspired by the writing of the Boston organizational development thinkers, we have had little direct support from them. In fact, we utilized a consultant from Goree Institute in Senegal to

help us mainstream the learning organization concepts as he had experience using them as I did in a developing country context.[21]

Stage two of the transformation process was launched in 1999/2000. It provided a more immediate focus on further program coherence, and adapting structures and systems to the new strategy.[22] There was also a new exercise to explore the potential of an advocacy approach using a basic economic and social rights framework to guide Oxfam America's work. In phase two, the senior team recommended moving away from longer-term planning to more dynamic and flexible three-year rolling plans.

One of the results of the transformation is that Oxfam America now has a core staff working on internalizing learning and strengthening approaches to global advocacy. This process entails, among other things, reflection by managers and staff throughout the organization on what is working well, where mistakes have been made, and how to seize the opportunity to learn from that process to devise operational changes. According to Offenheiser, achieving behavioral change and internally owned commitments to a learning process to guide change will help Oxfam America reposition itself for more long-term sustainable improvement.[23]

World Vision US

World Vision began its major organizational transformation efforts later, in 1997. As at CARE, the first major change was the physical relocation of headquarters—from Southern California to Federal Way, Washington, to try to gain cost savings. Also as at CARE, major vision and reengineering work did not move into full swing until a new president, Rich Stearns, joined the organization. Unlike CARE's and Oxfam's presidents, Stearns came from the private sector (Lenox China), where he had witnessed and led reengineering efforts. Stearns's efforts were backstopped by a planning team that included John Reid (who had participated in CARE's transformation earlier and became the chief operating officer at World Vision in 1999).

Like Oxfam America's, the World Vision process was a two-step effort. It began with reconsideration of the mission and values of the organization. Unlike the Oxfams and CARE, however, World Vision US relied more heavily on market research by consultants.[24] Also unlike either the Oxfams or CARE, the effort focused more squarely on reengineering systems, structures, and processes, and less on extensive mission redefinition. The motivation for reengineering was not external financial pressure and competition, but rather the previous experience of the president, board interest in reducing the overhead rate, and an external peer review.

According to Reid, his approach to reengineering was adapted on the basis of learning from what had worked effectively and what had worked less well at CARE.[25] The World Vision approach developed a few highly focused goals, such as bringing down overhead as a percentage of cash from 32 percent to 25 percent, and increasing revenue by $30 million a year over a five-year period. CARE's goals had been more extensive and diffuse.[26] Like CARE, however, World Vision identified key problems and organized working groups that included outside consultants as well as staff. Unlike CARE, which had used multiple consulting groups, World Vision used only one outside consultant, Arthur Andersen, to provide overall project coordination and industry best practice methodology and information. Finally, World Vision completed its planning and implementation over a thirteen-month period. The CARE process was longer and less clearly coordinated.

World Vision's working groups focused on: change management, fundraising portfolio analysis, promoting workforce excellence, improving the fundraising telephone call center, increasing fundraising productivity, reducing donor attrition during child-sponsor replacement, developing a pricing model for child sponsorship efforts, and developing an organization-wide balanced score card. Staff development, too, had become a priority.

Reid noted that the task requirements of World Vision US, whose primary mission is fundraising for the larger family, made systems reengineering more important than it turned out to be at CARE or Oxfam. By October 2000, the overhead rates as a percentage of cash had moved from 32 percent to 29 percent, and income in the first year had increased by $20 million. According to Reid, some of the things that worked less well included: starting the process during other changes related to the CEO transition, having to wait for many new senior-team positions to be filled, and the fact that some of the private-sector reengineering approaches clashed with NGO staff culture. He noted that one of the hardest tasks proved to be conveying, in a faith-based NGO, that:

> Accountability and maximum effectiveness of private donations is not a private sector secular issue. Getting maximum funds available to help people in need ought to be motivated by the same spirit of religious commitment as program delivery.[27]

PLAN International

Like World Vision, PLAN International has transformed itself under a succession of CEOs with international private sector backgrounds (the most recent of whom is John Greensmith who came to PLAN from British Petroleum). The transformation over the past six years has been twofold—both clarifying its programmatic values and approaches through the development of Program Principles and Domain Guidelines, and restructuring its operational country units. Unlike Oxfam, or Save the Children, or MSF, or World Vision, PLAN makes a distinct separation between fundraising and field (within-country) operations. Fundraising is done through fourteen independent National Organizations that direct the funds to the International Headquarters—in Surrey, England—while the field country offices focus on operations. PLAN's senior leadership wanted not only to restructure and regionalize the field operations to increase efficiency, but to introduce a fully professional quality evaluation system that would be deployed consistently across all regions. The heart of this system was to be driven by carefully focused performance indicators serving as the core of the evaluation process.

PLAN has also continued to make changes to its program portfolio. As many child sponsorship organizations have over the years, development programs replaced individual handouts in recognition of the real needs within communities and localities that impact on children. In PLAN's case this process began in the early seventies in Southeast Asia. Each country office since then has become community development driven. The introduction of the Principles and Domains Guidelines has provided PLAN with an overall, organizationally agreed framework with which to ensure programmatic consistency.

Since these programs now represent the bulk of the field activities, the workload has grown considerably. Child sponsorship is demanding to manage. Children and their sponsors expect regular correspondence, the traffic for which goes through the local office. With more than one million sponsored children, this traffic comes with opportunities as well as requiring some management. The opportunities come in providing a sponsor with a firsthand understanding of the particular development challenges faced in the child's environment. Over time a constituency of people not otherwise familiar with the impact of poverty can be reached.

Structurally, however, becoming more of a coherent development organization via the modality of child sponsorship means that more technical specialists are needed, more localized and integrated programming is undertaken, and regional strategies must be set out. Technical specialists have been added to PLAN's staff, almost all of whom are nationals from within the country of operations. Only rarely do they hire expatriates. For example, the country office in Kenya has some three hundred staff, and all except three are local hires. PLAN has also been changing its approach to auditing and monitoring. Monitoring in order to more effectively measure impact has meant getting agreement globally about the indicators to be used. Gathering and using the same data globally is one of the major initiatives currently underway.

The system for doing this is only now being rolled out. It will enable PLAN to monitor globally their programs and their financial situation. But it has not all been plain sailing. There was considerable discussion with country staff to ensure that the local context was properly represented. A data system that combines the need to accurately reflect local realities with the efficiencies of standardized reporting was ultimately achieved. We will return to this issue in Chapter 8 below when discussing accountability.

Progress and Bumps in the Road

Despite differences in their approaches to mobilizing change, the relief and development NGOs have some common perceptions of which areas of change have resulted in the most progress and which have been more difficult.

Mission and Values

Almost all of the senior team members interviewed report that they have held major, successful exercises to formally redefine or at least adjust their organizations' missions and core values to new challenges. These exercises have taken place with the greatest intensity and redefinition at MSF, followed by CARE and Oxfam. At World Vision, Save the Children, and PLAN International, the effort has been more one of fine-tuning.

Before 1990, few of the organizations discussed here paid extensive attention to the highly explicit definition of core values. Today all of the organizations have prepared statements of values and engaged in values-clarification exercises. The discussions of core values and the relation of these values to program strategy and outcomes appear to be most intense and heated at MSF. However, discussions of mission and values have been very important in mobilizing renewed enthusiasm among staff and stakeholders in all organizations. In fact, working on the redefinition of mission and values is perceived to be one of the areas where it has been easier to gain stakeholder involvement and interest as well as organizational transformation. Our informants also report that taking this transformation into the deeper organizational culture and across country offices has proved to be much slower and more difficult.

Relief and Development Programming

In addition to transforming mission statements and defining core values, most of the organizations report that they have reformulated program strategies and priorities in important ways. The approach to emergency response has been redefined and redesigned in the era of intrastate conflict and in response to new ethical, operational, and strategic dilemmas (as Chapter 3 discusses in detail). Greater attention is now given to the interrelated nature of relief, rehabilitation, and development work. Development programs have moved from separate, fragmented, sectoral activities to more comprehensive household- and community-based approaches (see Chapter 4). Many of the organizations have conducted exercises to move resources and staff to countries and regions with greater poverty and to close offices and activities in middle-income countries. Some have introduced benchmarking, quality circles, and best-practice reviews into their efforts at program improvement.[28] More of the organizations are prepared to consider both operational work and advocacy simultaneously (see Chapter 7).

Perhaps the greatest program changes have occurred in the area of emergency response, and in more integral programming. What has proved more difficult is reorienting global portfolios toward areas of greater need. Vested interests among staff committed to particular sectors like health or agriculture have made resource shifts to new sectors or to more integral approaches slower to achieve than initially imagined. Finally, participative approaches to program analysis and redesign based on best practice have proven more lasting than those involving only external evaluators or headquarters staff. For example, one of the many things learned by CARE leadership in this process was just how difficult it is to help staff take a more analytical approach to their work. In the course of negotiating this change, one of the strengths of NGOs—highly value-centered staff—came into conflict with what the external environment required: a look at the implications of competitiveness through a more detached analytical lens. For example, some of the techniques used in the private sector—benchmarking and portfolio analysis—were not easy frameworks to adapt for the nonprofit world.[29] Peter Hall points out in his work on the wider field of nonprofit management that value-centered staff feel very conflicted when asked to assume a more businesslike perspective.[30]

Service and Support Systems

The transformation of mission and programs has often proved to be exciting as well as motivating to NGO staff; transformation of the service and support systems has been slower as well as more difficult. Yet there has been progress and (for better or worse) more progress than in other parts of the nonprofit sector, which we believe may be more shielded from the pressures of globalization. Virtually all of the organizations have made important changes in the use of the most basic forms of new information technology—hardware and software. Most have connected their offices globally through e-mail and the Internet. Most have moved to more standardized software use, although there is considerable variation in the quality of computer hardware around the globe. Most of our informants' organizations are today capable of exchanging electronic files—something unheard of a decade ago. Many staff can file on-line reports with computerized tabulation from remote locations. Most organizations are also moving away from customized financial, personnel, and marketing software to more standardized packages. When asked about the pace of change within different support areas, our informants rank human resources management and marketing operations among the hardest to transform and the most basic management information and financial management as areas where improvements have come more quickly.[31] They cite less progress in moving beyond basic information technology to deeper and more indicator-based performance measures and information systems.

National Boards and Global Family Governance

Looking across the range of changes that an NGO attempting transformation might undertake, one would expect board changes within national boards and global family governance structures to be high on the list. Senior staff emphasize that such changes are important. But it is hard to document extensive changes in national board membership within global family networks in actual practice. All of the senior teams of our six global family networks report intensive discussion and action in restructuring global governance (Chapter 5 explores this topic in detail). One of the major innovations, and a part of the process of "becoming global" in the last several years, has been the establishment of international network offices (for example, the International Save the Children Alliance, Oxfam International, or CARE International) charged with increasing the collaboration among the national offices and providing, in some cases, some services common to all. Each of these international units functions differently; the commonality is their commitment to having the sum of all the country offices' impacts mean more than just the sum of their various parts. They also share a common reality: in general, international units have little power and thus only whatever influence or moral suasion they can bring to bear to achieve coordinated action. Power still resides in national units, and, depending upon the history of the particular NGO, national power varies greatly among the members of the family. This means management by persuasion, innovation, or inspiration if joint work is to be accomplished. In the words of Ernst Ligteringen, executive director of Oxfam International:

> We are small and do not expect ever to be large. We started with five people and expect to be seven next year; in addition there are the four people in Washington who do the international advocacy work. So we have to think carefully about how to work through

existing capacities and in different kinds of ways. So we work in virtual teams—we think of ourselves as a series of concentric circles with responsibility for mapping out what Oxfam would be doing together around four major areas—advocacy; programmatic collaboration; market-outreach; media, information, and communication. A senior staff member assigned to these teams has to be someone who can make decisions on behalf of that function. They stay in touch via email constantly. (But some executive directors don't like email as much as do younger staff—but that's just a generation difference.)[32]

The International Save the Children Alliance is similarly a lean, small staff leveraging synergy among twenty-six Save the Children offices worldwide. They, too, stay in communication with one another via e-mail, with taskforces on specific issues or needs, and occasional CEO-forum phone conferencing. Much of the focus of the international unit has been on helping individual members increase their local fundraising capacity—often by sponsoring major fundraising events that the international office helps make happen, such as the British Telecom–sponsored Around the World Sailing Race.

Partnerships beyond the Family

There is less change under way than one might expect in developing partnerships beyond the particular NGO family (see Chapter 6). The arguments about what kinds of agreements should govern partnerships are many, and, of course, contingent upon the nature of what that partnership is to accomplish. Many partners want to be equal players at the table with reciprocity as the norm. Some Northern partners require, however, that Southern partners become equal players at the table only when they have become financially self-sufficient. Even when they are "equal players" in rhetoric, old habits in partnering relationships seem to have a life of their own in spite of evidence of the need for change. To date, it can only be said that competitiveness, not cooperation, is the norm among the growing numbers of nongovernmental organizations. Calls for cooperation, especially Northern-Southern NGO cooperation, are plentiful but, in practice, full cooperation and felicitous formal agreements between Northern and Southern NGOs are not easy to identify. This is in part due to the growing pressures and identity crises that Southern NGOs are experiencing. They, too, are going through very turbulent times, given the political transitions in most regions of the world.[33] While it is difficult to identify a rich field of productive North-South partnerships there is evidence of innovation in the development of unusual public, private, and nonprofit partnerships (see Chapter 6).

Broad Constraints on Transformation

Although much transformation is under way, that change is not always apparent, especially not from the outside. Turning an ocean liner is not like changing directions in a motorboat. Change is incremental, and even very hard work leverages little movement. That said, it is worth looking in more detail at the nature of the constraints.

Middle Managers

Implementing the iterative negotiations, working through disputes in seemingly endless meetings, and solving the consequent problems of each incremental step grinds down the resolve of many managers, especially those in the middle. In part this is because they have only a partial view of how their work fits into the whole, and far fewer top leadership incentives for driving change, since they have much to gain from collegiality—knowing they will change roles and wear different hats in the future. It is interesting in this regard to consider how one becomes a president in the particular NGO family, and where presidents go after turning over the reins. For remaining at work in the organization in a different role when no longer president carries implications for navigating change while in authority. MSF assemblies of national members elect presidents who often remain within the organization after their terms have expired. Far more frequently, however—for example, at CARE, World Vision, and PLAN International—boards and search committees conduct national and international competitive searches. In those cases, past presidents rarely stay on. In one case (CARE USA) the board president became the organization's president.

Structures of NGO Families

The Northern relief and development NGO families (except for World Vision and PLAN International) largely exist as horizontally grouped networks with little hierarchy that can be used to deploy network-wide restructuring. As we will discuss in Chapters 5 and 6 in greater detail, some networks have moved away from loosely linked confederations to more centralized relationships through a negotiated agreement, only to find that they later back up and move toward more loosely configured relationships. Others are confederations with relative readiness to discuss the features that come with a common logo and issues of enforcement.

In those that are loosely linked, decentralized operations affect the pace and the nature of transformation. There are instances of different national offices within the same Northern NGO family—and not necessarily rogue units—having multiple projects in the same country. Pressures prompting this to happen are greatest in the case of emergency operations. Thus it is all the more noteworthy that the International Save the Children Alliance negotiated an agreement across Alliance members for the coordination of their work in Kosovo—and that the agreement worked.

Although there is concern about duplication by a network within any given country, this is not easy to prevent. Each national member has different partners in countries of operation, and these in turn have different sectoral capacities. Moreover, without a center, it is difficult to enforce (or even negotiate) quality control and coordination, as these must in such a setting rely on interpersonal skills, not organizational authority. International offices are relatively new and work through limited modalities that would not necessarily prevent duplication in field operations. In the case of complex humanitarian emergencies, several different members of the same family do come to undertake refugee relief work. It is all the more worrisome when rogue entities appear claiming to be part of a recognized NGO family.

Given the nature of relief work, there are real pressures for any given national office to be seen and known to be effective. For example, people in New Zealand want to be assured that their money contributed to Oxfam New Zealand is helping in Kosovo. In fact, however, the Dutch Oxfam, NOVIB, along with Oxfam GB, has a greater in-country presence. Oxfam International has worked on this problem, developing videos for use back in country news and media offices (for example, New Zealand) in order to demonstrate what Oxfam is doing in Kosovo without specifying which Oxfam national unit is on location in that country. This is fair enough, for contributors also want to know that scarce resources are not being wasted through duplication. But all too often international offices do not have the capacity, technical resources, mandate, or clout to undertake even that level of coordination.

The private sector refers to these problems as brand and logo control issues; the analogy, then, is to private for-profit franchising. But the analogy is of limited utility, given the way that national units of Northern NGOs evolved; it often does not have the same legal clout as franchises do. Moreover, while there are wide variations in control over national units, such control is not as complete as is the case with licensed or franchised operations. Some national units, such as NOVIB in Holland, may well have developed their own processes, projects, and stakeholders and then later joined the Oxfam family—keeping their own name, like NOVIB. In many cases, the name of the national member was registered nationally, not licensed from a network. While lawsuits can be brought to enforce network standards (MSF has been through one of these with a previous national member in Greece, and the Greek courts ruled in MSF France's favor), there is not nearly the body of case law that exists in the private sector to back enforceability.

Donor Pressures

While support for Northern NGOs has been growing, largely from individual donors, public support for official development assistance has been declining, particularly in the United States. These budget cuts invariably have led to staff cuts in the bilateral agency. With each reduction in staff, the pressure to contract the implementation of projects and programs to NGOs increased. NGOs, in turn, were in some instances glad to be repositioned in order to enhance their access to resources. But there is a serious "downside" for NGOs in that situation; they are at risk of being used much like a consulting organization that provides services for a fee without much influence over the policy directions or objectives. Over time, they can be pulled away from their own missions and experience undermined credibility for their claim to be close to the grassroots. When accepting large contracts for relief work, there can be greater fallout. For example, toward the end of the Rwanda War, when NGO mistakes confounded their own staff and leaders as much as it did public opinion, NGOs came under heavy public and academic criticism.[34]

Unpredictable External Environment

There are few ways for NGOs to anticipate the changing nature of the international context for their work or fundraising. Their limited resources for research must, rightly, be devoted to other areas. They cannot avoid being driven in large part by international turbulence. Few international economists predicted the Asian financial crisis of the mid-1990s; little is known as yet of when or even whether Russia's faltering economy and fragile political balance will lead to more problems. Given its strategic geopolitical position, how the European Union (EU) will thrive in the years to come remains uncertain. Since so many more of the national members of these NGO networks are European-based, changes in the EU will matter more than is commonly acknowledged by the U.S. public. The downside of the increased international interdependence is precisely that economic crises in one place have far-flung consequences for others—often even those at great distances.

Staff Motivation and Organizational Culture

Many of the scholar-practitioners writing about managing strategic change are most preoccupied with behavioral constraints. Motivation and mindsets immediately affect how well or fast staff or line managers adapt to change. Organizational cultures are real—especially in highly normative organizations such as NGOs. Not surprisingly, staff surveys in the 1990s reflected serious morale problems, especially U.S.-based NGOs; there was then a climate of criticism of development and no sign of any sources for increasing support, or for finding more constituencies. Moreover, NGO staff could see the changes brought about by globalization and the decline in state capacity; they also knew that the skill mix—including their own skill mix—had to be reconfigured. Thus both external and internal drivers met and caused pain for staff motivation.

NGO staff derive psychological rewards from their work and from their belief that they are trying to make a difference. This has certain implications for leaders endeavoring to transform organizations. One of the most important barriers to change in NGOs is the strong individualistic and independent style of staff. "It's like trying to herd cats," say some key informants. Moreover, managers must be cautious about references to standard incentives, like salaries. The value system around their independence means that salaries as an issue function differently than in the private sector, nor are they excited about business school training in management. For example, people join CARE because they want to make the world a better place. If they had wanted to earn significant income, they would not have joined an NGO. Their motivation is grounded in a sense of urgency about global problems and a desire to help.[35] Staff therefore resisted borrowing management concepts from the private for-profit sector. For them, paying attention to competitiveness was antithetical to their core principles. The distinctiveness of this sector is frequently reasserted. Only when private-sector managerial techniques were customized for use in a differently motivated sector did they become useful.

Some of the greatest tensions have been around reengineering and downsizing efforts driven by cost control in a more competitive environment. Many of the organizations have attempted to reduce health benefits and have asked their staffs to pay more of their share. Some organizations have carried out early retirement programs, as well as actual downsizing after reorganization. These efforts have been painful for staff, some of whom saw employment and benefits as an entitlement for their dangerous work with low pay compared to the private and even the public sector. Senior managers have found themselves buffeted between the recommendations of reengineering consultants with largely private-sector experience and some of the values of compassion for staff that are embedded in NGO culture.

Ethnology and Beyond

What leaders and staff are saying about their transformation processes is hard to empirically verify if one wants to meet the standards of current social science research. Our major informants are the members of the senior management teams; we clearly do not have the views of those working in the countries where all of these NGOs have major programs. As these NGOs cumulatively work in a total of over 120 countries, that research scale was well beyond our means. Furthermore, these are private organizations that are not subject to rules of transparency—especially not in regard to their strategic change processes. Moreover, even when, as was often the case, staff were very candid and forthcoming, there was little way to ascertain the costs and benefits of an internal change process.

Despite these limitations, there is empirical evidence that an important transformation process is taking place. Within each of the NGO families studied here, one can find and read new mission statements and declarations of values. These declarations are in fact different from those of a decade and even a half-decade ago. Record reviews reveal that program design and portfolios in many of these organizations indeed reflect the new conceptions. For example, a review of the country-level strategic plans and program portfolios of CARE USA clearly reflect a change to household livelihood security programming between 1994 and 1997. CARE program evaluations provide empirical evidence that most sectoral portfolios had a higher proportion of programs closer to "best practice" in 1997 than 1994–96.[36] It is a fact that all six of the NGO families now use e-mail and have offices with faster global communications than a decade ago. They all have Web pages that receive thousands of "hits" every day and are moving away from customized financial software to more standard packages.

It is harder to document the assertions that change has been slower in the areas of human resources and development than finance and management information systems. Comparing lists of board members today with those of a decade ago confirms the perception that substantial multinationalization of boards has not yet taken place. There is evidence that new global structures have been created, at least on a formal basis. One can visit new offices of CARE, Oxfam, and PLAN International that did not exist before and talk to new directors of Oxfam and Save International about their aspirations and problems.

But it is beyond the scope of methods used in this study to really verify how deep and far-reaching the changes have been within each of the organizations and at the staff level. What was observable, and striking in its effect, was the energy and commitment that all the staff who were interviewed displayed about the various change processes. As noted, it is known that there had been morale problems in several large NGOs in the 1990s. That the staff we interviewed were highly motivated and apparently candid about the changes was impressive. Their real efforts to implement changes through meetings and endless negotiations in the field spoke volumes. It was also inspiring. In some instances, we noted that staff are perhaps more excited by the changes than some senior leaders.

It is our sense that many of the organizations are involved in serious transformation. An interesting issue is whether the changes they are making will be enough to keep them at the cutting edge. For example, there is ample evidence that the transformations have been accompanied by the growth of their budgets and resources. In spite of critics' dire predictions about impending obsolescence, NGOs are much more financially solvent than before. However, it is not yet clear that they have become more flexible and adaptable as opposed to simply big. Nor have they made themselves more accountable by opening their boards and governance structures to people from the countries and communities they serve.

In spite of continuing questions about whether their change process is comprehensive, they continue to inspire the world community. This can be seen by the Nobel prizes awarded in 1999 to MSF and in 1998 to the international campaign to ban landmines (in which many of the organizations studied here participated). Additionally, the Hilton International Prize was awarded in 1977 to the International Rescue Committee (an organization similar to those whose story appears here) for its work with refugees and internally displaced people.

Motivations Not Explicitly Discussed

What would motivate leaders and senior teams to embark on large-scale organizational transformation? This is a particularly difficult question to address. Achieving strategic change requires drawing upon some of the most deeply held and compelling motivations. In most cases, our informants reported that these transformations were necessary to maintain relevance in a changing world. Outsiders might argue that the senior teams had no choice but to transform their organizations and to streamline and cut costs in the wake of increased competitive pressure for funding. Yet transformation efforts are taking place in World Vision and PLAN International—the two NGOs in our study least subject to the very fiercest competitive pressure. These two organizations are in fact the least financially dependent on governments and have the strongest private fundraising efforts. Perhaps their presidents, who come from the private sector, believe that "doing good can be done even better" even in the absence of the stronger external drivers the other organizations face.

We cannot claim to know the motivations not discussed. Hazarding guesses, it is apparent that specific NGO leaders' backgrounds—where they are in the life cycle, their previous careers, and their religious as well as secular humanist traditions—reveal some patterns. But these are not the only factors affecting their steerage of strategic change. Thus this response must perforce be speculative. It is likely that all are, in different ways, concerned about what tracks their leadership will leave in their organizations, and how their work is and will be interpreted by their peers, their major (especially deeply valued) stakeholders, and their staff. They wonder, and sometimes worry, about how some actions, decisions, and choices will be read in the future. That said, some enjoy policy leadership and their advocacy work more than others. Some are more concerned with professionalizing their organizations—with achieving special efficiency in a sector where that is particularly daunting to measure. Still others take pride in improving the financial security of their organization through prowess in fundraising—especially where financial insecurity had been an issue for their predecessor.

Further Details

A number of areas on which our informants did not comment in detail due to limitations of time could easily be areas of additional interest. For example, why is the globalization of national boards moving at a slower pace than other changes? Or are multi-sectoral partnerships developing more quickly than North-South partnerships? It is worth at least speculating about some of the reasons for the slow pace of change in internationalizing national board membership. (We devote all of Chapter 6 to the issue of emerging partnerships.)

One might initially be surprised that internationalizing board membership did not seem to be happening. But each contextual story carries some of the explanation of this situation. First, NGOs vary significantly in what they want from their boards. Some chief executive officers are in close communication with boards, drawing upon them for input and advice as often as once a week. They have not yet capitalized on new communications technologies well enough to permit frequent globally connected board discussion. Thus, it may be easier to find board members around the corner. Others find boards more useful for drawing in further legitimacy for their work in their country of residence. It is possible that local board members simply have more name recognition.

Some NGOs are more careful than others to ensure that the personal characteristics of board members convey their commitment to diversity. This is often achieved by simply including people from other countries who have become naturalized citizens of the country where the NGO headquarters is located. This is distinguishable from a purposeful search for board members among partners—or among leaders in the countries where there are large programs. This latter strategy is not yet high on the agenda. Board development, however, is getting attention. More use is being made of organizations such as the National Center for Non Profit Boards, based in Washington, in order to deepen and strengthen board capacity.

Boards vary in their roles and contributions, echoing the diversity we have already seen among the NGOs themselves. Many NGOs have held their boards at arm's length, or used them less intensively than, for example, secondary schools or hospitals in the domestic nonprofit sector. This may change, however, given the increased needs of NGOs. Expectations about what an institution needs from its board vary. Oxfam GB, for example, decided that it wanted a smaller but more active board. They hoped that smaller size would result in more board member engagement in critical Oxfam issues. In general, however, there appears to be a view that at this time, with other changes underway, board stability is more needed than board change. There is a complex interplay of issues for chief executive officers and their senior staff surrounding what their organization needs, and gets, from boards.

MSF's boards are different from those of most other NGO families, as MSF national members often draw in senior staff from fellow MSF national members to serve on their board. For example, the senior finance officer of MSF France serves on the board of MSF US. Queried about this process, MSF leaders said that they found it easier to achieve more collaboration by embodying that collaboration through board appointments. Some might wonder whether such multiple roles do not create some conflicts of interest. It is interesting that for MSF this does not seem to be an issue. Rather, it is taken to mean that a wide-ranging cadre of senior staff know more about other national members' work, and therefore have a great sense of the whole of the movement and its many working parts.

Given the subtlety of the interests and stakes around this interplay of issues, it is most likely that board changes come about only when the senior leadership of an NGO become more focused on what they need and want from their board. As noted, Oxfam GB concluded that the board should be smaller and more actively engaged in assisting Oxfam with hard choices. Therefore it was also decided that Oxfam GB would continue to draw its board members from residents of the United Kingdom—since that would ease the costs of more frequent meetings for all board members. In the past, board membership was more likely to hint at representativeness—at having some members come from some of the countries in which Oxfam was working. But that meant less frequent meetings and less engagement.

Emerging Trends

The pace of change is quickening in these NGOs. They are both learning more and doing more. Some of them are now also beginning to be more adept at learning from one another; this outcome was strengthened at our NGO conference, where leaders have been able to come together to share their reflections on their experience.

There is every indication that the larger Northern NGOs will continue to grow, although perhaps more slowly than they did in the 1990s. There is an even higher probability of mergers, new alliances with smaller NGOs, multi-sectoral partnerships, and more truly *global* actions—reflecting not North-South in the old sense, but creating networks and alliances from the North, East, South, and West, perhaps working not only vertically but also horizontally.

It is plausible that the division of labor among global network members will change dramatically. For example, Northern organizations may have a special role to play in advocacy in Northern power centers, perhaps because of their proximity to these centers of decision-making as well as their special understanding of the context. It is fashionable to say that Northern organizations will have less of a role to play in service delivery in the developing world. A more probable statement might be that national organizations in every country have a special comparative advantage in program delivery in their own country compared to outsiders—due to their unique understanding of the context. However, much of the Northern NGOs' credibility in advocacy and fundraising within their own countries is based on the credibility that their operational field presence provides; they are perceived by donors and the public to speak on the basis of real field experience. So the exact nature of the comparative advantage of different network members is not yet clear.

It is undeniable that the technological revolution of the past decade has had an impact on every international NGO studied in this book. This impact looks more extensive than in many national NGOs. But its full implications are only beginning to be explored in the global relief and development community. For example, how successful can global Internet-based fundraising become? What methods might be most effective? Could global advocacy be made more effective through the use of Internet-based campaigns? How might new technology be harnessed to make global emergency response efforts more successful? We are only beginning to see Internet-based efforts to speed up procurement of emergency supplies, register refugees and issue identity cards quickly as they come across borders, and put pictures of lost family members on the Internet for other refugees to see. What else might be possible?

Nor do we understand the implications of new technology for NGO global organizational structure. All kinds of principal-agent problems change when field and headquarters can reach one another via the Internet and cell phones. Given the remoteness of the locations in which these groups work, it is difficult to overestimate what this change will mean for the shifts in authority within organizations. Field independence could diminish; information overload could increase at headquarters. Board strengthening—getting little attention now—could become increasingly salient. Boards are intrinsically conservators; it seems to come with concepts of trusteeship. But they will also need to become better at helping guide strategic change processes.

Notes

1. Oxfam US Program Team, *The Oxfam America Plan 2001–2005*. The phrase is a more authentic version of the proverb, "A thousand mile journey begins with one step."

2. Oxfam US Program Team, *The Oxfam America Plan 2001–2005*, 1.

3. Michael Edwards and David Hulme, *Beyond the Magic Bullet: NGO Performance and Accountability in the Post–Cold War World* (West Hartford, Conn.: Kumarian Press, 1998).

4. Edgar Schein, *Organizational Culture and Leadership* (San Francisco: Jossey-Bass, 1985). For the best discussion of transaction costs see Douglass North, *Institutions, Institutional Change and Economic Performance* (Cambridge: Cambridge University Press, 1990).

5. Steve Commins of World Vision US, paper presented September 1998, Bellagio, Italy.

6. David Bryer and John McGrath, "New Dimensions of Global Advocacy," *Nonprofit and Voluntary Sector Quarterly* 29, no. 1 (Supplement 2000): 168–77.

7. Sharon M. Oster, *Strategic Management for Nonprofit Organizations: Theory and Cases* (Oxford: Oxford University Press, 1995).

8. *Managing Organisational Change*, ed. Somnath Chattopadhyay and Udai Pareek (New Delhi: Oxford University Press and IBH, 1982).

9. *World in Crisis: The Politics of Survival at the End of the Twentieth Century*, ed. Julia Groenewold and Eve Porter (London and New York: Routledge Press, 1999).

10. Rony Brauman, Foreword, in *The World in Crisis*, ed. Groenewold and Porter (London: Routledge Press, 1999).

11. Ian Smillie and Henny Helmich, *Stakeholders: Government-NGO Partnerships for International Development* (London: OECD and Earthscan Publications Ltd, 1999).

12. Smillie and Helmich, *Stakeholders*.

13. Peter Senge et al., *The Fifth Discipline Fieldbook: Strategies and Tools for Building a Learning Organization* (New York: Doubleday, 1994). This book builds upon the conceptually rich book *The Fifth Discipline: The Art and Practice of the Learning Organization* (New York: Doubleday, 1990), conveying the field experience of the team reflected in its authorship. Peter Senge is director of the Center for Organizational Learning at MIT's Sloan School of Management.

14. Neal Keny-Guyer, president of Mercy Corps, interview by Marc Lindenberg, June 2000, Seattle, Wash.

15. John Reid, Senior Vice President of Strategic Support, World Vision US, interview by Marc Lindenberg, October 2000, Seattle, Wash.

16. Following the NGO Leaders Conference in Bellagio, there was a second NGO Leaders Conference in Seattle, Washington, May 6–8, 2000. The Third NGO Leaders Conference took place at Balliol College, Oxford, July 1–4, 2001. It was sponsored by the Daniel J. Evans School of Public Affairs at the University of Washington with the assistance of the Economic and Political Development Program, School of International and Public Affairs, Columbia University, and supported by, among others, the Bill and Melinda Gates Foundation.

17. See Tim Frankenberger, "Measuring Household Livelihood Security: An Approach for Reducing Absolute Poverty" (paper prepared for the Applied Anthropology Meetings, Baltimore, March 1996). See also the following documents, "CARE Kenya: Rapid Food and Livelihood Security Assessment," working paper, CARE USA, Atlanta, Ga., 1996; "Food Security Policy and Guidelines," working paper, CARE International, Atlanta, Ga., 1995; and "Preparing for a Rapid Livelihood Security Assessment (RSLA) Guidelines and Checklist," working paper, CARE East Africa Region, Atlanta, Ga., 1996. For a broader look at the relevance of using a focus on assets when undertaking poverty work, see Carolyn Moser, "The Asset Vulnerability Framework: Reassessing Urban Poverty Reduction Strategies," *World Development* 26, no. 1 (January 1998): 1–19. Note also that there is increasing discussion in the newer approaches to political economy of reopening the discussion of increasing access to assets as a major part of poverty reduction. See DeJanvry, Sadoulet, and Thorbecke, "State, Market, and Civil Organizations: New Theories, New Practices, and Their Implications for Rural Development," Special Section, *World Development* (April 1993): 565–66.

18. This was the mandate that David Bryer, executive director of Oxfam GB, gave to those charged with undertaking the peer review as part of the larger strategic review.

19. Chris Roche and Christy Cannon Lorgen, "NGOs in an Interdependent World: The Case of Oxfam," paper presented at the Conference, *NGOs in a Global Future,* January 10–13, 1999, University of Birmingham, England, 2.

20. Ernst Ligteringen, executive director, Oxfam International, interviewed by Coralie Bryant and Christina Kappaz, March 30, 2000, Oxford, England.

21. Harvard Business School, *Oxfam America,* January 1998, no. 9-798-036 reviews the options put to the board.

22. Oxfam America Program Team, *The Oxfam America Plan 2001–2005* (Boston: Oxfam, 2000).

23. Ray Offenheiser, president of Oxfam America, interviewed by Marc Lindenberg, June 1999, Boston, Mass.

24. John Reid, Senior Vice President of Strategic Support of World Vision US, interviewed by Marc Lindenberg, October 2000, Seattle, Wash.

25. John Reid, Senior Vice President of Strategic Support of World Vision US, interviewed by Marc Lindenberg, October 2000, Seattle, Wash.

26. P. Bell, "Memo to the Board of Directors on Decision to Date on Structural Review," paper presented to Board of Directors, CARE USA, Atlanta, Ga., June 1996. See also P. Bell, "Structural Review Decisions for Program and Marketing Divisions" (Atlanta, Ga.: CARE, June 14, 1996).

27. John Reid, Senior Vice President of Strategic Support of World Vision US, interviewed by Marc Lindenberg, October 2000, Seattle, Wash.

28. See Marc Lindenberg, "Are We at the Cutting Edge, the Blunt Edge, or the Wrong Edge?" *Nonprofit Leadership and Management* 11, no. 3 (March 2001).

29. Christine Letts and William P. Ryan, *Managing Upstream: The Challenge of Creating High Performing Organizations in the Nonprofit Sector* (New York: John Wiley and Sons: 1998), chs. 1 and 5.

30. Peter Dobkin Hall, *Inventing the Nonprofit Sector* (Baltimore: Johns Hopkins University Press, 1992).

31. See Lindenberg, "Are We at the Cutting Edge?"

32. Ernst Ligteringen, executive director, Oxfam International, interview by Coralie Bryant, June 18, 1999.

33. See Anthony Bebbington, "Mediators of Sustainability/Intermediaries in Transition?" in *Mediating Sustainability,* ed. Jutta Blauert and Simon Zadek (West Hartford, Conn.: Kumarian Press, 1998), 55–74.

34. Peter Uvin, *Aiding Violence: The Development Enterprise in Rwanda* (West Hartford, Conn.: Kumarian Press, 1998), and Michael Bryans, Bruce D. Jones, and Janice Gross Stein, "Mean Times: Humanitarian Action in Complex Political Emergencies—Stark Choices, Cruel Dilemmas: Report of the NGOs in Complex Emergencies Project, Program on Conflict Management and Negotiation, Coming to Terms," vol. 1, no. 3 (Toronto: Centre for International Studies, University of Toronto, January 1999).

35. See Lindenberg, "Are We at the Cutting Edge?" See also Christine Letts, William P. Ryan, and Allen Grossman, *High Performance Nonprofit Organization* (New York: Wiley, 1999). See chapters 1 and 5; this point was also echoed in an interview with John Greensmith, international executive director, PLAN International, interview by Coralie Bryant, May 1999, Seattle, Wash.

36. Tim Frankenberger on the impact of HHLS in country programming at CARE, phone interview by Marc Lindenberg, March 2000.

NGOs, Complex Emergencies, and Humanitarian Action

Humanitarianism is not a tool to end war or to create peace. It is a citizens' response to political failure. It is an immediate, short-term act that cannot erase the long-term necessity of political responsibility.

And ours is an ethic of refusal. It will not allow any moral political failure or injustice to be sanitized or cleansed of its meaning. The 1992 crimes against humanity in Bosnia-Herzegovina. The 1994 genocide in Rwanda. The 1997 massacres in Zaire. The 1999 indiscriminate attacks on civilians in Chechnya. These cannot be masked by terms like "Complex Humanitarian Emergency" or "Internal Security Crisis." Or by any other such euphemism— as though they are some random, politically undetermined event. Language is determinant. It frames the problem and defines response. It defines too rights, and therefore responsibilities. It defines whether a medical or humanitarian response is adequate. And it defines whether a political response is inadequate. No one calls a rape a complex gynecologic emergency. A rape is a rape, just as a genocide is genocide. And both are a crime. For MSF, this is the humanitarian act: to seek to relieve suffering, to seek to restore autonomy, to witness to the truth of injustice, and to insist on political responsibility.

— James Orbinski, President, MSF International
Nobel Peace Prize Acceptance Speech, 2000

M OST OF THE NORTHERN NGOs featured in this book were founded in response to the horrors of war and famine between World War I and the Korean War. They captured the world's imagination as they sent, for example, CARE packages to hungry families in post–World War II Europe and Japan. During most of the second half of the twentieth century, warring nations viewed humanitarian agencies like the International Committee of the Red Cross as respected neutral parties that aided civilians and refugees.

As we enter the new millennium, these organizations must respond creatively to disasters that accompany and follow the new kinds of wars. In recent years, the complex man-made emergencies more frequently have been civil wars catalyzed by internal ethnic or religious strife than by conflicts between nations. During such civil wars, the NGOs are compelled to aid increasing numbers of internally displaced people who fear for their lives because they fall outside the international system's post–World War II mandate to protect refugees—that is, those who cross a border to escape conflict or persecution. In today's world, however, neither relief organizations nor civilians are safe from belligerents. In the Kosovo crisis, for example, there were in fact few military casualties; the majority of those who died were civilians.

In the past decade, the treatment of refugees has changed as well. Refugees frequently become pawns in the hands of warring factions. It is increasingly difficult to separate civilians from insurgents. Women and children more frequently become victims of intimidation. Rebel armies extort food from civilians and use them as "human shields." Open access to refugees must now be fought for rather than guaranteed. NGO workers are called upon to provide medicines, food, and safe drinking water where no nation will send its troops. Moreover, new types of military actions, ironically labeled "humanitarian interventions," have blurred the roles of soldiers and humanitarian workers.

The new complex emergencies have forced a radical rethinking of NGO and world community responses. This chapter sketches what our informants believe are the external challenges presented by these new kinds of emergencies and outlines how NGOs have begun to respond to the operational, structural, ethical, and system-wide dilemmas.

The New World of Complex Emergencies

Our informants believe that in the past decade, the number of internal armed conflicts around the globe has increased dramatically. They believe that these conflicts have their roots in scarcity, as well as in ethnic, religious, and cultural differences. They cite evidence that in 1997 alone, forty incidents sometimes spoken of as "complex emergencies" resulted in more than 13 million refugees fleeing to other countries and 20 million people internally displaced within the borders of their own countries.[1] Literally one person in every 133 was in flight. In 1997, more than 68,000 civilians died in such conflicts, many were wounded, others went hungry, and in refugee camps had little access to education for their children or to health services. In addition, the four hundred natural disasters reported in 1998 resulted in 90,000 deaths, 5 million temporarily displaced persons, and more than 144 million people affected.[2] In 1998, the governmental donor community spent more than

Figure 3.1. Worldwide Humanitarian Response in 1998
Rough Estimate of Global Humanitarian Aid ($)

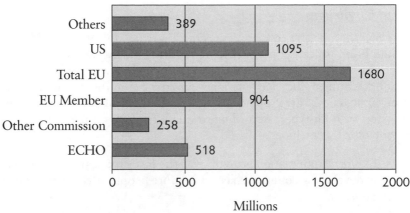

Millions

Source: Adapted from *European Community Humanitarian Office Annual Review* (Brussels, 1998), 29.

$3 billion responding to the immediate effects of natural disasters and man-made emergencies (see Figure 3.1).

Both natural disasters and man-made crises cause not only immediate human suffering but also damage to property and infrastructure. For example, the International Federation of Red Cross and Red Crescent Societies (IFRC) estimated that property damage from natural disasters in 1998 amounted to more than $70 billion.[3] In the case of conflict-related disasters, the social fabric is weakened as trust in societies breaks down. The Kosovo War in 1999 resulted in more than a million refugees and a global geopolitical problem that created new tensions between Russia, NATO, and the People's Republic of China. The costs of this war have been estimated at $15 billion. The relief effort has cost more than $1 billion. The cost of postwar reconstruction in the Balkans as a result of this crisis is yet to be estimated.

Against this backdrop of human tragedy, our NGO leader informants emphasized the persistence of two very difficult problems. First, there continues to be a critical need to help refugees and internally displaced people stay alive and protected in times of conflict. The global players in this process often function like uncoordinated volunteer fire departments; responses are inadequate in terms of speed and efficiency as well as quality. Second, there is little systematic effort to redress the causes of such conflicts or to develop early-warning mechanisms that would make emergency response less necessary. With respect to natural disasters, there is as yet no systematic effort to examine how global ecological damage, such as massive deforestation, has contributed to the severity of recent natural disasters like floods.

New Challenges

The past decade, when many expected that the end of the Cold War would bring peace, served to heighten worldwide awareness of the impact of both natural disasters and the calamitous new types of conflicts that have broken out. The outcomes experienced in the past may, however, appear less catastrophic than those brought about by the recent disasters of both types. According to our informants some of the main reasons for this include:

- Explosive population growth over the last fifty years, particularly in developing countries, has led to more people affected in any one disaster.

- The collapse of the Soviet Union and the end of the Cold War have produced a wave of new complex emergencies marked by intrastate ethnic conflict in places like Bosnia, Chechnya, Kosovo.

- The media plays a powerful role in "bringing such disasters into people's living rooms around the world."

- These complex emergencies have produced large numbers of internally displaced people, who now outnumber the refugees who have fled across borders.

- The current international response system developed at the end of World War II is ill-equipped to respond to the needs of internally displaced people and these new complex emergencies.

- Ecosystems have become fragile, magnifying the impact of disasters as refugees cut down trees for firewood and compete with local communities for food, water, and basic services.

- While in some countries governments are quite unwilling to allow international humanitarian response, in others the state has collapsed partially or completely and global humanitarian response has been summoned to fill the vacuum.

- Finally, a new doctrine called "responsible sovereignty," developed under the auspices of the UN Secretary-General, has not yet provided a context for international response where states are able or willing to protect civilians, refugees, and internally displaced people in conflicts such as that in Kosovo. Furthermore, the full implications of global application of such a doctrine are not fully understood.

Figure 3.2. Complex Emergencies Challenge Traditional Roles

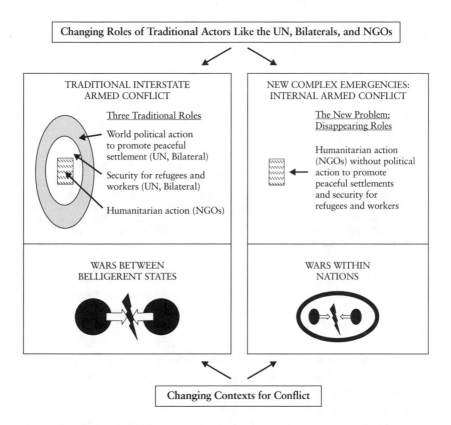

Man-Made Crises

The new, largely internal, armed conflicts have changed the world of humanitarian response in which NGOs work. Figure 3.2 highlights the critical differences between the world of traditional international armed conflict and the new reality of complex emergencies.

As Figure 3.2 shows, the traditional international humanitarian response system to man-made disasters was based on a model of struggles for territory between two belligerent sovereign states. Within this conflict context, three major roles were played. First, at the level of world political action, either the United Nations or specific nation-states attempted to bring warring parties to the bargaining table to end such conflicts. Second, security for refugees and humanitarian actors like the International Committee of the Red Cross (ICRC) was provided under specific UN protocols, or negotiated so that refugees' needs could be met, prisoners of war could be visited, and services provided. The belligerents themselves often provided the guarantees of safe access. Fi-

Figure 3.3. Comparative Forced Displacement: IDP and Refugees, 1965–99

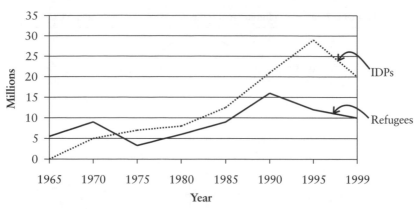

Source: Global IDP Survey and Norwegian Refugee Council, *Internally Displaced People: A Global Survey* (London: Earthscan, 1998), 28.

nally, UN organizations like the UN High Commissioner for Refugees (UNHCR), or the NGOs, supervised or provided direct humanitarian action through the delivery of food, medical services, water, sanitation, and refugee relocation.

The post–Cold War world of heightened intrastate ethnic, religious, and political conflict provides a radically different context for conflict and for humanitarian action. This context is not adequately addressed in the existing international protocols that govern humanitarian response during conflict between nations. For example, in the world of totally failed states such as Somalia in 1993, more than five clan factions and militias replaced the world of stable belligerent states in conflict. Thus, all humanitarian actors had to negotiate with a bewildering number of coalitions whose territory shifted rapidly. Existing protocols also provide few guarantees for internally displaced people who are often the major civilians at risk during conflicts within nations and whose numbers have increased dramatically (see Figure 3.3).[4] Furthermore, in the world of collapsed states and multi-faction armed struggles, the new leaders and soldiers often know little of international law or have little incentive to cooperate with humanitarian actors. In addition, as the number of child soldiers (for example, in Liberia, Somalia, Rwanda, the Democratic Republic of the Congo, and Sudan) has greatly increased, problems of discipline have soared dramatically. Finally, in many parts of the world, regularly established armies have not honored the rights of refugees, civilians, and internally displaced people.

In addition, the post–Cold War politics hindered the nature of response by the international community in the 1990s. The United

Nations, the international community, and individual nations like the United States or France have been less willing to undertake diplomatic action to bring belligerents to the bargaining table in Africa. The result has been poorly defined roles for "peacekeeping" forces that have been extremely hard to implement. It has been increasingly difficult to get the UN or other actors to guarantee security for refugees or aid workers. Troops were assigned in Bosnia and Somalia to provide safe corridors, but this was the exception rather than the rule.

As a result, in the new world of complex emergencies, humanitarian action by the NGOs and ICRC has been provided without adequate security and without world pressure to bring belligerents to the bargaining table to get them to accept international human rights protocols, anti-genocide protocols, or normal guarantees to refugees and innocent civilians. In conclusion, many in the NGO community believe that humanitarian action has been used as a less expensive substitute for long-term international action to deal with causes of conflicts and to bring warring parties to the bargaining table.

Natural Disasters

Since the early 1980s, the population affected by natural disasters—drought, famine, floods, hurricanes, earthquakes, blizzards, tornadoes, volcanic eruptions, and forest fires—was an average of 144 million a year.[5] Of the 90,000 fatalities worldwide the largest number were caused by drought and famine, with earthquakes and floods ranking next. Asia and the Pacific is by far the hardest hit region, with 64 percent of the total number of people affected, followed by Africa at 31 percent.

The Global Relief System

The Actors

The global humanitarian and natural disaster organizational network forms a complicated web. Each actor participates in complex overlapping roles, making the system difficult to map. The actors can be clustered in four groups: resource suppliers, coordinating organizations, operational response agencies, and the media, advocates, and peace builders.

Resource Suppliers

In 1998 more than $3 billion came from a tiny group of public donors, notably the European Union, individual European countries, Japan, and the United States. In addition, many individual, private foundation, and corporate donors provide another $500 million in times of crisis. The process of resource mobilization is critical to making emergency response possible.

Coordinating Organizations

Headquarters and field coordination is performed by UN agencies, national governments, and the NGOs themselves. Within NGO confederations, governing bodies try to coordinate. Within the NGO community itself coordinating bodies like the International Council of Voluntary Agencies (ICVA) and the Steering Committee on Humanitarian Response (SCHR) attempt to set response standards and coordinate overall efforts. Such coordination is necessary to help match refugee needs with staff, supplies, and financial resources.

Operational Response Agencies

Roughly twenty international nonprofit organizations like the Red Cross, MSF, CARE, the International Rescue Committee, World Vision, Oxfam, Save the Children, as well as national governments provide most of the "on the ground" operational services. Depending upon the situation, international and national military forces provide not only security but also food, emergency medical services, water, and shelter.

Media, Advocates, and Peace Builders

In addition, the media, advocacy groups that favor a particular side in a conflict, as well as peace and conflict resolution institutes play an active role in how emergency response is carried out. Given global communications technology, the media often dramatize conflicts and bring them into living rooms around the world. Sometimes their coverage is so important to conflict visibility that conflicts are highlighted or forgotten depending on the level of media attention they get. Advocacy groups also dramatize the issues by bringing media attention to bear on problems—getting legislative and citizens' groups to take positions or mobilize resources. Finally, institutes like the Carter Center or the Institute for Multi-Track Diplomacy attempt to identify and avert budding conflicts and also to work in conflict resolution and post-conflict reconciliation.

The System

The elements of the global relief system are also complex, overlapping, and by no means sequential. A simplified flow chart of response phases is shown in Figure 3.4 but it is rare for an emergency to move from early warning to mobilization to operational response and post-conflict reconstruction. More often than not, there are substantial reversals— for example, in Angola, where combatants recently moved from war to peace agreements and then back to war again. In other cases, decades of calm can be interspersed with explosions of bitter ethnic or religious strife. In still others—for example, Sudan or Somalia—conflict appears to continue indefinitely.

Figure 3.4. The Key Players in Emergency Response

HOW DO CURRENT RELIEF ACTIVITIES REALLY WORK?

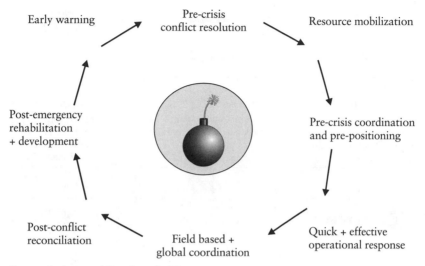

Early warning

Pre-crisis conflict resolution

Resource mobilization

Post-emergency rehabilitation + development

Pre-crisis coordination and pre-positioning

Post-conflict reconciliation

Field based + global coordination

Quick + effective operational response

Source: Authors and San Cornelia Ng.

A second way to view the system is from the perspective of the families whose livelihood is impacted along what some call the "relief-to-rehabilitation-to-development" continuum.[6] The idea is that a family can be in equilibrium when its income and assets are in balance, and that it can actually improve its well-being when its income and assets are expanding. During war and famine, families disinvest in assets; they often flee with only the clothes on their backs. During food shortages, they may be forced to sell livestock, or property, or to expend their savings.

The framework is useful because it helps relate what is happening in the broader environment to families and their needs. For example, during war and famine, the emergency provision of resources such as food, shelter, and medicine can be essential. During rehabilitation, protection of assets and income can be stimulated by reconstruction activities that involve food and cash for work. In development phases, programs to promote new income and assets can be pursued (see Figure 3.5 on the following page).

This figure is not meant to imply systematic movement from relief to rehabilitation to development. Just as societies lurch from war to peace to war again, or from good rainfall and harvests to drought and back again, families, too, may move in and out of poverty and deprivation in a more cyclical way.

Figure 3.5. The Relief and Rehabilitation to Development Continuum

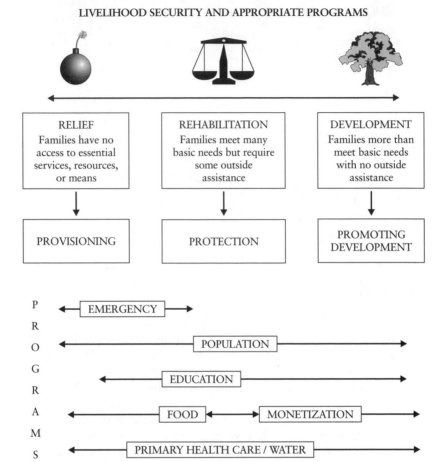

LIVELIHOOD SECURITY AND APPROPRIATE PROGRAMS

Source: Based on work by Tim Frankenberger, CARE 1997.

Major Impediments to
Complex Emergency Response

Our key informants also identified the most important operational, ethical, and structural impediments that they believe they face in keeping people alive during war and famine.[7]

Operational Problems—The Global Volunteer Fire Department

The NGO senior team members interviewed identified five operational obstacles that still make global emergency response a patchwork of well-intentioned but ad hoc efforts that sometimes gets labeled a "global fire department." The deeper, underlying issue is that, in the era of economic globalization, it is hard to provide global public goods like emergency response to meet the needs of large-scale movements of refugees or internally displaced people.[8]

Perverse Funding Dynamics

Because emergencies occur sporadically, the operational NGOs have trouble maintaining the resources for readiness capacity in non-emergency periods. Public funding is disbursed by a few large organizations like the European Union and bilateral donors. These public donors provide most resources only *during* emergencies and largely for field operations. Private donors get involved only after an emergency is well under way. They show little interest in maintaining installed operational capacity. The results of these perverse funding dynamics add up to a slow NGO response due to lack of installed capacity and preparedness.

Low Levels of Emergency Staff Preparation and Staff Retention

Many of the operational nonprofit organizations complain of high yearly emergency-staff turnover (the Red Cross, 25 percent; CARE, 35 percent; MSF, 50 percent). They attribute this not only to the lack of resources to maintain installed capacity, but also to the high stress of emergency work as well and the personal characteristics of relief workers. Many emergency staff view relief work more as an experience than as a career. Low staff retention results in waste of training resources and inability to mobilize experienced emergency teams quickly. Inexperienced emergency response teams often repeat the same operational mistakes again and again as new staff do old things for the first time.

Outdated Technology

Most of the relief organizations use antiquated technology. Communications systems are poor. Registration and family-tracking systems are often "paper-based," and archaic emergency-response teams utilize large quantities of medicine, food, and clothing. Yet there is little good software for purchasing, inventories, and logistics. Outdated technology affects the ability to save lives and relieve suffering more quickly. The implications of new Web-based solutions to registration, finding lost families, monitoring human rights violations, and managing food inventories have yet to be fully explored.

Inadequate Coordination

Our respondents complain of duplication among operational NGOs. Simultaneously, they lament the lack of clarity of roles among UN agencies, many of which compete for resources and for control of emergency operations. While emergency work is usually perceived as "organized chaos," such chaos is exacerbated by poor coordination. The consequence of poor coordination is the waste of resources due to replication of costs and systems. A far more severe consequence may be the loss of lives due to the slowness of response caused by long quibbling about the clarification of roles and discussion of which groups will work where.

Little Attention to Preventing Conflicts, Facing Forgotten Wars, and Post-Conflict Rehabilitation

Once wars start, the human costs and the destruction of physical infrastructure are enormous. Sometimes a generation is deprived of its brightest people. We need only imagine the benefits of successfully averting even one of the forty "complex humanitarian emergencies" that occurred in 1998.

While conflict early warning and conflict prevention through negotiations are widely perceived as lofty goals, many skeptics continue to shy away from peace building because it is hard to know what to invest in and whether it matters. The world community, the United Nations, and regional bodies often lack the political will and the organizational mechanisms to identify potential conflicts and to bring belligerents to the bargaining table. In addition, once media attention shifts to new conflicts, costly forgotten wars often continue for decades. Moreover, as soon as a conflict ends, it is extremely difficult to find resources for physical and social reconstruction. Normally, donor-funding windows are organized around either relief or development. Vital support for physical reconstruction and social healing is often unavailable when it is most needed.

Ethical Dilemmas

The toughest dilemmas for NGOs working on complex emergencies revolve around whether actions that save lives help perpetuate conflict in insidious ways. "Moral calculus" is not a highly developed form of mathematics. It is hard to know whether one hundred lives saved is worth the price of having inadvertently helped to prolong a conflict by a month. It is even harder to document the numbers of lives lost and saved in such situations. Furthermore, the operational choices that NGOs must make to reach people create complex ethical issues. What follows is a list of some of the more common difficult dilemmas that could easily paralyze any well-meaning person. While many of these problems are as old as war itself, the new context of today's complex emergencies has made them conspicuous enough to be mentioned by our informants.

Supporting Forced Population Movements

NGOs may find themselves being asked to work with people who have been forcibly moved to refugee or internally displaced persons' camps. These refugees may be either loyal supporters whom a government is trying to protect, or dissidents that a government is trying to control. The NGO may be able to help large numbers of innocent civilians in such camps, but it may also inadvertently help the war effort of one belligerent at the expense of another—by providing food, clothing, and shelter that allows the other belligerent to use its own resources for other purposes. It may also assure that a belligerent maintains access to, control over, and manipulation of large numbers of civilians, internally displaced people, and refugees.

Falling Victim to Food Diversions, Looting, and War or Protection Taxes

Where access is a problem, NGOs can find their supplies looted at gunpoint. They may find that political elements in camps extort war taxes from refugees after food distributions take place, or that political groups try to control the distributions themselves. The NGOs may be asked to pay protection taxes to move their supplies through particular territories, or to take on armed guards from a particular faction. Rebel factions may locate near refugee camps and divert food and supplies to maintain their armed struggle.

Perpetuating a War Economy

Warring factions may sell refugee supplies to buy guns. Relief efforts can allow factions to use their own resources for continuing the war while the international community takes care of their civilian population. Importing food or other supplies may provide disincentives to the reactivation of agriculture or other key sectors.

Heightening Conflict and Competition

High media visibility often puts the spotlight on refugee populations at the expense of equally needy residents of communities located near such refugee camps. Favoring refugees over residents can lead to jealousy and violence. Aid providers can also inadvertently provide unbalanced assistance by favoring some ethnic, religious, or racial groups over others.

Weakening Local Capacity

While there are many examples of excellent partnerships between international relief groups and local organizations, outside aid delivered by expatriates can weaken the capacity of local institutions like local self-help organizations, community or tribal organizations, and local NGOs.

Structural Problems—Outmoded Global Institutions and Mandates

According to our key informants, the international response system to the new kinds of emergencies has serious structural flaws. For example, many important new problems like the protection of increasing numbers of internally displaced people fall outside existing organizational mandates. In other cases institutions, well designed for the immediate post–World War II period, have serious problems coping with the number and complexity of recent emergencies.

Responsibility for Internally Displaced People

The Office of the UN High Commissioner for Refugees was established in 1950 in response to the special problems of those fleeing across borders to seek safety and avoid persecution during war. Its mandate was to protect refugees and seek durable solutions to their plight. This mandate did not, however, include protection of those who fled civil war and persecution but stayed within their country's borders. The exclusion of internally displaced people from the UNHCR mandate probably took place for two reasons. First, those involved in discussions of the new institutions were primarily exposed to wars between nations, not civil wars. Second, and probably more important, the new United Nations was built by consenting sovereign states, each of which protected its right to the legitimate monopoly on the use of force within its own boundaries. Protecting internally displaced people would have run counter to the UN Charter principle of non-intervention by sovereign states in the internal affairs of other sovereign states.

Today, however (as shown in Figure 3.3), the number of internally displaced people far exceeds the number of refugees in any given year. The protection of such people does not fall under any current international organizational mandate. The world system does not have an effective umbrella to protect increasingly large numbers of internally displaced people whose lives are at risk.

Humanitarian Action without Security

Humanitarian action in the absence of security or broader peace-making efforts deals only with the most life threatening symptoms of problems. Bandages and biscuits are not a substitute for negotiated political solutions or dealing with root causes of problems. But in the post–Cold War period, UN members have been unwilling to provide troops or fund effective peacekeeping operations. It took Secretary-General Kofi Annan almost two weeks of pleading with the international community before

Australia stepped forward to provide troops to protect citizens in the violent aftermath of the East Timor elections in September 1999. Given the unwillingness of the international community to provide security to refugees and internally displaced people, their safety has become even further compromised.

Mixing Civilians and Soldiers

In many places, the inability to separate civilians and belligerents in refugee camp situations became the rule rather than the exception. For example, many innocent people in camps in Rwanda found themselves mixed with soldiers and officials of Rwanda's Hutu-based government in exile—with their lives thereby at risk even if they wanted to return voluntarily to Rwanda. Some were even killed because they publicly expressed a desire to return to Rwanda. Although current UN agencies like UNHCR have a mandate to protect refugees in camps, they have no security forces and are very ill-equipped to do so.

Protecting Aid Workers

A fourth problem has been security for humanitarian workers. NGO and Red Cross workers are no longer viewed as neutral helpers. Warring parties have been increasingly willing to target aid workers and to capitalize on their deaths for political purposes. For example, in 1996 and 1997, seven ICRC medical personnel in Chechnya, three Médecins Sans Frontières staff in Rwanda, and three UN human rights monitors were assassinated in Rwanda.[9] Since 1979, CARE has lost seventy-four workers—most recently to landmines and gunfire.[10] Furthermore, even if factions had wanted to guarantee security this is difficult to do in a multi-factional internal war. In the last two weeks of September 2000 four UNHCR workers were killed. Since 1992 eleven UNHCR staff have died during emergency operations and many more have been wounded.

Gaining Access to Refugees

Access, too, has been a problem. In a world where sovereign nations were at war, it was often feasible to negotiate access to refugees. Although this was done successfully in Bosnia and in south Sudan, more frequently than not, warring factions have been either unwilling or unable to guarantee the delivery of humanitarian supplies. In the absence of stronger world community responses, refugees can go unassisted for months at a time.

Increased Involvement of the Military in Humanitarian Responses

The recent UNHCR evaluation of the NATO involvement in refugee relief in Kosovo points out the dangers of blurring the role of armed forces participating in a war while simultaneously participating in relief activities.[11] The report states that, while military forces might be perceived to have a comparative advantage in flight logistics, construction, and water and sanitation for large numbers of people, the danger for refugees is that the military role in combat takes precedence and can put refugees at undue risk. For example, when faced with a choice to use air transport to move soldiers into combat or to move refugees to safety, refugee protection can become the second choice. Belligerents may also be more willing to attack refugee camps run by their foes than those run by a UN agency or an NGO.

Tough Choices for the NGO Community

In light of the new problems and dilemmas, many international NGOs— CARE, Catholic Relief Services, Médecins Sans Frontières, the International Rescue Committee, Oxfam, Save the Children, and others—are re-evaluating their roles and responses. Four potential responses are often mentioned (and will be discussed in more detail in the mini–case study of CARE later in this chapter).

Withdrawal

One possible choice for NGOs is to withdraw from any form of operational response to such complex new kinds of emergencies. Advocates of this viewpoint might argue as follows.[12] War is a reality, and internal state conflict makes work with refugees and civilians impossibly difficult. Given the fact that NGO work is often manipulated by belligerents, it probably does more harm than good in the short term. It is better to refrain from operational response and work instead on conflict resolution or advocacy to get groups to the bargaining table. There is no point in putting major resources into programs that simply deal with the *symptoms* of problems. It makes more sense for NGOs to wait until conflict is over, and then work on rehabilitation and development efforts or to use resources in places where development is possible. But none of our respondents' organizations favor this choice.

Neutrality

Those who adhere to a doctrine of neutrality might say the following: War is a reality. Regardless of the difficulties, we have a responsibility to work operationally on behalf of the victims. We can work best by negotiating access with the belligerents and simultaneously maintaining a neutral position on the conflict itself. We will not publicly judge the actions of the belligerents. Operational work should be based on three principles. First, we are neutral. We take no public stands on the actions of the belligerents. We will not comment on their respect for human rights or treatment of civilians, internally displaced people, or refugees. If we did so, we would never have the access to permit us to save innocent lives. Second, we will respond to victims' needs impartially, on the basis of areas of greatest need. Third, we are independent. We reserve the right to respond as we see fit given our own diagnosis.

The organization that most clearly reflects much of this viewpoint is the International Committee of the Red Cross (ICRC).[13] ICRC has a proud tradition. Its role is specified by the Geneva Conventions and a series of special UN protocols. ICRC has a special mandate to work with prisoners of war. Until recently, it did not advocate the use of any form of security in its warehouses or logistics operations. ICRC believes that to maintain neutrality a clear division of labor is necessary between advocacy groups, human rights groups, and those engaged in operational humanitarian response.

Active Humanitarianism

Many within the NGO community who initially believed that their organizations could play neutral roles in complex emergencies have begun to revise their views. After experiencing the special problems of negotiating with belligerents and those of service delivery during conflict, they have concluded that they may have exacerbated conflicts by not thinking more carefully about the implications of their work. However, they still believe that operational response is necessary when innocent people face death in complex emergencies. They believe that they can work positively and constructively to help reduce suffering with actions that minimize conflict and build the conditions for peace. Some of the principles for action are:

1. Take a long-term comprehensive view of the conflict.

2. Understand the social dynamics and political factions in any situation.

3. Consider how each program or action will either contribute to or reduce conflict.

4. Act but choose actions that contribute to conflict reduction.

The most articulate advocates of active humanitarianism are Mary Andersen, Peter Woodrow, John McDonald, and Louise Diamond.[14] Virtually all of the organizations represented in this book are beginning to align their emergency response efforts more closely to the philosophy of active humanitarianism.

Clear Partisanship

Some NGOs believe that war is a reality and that neutrality is impossible. They believe that one group in a conflict has a more just cause than another. Therefore, operational NGOs should take sides based on human rights records, ethnic views, and religious, political, or ideological beliefs. Such NGOs are willing to mix advocacy activities with operational work. Under appropriate circumstances, they forge alliances with the military and security forces that protect the group whose side they have taken. We will return to NGO responses to these tough choices after looking at their responses to the operational, ethical, and other structural challenges first.

NGO Responses to Operational Dilemmas

Our earlier discussion identified five major operational problems that inhibit effective global emergency response. Our respondents noted that they are currently taking or considering the following corrective responses as well as asking foundations and other donors to provide resources for them.

Overcoming Perverse Funding Dynamics

Fast-Disbursing Emergency Rotating Funds

Many NGOs have developed what they call emergency rotating funds. When an emergency takes place, the organization supplies initial disbursements for initial assessment teams, and then preliminary as well as full-scale emergency response. The fund is then replenished through private fundraising. It is also used as match money for grants and contracts from UNHCR, WFP, DFID, and other organizations.

Rapid Response, Forgotten War, and Post-Conflict Endowment Funds

Such endowment funds would accomplish the same purpose as rotating funds but would also provide more stability, since the interest from these funds could be used immediately without replenishment through fundraising. Endowment funds make more sense to help provide services in forgotten wars and post-conflict situations, for which public and private fundraising is not easy.

Advance Positioning of Supplies

Catholic Relief Services and the Church of Jesus Christ of Latter-day Saints have begun to pre-position standard medical, water, food, and clothing kits around the world as well as in the United States. They can then move them quickly from regional sites to particular emergencies.

Special Multilateral or Bilateral Agreements

Some donor organizations—for example, USAID, the World Food Program (WFP), and the European Union (EU)—have begun to look for alternatives to slow, cumbersome contracting with NGOs at the moment of an emergency. The alternatives they have discovered are framework agreements and indefinite quantity contracts. In each of these mechanisms, the direct and indirect cost parameters, quality standards, and disbursement mechanisms are pre-negotiated. During an emergency, donors can mobilize such agreements and disburse funds rapidly to the NGOs with which they have the contracts.

Enhancing Staff Quality and Staff Retention

Training, Certification, and Staff Development

To help overcome the problems of inexperienced staff serving poorly in emergencies, many NGOs are working to provide additional training for staff. Organizations like CARE are considering certification processes for employees in which staff cannot work in emergencies in key positions without completing training, passing an examination, and having a formal certification. In addition, because of the high level of stress that staff experience during emergency work, many organizations are also beginning to limit the length of assignments during emergencies. They have also begun to develop policies of staff rotation that move people from emergency to non-emergency assignments. Finally, some groups offer staff the option of having access to psychological counseling after particularly difficult emergency assignments.

Developing and Using Industry-Wide Standards

Within the NGO community, discussions are being held within umbrella organizations like InterAction and the International Council of Voluntary Agencies (ICVA) to develop general quality and cost standards for emergency responses. Although it is difficult to get enforcement through umbrella organizations, such attempts at setting standards are a good beginning. The Sphere Project co-sponsored by the Steering Committee on Humanitarian Response and InterAction is another example of global standard setting.

New Roster Systems

Many organizations—for example, the International Rescue Committee (IRC)—use roster systems in which professionals from outside the organization volunteer to be available for work of short-term duration, for example, one to three months. Other organizations, such as Save the Children and Oxfam, use a duty-roster system. In this system, regular staff from headquarters and country offices are placed on the roster for several months during the year. If there is an emergency during the months when their name is on the roster, their unit or country office must release them.

Building Local Capacity

Some donor organizations have provided umbrella grants to NGOs to permit training and capacity building in local emergency-response organizations and community groups. The potential of such capacity building is important in building stronger community infrastructure. Examples of this approach can be seen in Save the Children's administration of capacity building umbrella grants for local NGO strengthening in the former Soviet Union.

Humanitarian Volunteer Program

Some foundations, such as both the Bill and Melinda Gates Foundation and the Microsoft Foundation, have considered developing humanitarian volunteer programs. In one proposed program, Microsoft staff could serve as technology volunteers after certification. They would be assigned to short-term emergency response teams and handle their technology needs. In more extensive programs, general student volunteers would get training and work in operational or coordinating organizations for one to two years. Student loan forgiveness and opportunities for graduate study after volunteer service might make such programs even more attractive.

Experimenting with New Technology

Technology Pilot Innovation Grants

Such grants could help link technology experts with relief staff to carry out needs assessments, design new solutions, and experiment with them. Examples of recent successful efforts have been the Microsoft grant to UNHCR to set up an electronic registration system for Kosovo refugees, and a solution called "people finder" that puts pictures of missing refugee children on the Internet so that families could search for them.

Technology Training and Multiplication Grants

Such grants could be provided to help organizational networks train staff from many organizations and broaden technology use.

Improving Internal and External Coordination

Clear Division of Labor among Affiliates of the Same Organization

One of the biggest problems within global organizations—World Vision International, Save the Children, CARE, Médecins Sans Frontières, and others—is the duplication of costs, support structures, and services by affiliate members of the same international organization. In the worst case scenario, five national affiliates from the same international organization arrive on the scene and deliver the same services. They set up

costly parallel logistics operations, financial systems, and project management groups. Recently many organizations searched for ways to cut
costs and gain economies of scale. One method has been the development of a division of labor among local affiliates. For example, one
national member may specialize in primary health care or emergency
medicine, while another may take water, sanitation, or education. A
second example is to provide one umbrella organization to coordinate
the combined operations of other organizations. In the case of CARE
International, a national lead, or coordinating, member is named to set
up the administrative infrastructure. Other members contribute to the
costs of the infrastructure and then their field programs are directly
overseen by the coordinating member.

Regional Plans That Include Other NGOs

In the wake of the recent crises in the Horn of Africa, many NGOs
have begun to plan coordinated responses for their own members and
affiliates. This has resulted in the pre-positioning of supplies. Donors
like USAID have sponsored multi-organizational planning through their
Horn of Africa Initiative.

Joint NGO Committees for Coordinating Operations

At the field level, implementing organizations have found it useful to
have weekly meetings to identify and resolve the ongoing problems of
operational response. These meetings have sometimes been stimulated
and chaired by representatives of UNHCR and sometimes have worked
independently of UN organizations. Joint fundraising—for example,
among agencies in the United Kingdom through a televised system called
Disasters Emergencies Committee—has proved useful.

Joint NGO Negotiations with Donors, Governments, and Belligerents

The NGO community has found it increasingly useful to form umbrella
groups or ad hoc coalitions to negotiate directly with donors, governments, and belligerents. For example, the NGO community met with
village elders in Baidoa, Somalia, in 1993 to announced their combined
withdrawal unless the elders could speak to their communities and control increasing physical threats to staff. The NGO community combined
to negotiate with UNHCR in Geneva about using common costs and
overhead rates for projects in 1996. All of these actions help lessen the
problem of NGO competition.

Linking Operations to Global Advocacy

While it is difficult for operational groups to also engage in global advocacy for conflict resolution, organizations like Oxfam and Médecins

Sans Frontières have worked on advocacy strategies that build on the operational realities they see in emergency response and advocacy to help highlight humanitarian problems and pressure the international community to respond appropriately. The effectiveness of the global advocacy coalition of two hundred NGOs in the Nobel Prize–winning campaign to ban landmines shows the power and potential of the new global advocacy.

Preventing Conflict and Facing Forgotten Wars

Despite pessimism about preventing deadly conflict, there are examples of successful efforts. For example, the Carter Center worked success-fully in Nicaragua to promote a peaceful election transition between the Sandinista Government of Daniel Ortega and Doña Violeta Chamorro. It required a high-level intervention by former U.S. President Jimmy Carter as well as UN and bilateral pressure. Success was also achieved in the UN handling of peace negotiations in El Salvador, Cambo-dia, and Guatemala. Finally, there are exciting successful experiments in post-conflict reconciliation like the South Africa Truth Commis-sion, human rights discussions, community reconciliation meetings, and trauma counseling. Every such success saves many lives and dollars.

Creative foundation responses in the areas of peace building and forgotten wars might include the following.

Famine Early-Warning Systems

In an effort to identify potential problems of natural and man-made disasters, organizations in Ethiopia have developed a food-security mon-itoring system to identify potential crop shortages region by region. Such systems permit better targeting of food resources to actual needs. For example, where people have food shortages for several months only, the extra food that is not distributed to them can be used elsewhere. At the same time, such systems allow early identification of serious droughts and potential famine conditions. The overall quality of operational response can be improved through such early assessment.

Rapid-Disbursing Peace and Mediation Grants, Forgotten War Grants, and Post-Conflict Grants

Such grants could help get high-level peace and negotiation teams into the field to search for solutions. Similar grants could help the United Na-tions and other appropriate organizations improve their own high-level early-warning systems as well as support regional networks to develop their capacity to identify and help mediate conflicts. Special efforts could also be made to bring combatants to the bargaining table in many of the forgotten wars like those in Sudan and Angola. Such grants could be useful, for example, for truth commissions and reconciliation projects as well as for building water systems, houses, and infrastructure. One of the most interesting examples of creative response to post-conflict is the development of a new concept called the "Strategic Recovery Facility" by colleagues at the Center for International Cooperation at New York University. The facility "attempts to combine both financial resources and expertise in a coordination mechanism that engages NGOs and intergovernmental and bilateral donor agencies in a common approach to conflict recovery even as conflict is abating and not yet settled. It is geared to common needs assessment to be undertaken jointly with local actors and to a rapid and collaborative field-based approach to meeting essential needs that are too often neglected between relief and development."[15]

Working along the Relief-to-Rehabilitation-to-Development Continuum

Organizations like CARE, Catholic Relief Services, and World Vision have found it increasingly important to design emergency programs with long-term community rehabilitation and development needs in mind.

NGO Responses to Ethical Dilemmas

There are no simple solutions to the ethical dilemmas that NGOs encounter as they work in the new complex emergencies. There have, however, been useful pragmatic responses to some of the problems outlined earlier.[16] These responses represent a step in the right direction.

Countering Manipulated Access

Many NGOs have gotten around the problem of serving refugees in territories of only one political faction by maintaining the principle of "balanced service." For example, CARE works with displaced people on both sides of the conflict zones in Sudan. They have programs in both Northern and Southern Sudan. In both Bosnia and Sudan, insisting on negotiated humanitarian corridors has allowed the NGO community more balanced access to people in need. Finally, when it has become impossible to reach groups in need through national territory, some organizations have set up cross-border operations—for example, from Rwanda into Eastern Zaire.

Reducing Diversions, Looting, and the Need for Staff and Refugee Protection

For some NGOs, the solution to looting and security problems has been hiring armed guards. Others, however, have felt that there are alternative ways to minimize security problems and theft. For example, it has been possible to ask the recipient communities themselves to guarantee the safe transit of goods. At times, subcontracting merchants and truckers and paying for actual quantities of commodities delivered has reduced NGO involvement in security. It has also increased the volumes of food arriving at final distribution points. Some organizations have also resorted to joint negotiation of standard rates with truckers to help keep costs down. They have also used the threat of withdrawal if there is violence. Some have tried a more indirect way of reducing diversions by staying out of food delivery entirely and relying on monetization—the sale of food and use of cash proceeds for relief operations. Standardizing delivery size and format—to ease checking—has been used to reduce theft. Finally, there is no substitute for professional inventory management systems and qualified staff to provide supervision.

Diversion has also taken place at the level of distribution. Some of the strategies that have worked to counter loss and help ensure that real needs are met have included: working toward more accurate beneficiary assessments, getting beneficiary lists with signatures on receipt, beneficiary cards, refusing to distribute food through paramilitary hierarchies in camps, targeting women and children directly, doing family distributions, and doing "wet" feeding (a term used to provide cooked food on the spot, instead of distributing dry commodities that can be sold on the black market).

The issue of security for staff and supplies is a difficult one for NGOs. Most recently, some organizations have begun to use security consultants to analyze the risks of current procedures like bringing large amounts of cash on a weekly basis into places where there is no banking system. Some organizations are hiring their own internal security staff as well as communications officers. Many organizations are also beginning to offer short courses and workshops on recognizing and responding to security problems in conflict situations.

Reversing the Incentives That Promote a War Economy

As NGOs have become more involved in responding to complex emergencies, they have begun to think more carefully about how to counter tendencies that might perpetuate war economies. Some of the responses have included: working not just on relief but also on advocacy to encourage the world community to hold belligerents accountable and to bring them to the bargaining table, promoting projects like seeds and tools programs to reactivate the economy, and resorting to barter shops to stimulate agricultural recovery. The CARE barter shops in south Sudan are an interesting example. In this model, CARE shops provide basic goods that are currently inaccessible in return for local agricultural products. This has helped to stimulate agricultural recovery. The newly produced agricultural commodities have then been sold to other NGOs that need them for relief food distribution. This has lowered the need to bring in outside commodities and also has allowed the barter shops to build up a cash reserve to repurchase goods. Finally, providing food or cash for work for road and infrastructure rehabilitation also helps with economic recovery.

Reducing the Risk of Conflict and Competition

One of the biggest concerns in the NGO community has been the intense media focus on refugees at the expense of equally needy civilian populations living right next to refugee camps. One alternative has been to attempt to provide balanced programs to refugees and the stable communities that exist side by side with them. Another has been to develop projects which assure balanced services to opposing groups that have been involved in conflicts, and projects bringing together soldiers who previously fought on opposite sides to jointly help implement activities. One of the more interesting recent examples of this is provided by the de-mining teams made up of people from formerly warring factions in Angola and the land titling programs for ex-combatants from both sides of the war in El Salvador. Another example is CARE Uganda's water program in northern Uganda: UNHCR funds CARE to bore holes and establish pumps in Sudanese refugee areas, while UNICEF funds CARE to do the same for the Ugandans in resettlement areas adjacent to the camps.

Reinforcing Local Capacity

Although external responses to emergencies are based on the premise that local institutions have been overwhelmed by the disaster, there are still opportunities to partner with local organizations, such as the local Red Cross or Red Crescent Society, church groups, and NGOs. There is also the opportunity to rely on traditional tribal structures or village structures for identification of people in need and for the distribution of supplies and crowd control.

Responses to Structural Problems

It is helpful to see how the United Nations, as well as one representative organization, CARE, has begun to change within its practices in response to the structural dilemmas posed earlier.

UN Systemic Responses

Key actors in the UN system have begun to take the challenges of the new world of complex emergencies more seriously by beginning to redesign their frameworks, mandates, and coordinating mechanisms.

The New Framework of Responsible Sovereignty

In an effort to meet the needs of increasing numbers of internally displaced people, a new framework called "responsible sovereignty" has
been developed by Francis Deng, special advisor to the UN Secretary-
General.[17] This concept—a controversial one—argues that when a
sovereign state cannot or will not effectively protect its citizens from
major persecution or the dangers of civil war, the community of nations
should step in to do so. Although this new concept is not fully accepted,
it is the subject of increased discussion in the world community and has
been more frequently advocated by the Secretary-General.

Revising Agency Mandates

The Office of the UN High Commissioner on Refugees has begun to
publicly present a broader interpretation of global responsibility for internally displaced people. For example, UNHCR's *Global Appeal for
1999* makes special reference to its right to protect internally displaced
people when the UN Secretary-General or the UN General Assembly ask
the organization to do so.[18] In February 2000, both Secretary-General
Kofi Annan and the UN High Commissioner for Refugees, Ms. Sadako
Ogata, approached the UN Security Council to open a debate about
bringing internally displaced people more fully within the scope of UN
responsibility. At the Security Council session, Mrs. Ogata said: "The
difficulty of having access to large numbers of people in insecure and
isolated areas is compounded by the complexity of assisting civilians
in their own country, where their own state authorities or rebel forces
are frequently the very cause of their predicament." The U.S. Representative, Richard C. Holbrooke, maintained that: "To a person who has
been driven from his or her home by conflict, there's no difference" between a refugee and an internally displaced person "in terms of what's
happened to them.... They're equally victims. But they're treated differently." Mr. Holbrooke further argued that the UNHCR is the most
logical agency to concentrate efforts. "What we must do," he said, "is
expand the definition of what is a refugee, erode if not erase the distinc-
tion between a refugee and a person who is internally displaced...."[19]
Although new discussions are taking place in UN bodies, there has been
no formal solution to the question of which UN agency might take on
broadened responsibilities for internally displaced people.

New UN Headquarters Conflict Early-Warning and Operational Response Systems

Several new UN headquarters committees have been formed to improve
conflict early warning systems as well as improve coordination of emergency operations. Figure 3.6 provides an organization chart of the new
system for conflict early-warning and subsequent operational emergency

Figure 3.6. New UN System Committees

AN EXAMPLE OF POLICY NETWORK MAPPING EMERGING
UN HUMANITARIAN COORDINATING NETWORK POST KOSOVO: OCT. 1999

Help Civilian Victims of Conflicts and Natural Disasters
through Coordination, Advocacy, Policy Development, and Operational Response

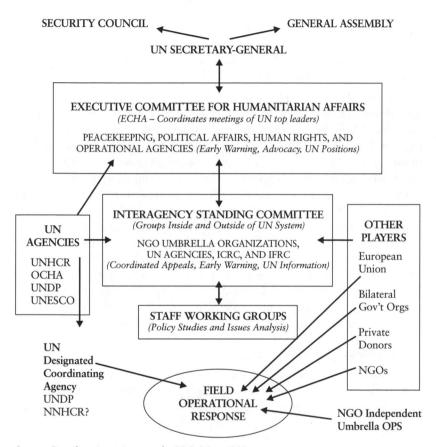

Source: Based on interviews at the UN, May 1999.

coordination. The UN Interagency Standing Committee provides special representation for NGOs along with UN agencies. The Office for Coordination of Humanitarian Action (OCHA) has major oversight responsibility for the new committees.

Field-Based Operational Coordination Mechanisms

Finally, the UN system has made some attempt to redefine roles and responsibilities of its own organizations in field-based, operational coordination. In earlier crises, operational coordination normally was managed by UNHCR. In 1999, UNDP was given the new responsibility for general field coordination of operations unless a special envoy or different lead agency is named by the Secretary-General. Under this new system, UNHCR, the World Food Program, and other agencies become part of the coordinated operation. Whether the new systems will work effectively is an open question, but there is no question that changes have been made.

An NGO Response to the Structural Problems: "Active Humanitarianism" at CARE

In 1996 CARE staff and leadership began a process of intense reflection about the organization's future role in humanitarian response. They considered whether to align their emergency work more closely with philosophies like neutrality, active humanitarianism, and partisanship or to withdraw from providing emergency services completely. There were few advocates of either withdrawal from humanitarian work or active partisanship. CARE staff said that total withdrawal from humanitarian work would be a negation of the organization's origins. Few staff advocated partisanship because of the difficulty in deciding whether any particular ethnic, religious, or ideological group had more "right on its side" during a conflict. They more easily identified with the need to respond to hunger, malnutrition, thirst, and physical injury. In 1997 the CARE community began realigning its emergency response to reflect the philosophy of "active humanitarianism" buttressed by some of the following general principles:

The Humanitarian Imperative

Civilians in conflict situations have the right to stay alive and survive in both natural and man-made disasters. Organizations like CARE have an imperative to help them rebuild their lives once emergencies are over.

Timely Operational Response

When there is a pressing need for humanitarian assistance, and a reasonable chance of having a positive impact, CARE will attempt to respond by using the combined resources of the CARE International System.

Assuring Humanitarian Access

Humanitarian response cannot take place without guaranteed relatively safe access to people in need. CARE will try to negotiate access when and where possible. When necessary, it will advocate that the UN system help provide safe access through humanitarian corridors, such as that which existed in Bosnia and south Sudan through Operation Lifeline.

Refugees, Internally Displaced People, and NGO Workers Have a Right to Safety

As an NGO, CARE is capable of providing emergency assistance. It is not, however, equipped to provide physical security or safety to refugees, or to effectively separate them from belligerents. CARE expects the UN system and the international community to hold belligerents accountable for respecting the Geneva Conventions and protocols concerning refugees. It challenges the United Nations and the world community to find ways to provide safety to refugees in camps, and to find creative ways to separate refugees from belligerents and to protect relief workers.

The Right to Withdraw

Although CARE will attempt to respond quickly to immediate human needs where it has reasonably safe access, it reserves the right to withdraw wherever it believes that innocent civilians have not been separated from belligerents, wherever it believes that refugees are being intimidated, wherever political groupings will not allow it to distribute resources to people in need, or wherever civil order cannot be maintained. In such circumstances, CARE will help organize as well as participate in coalitions with other NGOs to withdraw, publicize problems, and encourage authorities to resolve such problems.

Humanitarian Response Is Not Enough

CARE does not believe that humanitarian response is a substitute for efforts by the world community and the UN system to promote negotiated settlements of conflicts that get at the roots rather than just the symptoms of such conflicts. While CARE provides operational assistance, it will simultaneously advocate for strong international efforts in conflict resolution and for organized ways to achieve safe access and safety for refugees and humanitarian workers.

The Goal of Active Humanitarianism

Since 1997 CARE and many of the other organizations discussed in this book have continued to shape their work around the concept of active humanitarianism. A more active but loosely coordinated approach began in February 1997, when representatives of CARE International, Oxfam, Médecins Sans Frontières, and the International Committee of the Red Cross had an unprecedented opportunity to take their views about the problems of global humanitarian response to the international community. They participated in the first NGO testimony to the UN Security Council—followed by a special meeting with the then new Secretary-General, Kofi Annan.[20] What was to be a two-hour session turned into a four-hour one because Security Council members showed such a high level of interest. This has led to additional NGO Security

Council briefings on special problems (for example, Sudan and Ethiopia) and recently to the inclusion of regular NGO representation in the UN Interagency Standing Committee on Emergency Response.

Beginning in 1997, the United Nations as well as individual member states began to put a more comprehensive approach into practice. The Secretary-General named a special representative for the Great Lakes, Ambassador Mohamed Sahnoun, to promote a negotiated settlement of the conflict in Zaire (now the Democratic Republic of the Congo), to advocate for the safety and security of the refugees in the eastern part of the Democratic Republic of the Congo, to assist rehabilitation in Rwanda, and to promote attention to refugee issues in Burundi.[21] Not only representatives of the United Nations, but also President Nelson Mandela of South Africa and U.S. Ambassador to the United Nations William Richardson made efforts at personal diplomacy to bring President Mobutu Sese Seko of Zaire and Laurent Kabila, the leader of the opposition movement, to the bargaining table.[22]

During this period, the Secretary-General, the Special Ambassador Sahnoun, and the head of UNHCR, Sadako Ogata, pressured heavily for refugee access, safety, and repatriation in Eastern Zaire. They denounced massacres of refugees.[23] Between 1997 and the time of this book's publication the UN Secretary-General and many heads of UN agencies have been increasingly vocal about the needs of refugees, internally displaced people, and the safety of their own staff in places like East Timor, the Democratic Republic of the Congo, and elsewhere.

Ethnology and Beyond

Before leaving the theme of this chapter—the NGOs' response to the new complex emergencies—let us again step back for a moment to readdress the questions we raised earlier about the ethnology of the Northern NGO leaders' views. Which of the Northern NGO senior-team viewpoints can be supported by empirical data? What motivations may not have been explicitly discussed by our respondents? What nuances and details may have been known but not explicitly commented on? What emerging issues need further exploration?

Empirical Support

There is substantial empirical support for our senior team members' views that complex emergencies present tough new challenges. For example, clearly there have been more civil wars and internal conflicts since 1980 than in prior periods, and there are today more internally displaced people than refugees. More relief workers and civilians have been killed recently than in other times after the end of World War II. It is not difficult to document that both the NGOs and the UN system are changing their systems, structures, and perspectives to meet these challenges.

There may be nuances, however, that our informants did not mention—notably due more to lack of time rather than awareness. For example, perhaps the new viewpoint about the increased frequency of intrastate conflict and larger numbers of internally displaced people understates the horrors of earlier wars for civilians who stayed within their countries. For example, many civilians died in World War II as a result of the London blitz by the Germans, the bombing of Dresden by Allied forces, the invasion of Nanking by Japan, and the use of the atomic bombs in Hiroshima and Nagasaki by the United States. Perhaps the more comprehensive shift in the nature of conflict may be that in the new age of even greater "precision bombing" and less use of ground troops far fewer combatants than civilians have died. Nor did our informants mention that there were internally displaced people during the Cold War. They may have been harder to count due to less international access to independent information. Furthermore, the world community may have been less willing and able to intervene in the internal affairs of sovereign states within the communist bloc during this period.

Underlying Motivations

It is also important to consider possible motivations driving the NGO senior teams' reform suggestions. They propose, for example, that the perverse cycle funding of emergency operations be corrected so that global response can be improved. They clearly would be direct beneficiaries of such changes. Actors within the UN system also propose that they be given more resources to expand their own mandates and operations. While such suggestions would provide more resources for the existing delivery system, they may distract attention from new modes of delivery, which might actually diminish the roles of the current players. More explicitly, their reform proposals mention—but do not give special priority to—alternative delivery organizations like a global UN response team, the role of the military, or local Red Cross chapters. While our informants see building local capacity as an important option they did not single it out as a particular priority. Consistent strong local emergency response capacity across the whole community of nations might be one of the secrets of more sustainable long-term global response. Ironically, strengthening local capacity might make the role of Northern NGOs far less important or at the very least result in major changes in their roles.

Details and Nuances

Due to limits of time, the Northern NGO senior team members did not comment substantially on interesting implications of some of their suggestions. For example, there was little discussion of the comparative cost effectiveness of the provision of emergency services by national, regional, or international troops and peacekeepers. Nor did the group look at the comparative costs of strengthening local emergency response capacity instead of that of Northern NGOs and the UN system. Second, while it is easy to ask those in the UN system to provide better protection of refugees and aid workers, it is not all that easy to figure out practical ways to do this. Certainly more attention to realistic responses would be important and useful. Finally, while some of the new NGO efforts at coordination and standard setting will help rationalize response efforts, it is important to look for additional solutions.

Emerging Issues

A number of emerging issues were briefly touched upon by our informants. But they deserve much closer scrutiny by all parties interested in saving lives during complex emergencies. First, the full operational implications of the new doctrine of responsible sovereignty should be more fully explored. For example, to move from general philosophy to operational response requires specific guidelines. Could realistic global guidelines be developed? For example, what if the global community accepted that global intervention would be necessary if 5 percent of a nation's population was internally displaced in conflict and that the belligerents could not meet minimum standards for shelter, food, and health care? Would the world community really have the political will to intervene in every case? Would the resources be available even if there was the political will? Might this become another unfunded global mandate? Second, reshaping mandates to fit new circumstances is very important but has equally daunting operational implications. For example, if expanding the mandate of the UNHCR to include internally displaced people added 20 million new people per year to that organization's overall responsibility, where would funds be found to meet this need? What if belligerents attacked UN forces and NGOs who dared to intervene in their internal affairs? Would the world be willing to go to war to protect the rights of the internally displaced?

A third emerging issue worthy of fuller analysis is the role of the military in humanitarian response. NATO's Kosovo intervention raised a host of operational, ethical, and systemic questions that deserve closer attention. Even the recent UNHCR Kosovo evaluation acknowledges that military forces are better organized for rapid humanitarian response than the NGOs. They have immediate access to air and ground transport. They are accustomed to setting up large-scale logistics for troops that can be adapted to feed, clothe, and shelter people and to provide health, water, and sanitation as well as physical protection.[24] So far there have been few serious studies of the comparative costs and tradeoffs between military versus civilian and NGO humanitarian action. Furthermore, there needs to be a great deal more detailed analysis of the way the interests of national and regional military forces might run counter to the independent needs and interests of civilians. Finally, in an age of economic globalization, it is difficult to figure out how to produce global "public goods" like global disaster response, global social safety nets, and environmental protection. Such problems jump national boundaries, and as yet global responses are improvised and ad hoc. More attention needs to be paid to what global social goods are and who might best provide them. The roles of the nonprofit, public, and private sectors in providing them need to be carefully evaluated.[25]

We would like to extend our special thanks to Rick Barton, Peter Bell, Marc Cutts, Charles Denzell, Louise Diamond, Susan Farnsworth, Larry Fioretta, Shepard Forman, Dennis Gallagher, Paul Giannone, Harlan Hale, Andrew Jones, Uwe Koros, Jean Bernard Lindor, Aimable Uwizeye Mapendano, Abby Maxman, Appolinaire Mujawakigeli, Xaverine Mukansanga, Andy Pugh, Ron Redmond, Roland Roome, Eugene Rujikikiza, Abby Stoddard, and Margaret Tsitouris for their extensive contribution to the ideas in this chapter. I would particularly like to thank the Gates Foundation for a special grant to study the recent NGO responses to complex emergencies and for the helpful support of Jack Faris, William H. Gates Sr., Terry Meersman, and Patti Stonesifer—all of the Bill and Melinda Gates Foundation. Finally, our special thanks go to our research assistant San Cornelia Ng, who participated actively in the data collection and contributed important ideas to this chapter.

Notes

1. International Federation of Red Cross and Red Crescent Societies, *World Disasters Report: 1999* (Geneva: IFRC, 1999), 155–61, tables 14–16.

2. IFRC, *World Disasters Report: 1999*, 138–49, tables 1–10.

3. IFRC, *World Disasters Report: 1999*, 152, table 12.

4. Global IDP Survey and Norwegian Refugee Council, *Internally Displaced People: A Global Survey* (Geneva: Earthscan, 1998), 28, figure 1.

5. IFRC, *World Disasters Report: 1999*, 140.

6. Tim Frankenberger, "Indicators and Data Collection Methods for Assessing Household Food Security," in M. Maxwell and Tim Frankenberger, *Household Food Security: Concepts, Indicators, Measurements: A Technical Review* (New York and Rome: UNICEF and IFAD, 1992). See as well Tim Frankenberger, "Measuring Household Livelihood Security: An Approach for Reducing Absolute Poverty," paper prepared for the Applied Anthropology Meetings (Baltimore, March 26–29, 1996).

7. The data provided in this section is a result a research effort funded by the

William H. Gates Foundation and carried out by the Daniel J. Evans School of
Public Affairs at the University of Washington from June through December of
1999. Methods included in-depth interviews with senior organizational teams
and structured questionnaire responses from CARE, Save the Children, Oxfam,
World Vision, PLAN International, Doctors Without Borders, InterAction, and
the Steering Committee on Humanitarian Response, all featured in this book.
In addition the same research was carried out with other key organizations
like the International Rescue Committee, Catholic Relief Services, International
Federation of the Red Cross, International Confederation of the Red Cross,
Mercy Corps International, World Concern, International Medical Corps, and
Northwest Medical Teams.

8. Inge Kaul, *Global Public Goods* (New York: Oxford University Press,
1999).

9. *New York Times,* February 5, 1997, 5, and February 6, 1997, 13.

10. CARE Annual Report for 1996 (CARE USA, Atlanta, Ga., 1996), 1.

11. "The Independent Evaluation of UNHCR's Emergency Preparedness and
Response to the Kosovo Refugee Crisis," The Newsletter of the International
Council of Voluntary Agencies (ICVA) 2 (ICVA, February 2000), no. 1.

12. A number of the authors point out the negative aspects of NGO human-
itarian response. Some question whether such responses are appropriate at all.
See for example among them Michael Merrin, *The Road to Hell: The Rav-
aging Effects of Foreign International Charity* (New York: Free Press, 1997).
Others focus more clearly on the problems of NGO humanitarian response. See
for example *Life, Death and Aid,* ed. François Jean (London and New York:
Médecins Sans Frontières, 1993), see particularly chapter 15, "When Suffering
Makes a Good Story." See also John Pendergast, "Helping or Hurting? Human-
itarian Intervention and the Crisis Response in the Horn" (Center of Concern,
Washington, D.C., discussion paper #6, January 1995).

13. Pierre Perrin, "The Impact of War on Disaster Response: The Experience
of the International Committee of the Red Cross" (First Harvard Symposium
on Complex Humanitarian Disasters, April 9–10, 1995).

14. Mary Anderson, *Do No Harm: Supporting Local Capacities for Peace
through Aid* (Cambridge, Mass.: Local Capacities for Peace Project, 1996).
See also "International Assistance and Conflict: An Exploration of Negative
Impacts" (Cambridge, Mass.: Local Capacities for Peace Project, July 1994),
no. 1, 10. Mary Anderson and Peter Woodrow, *Rising from the Ashes: Development Strategies in Times of Disaster* (Boulder, Colo.: Westview Press, 1989),
see also "Disaster and Development Workshops: A Manual for Training in Capacities and Vulnerabilities Analysis" (Cambridge, Mass.: International Relief/
Development Project, Graduate School of Education, Harvard University, December 1990). Louise Diamond and John McDonald, *Multi-Track Diplomacy:
A Systems Approach to Peace* (Washington, D.C.: Institute for Multi-Track
Diplomacy, 1993).

15. Shepard Forman, Director of Center on International Collaboration, New
York University, phone interview by Marc Lindenberg, followed by e-mail,
December 2000.

16. For one of the best overviews of the issues of negative impacts see John

Pendergast and Colin Scott, "Aid with Integrity: Avoiding the Potential of Humanitarian Aid to Sustain Conflict," Occasional Paper Number Two (Office of U.S. Foreign Disaster Assistance, Bureau of Humanitarian Assistance, U.S. Agency for International Development, March 1996). See also John Pendergast "Helping or Hurting? Humanitarian Intervention and Crisis Response in the Horn," Discussion paper no. 6 (Washington, D.C.: Center of Concern, January 1995). Finally, see Larry Minear, "The International Relief System: A Critical Review," Parallel National Intelligence Estimate on Global Humanitarian Emergencies (Washington, D.C.: Meridian International Center, September 22, 1994).

17. Francis Deng, Sadikiel Kimaro, Terrence Lyons, Donald Rothchild and William Zartman, *Sovereignty as Responsibility* (Washington, D.C.: The Brookings Institution, 1996).

18. UNHCR, *1999 Global Appeal* (Geneva: UNHCR, 1999), 16–17.

19. Barbara Crossette, "U.N. Studies How Refugees Qualify to Get Assistance," *New York Times,* February 18, 2000.

20. See Marc Lindenberg, Senior Vice President for Programs, CARE USA, UN Security Council Briefing, "CARE International's Perspective on the Great Lakes Region," February 12, 1997.

21. Howard French, "Mobutu and Rebels Said to Agree to Talks," *New York Times,* 6, April 18, 1997.

22. Howard French, "Talks Between Zairian Foes Collapse Before the Start," *New York Times,* 1, May 7, 1997.

23. Steven Erlanger, "UN Refugee Chief Warns Zaire Crisis a Nightmare," *New York Times,* 1, May 4, 1997.

24. "The Independent Evaluation of UNHCR's Emergency Preparedness and Response to the Kosovo Refugee Crisis" (The Newsletter of the International Council of Voluntary Agencies [ICVA] 2, February 2000), no. 1, 18.

25. See Roberta Cohen and Francis Deng, *Masses in Flight: The Global Crisis of Internal Displacement* (Washington: D.C.: The Brookings Institution Press, 1998). See also UNHCR and NGO Partners, *Protecting Refugees: A Field Guide* (Geneva: UNHCR, 1999), and Alten Frye, *Humanitarian Intervention: Crafting a Workable Doctrine* (Washington, D.C.: Council on Foreign Relations, 2000).

– 4 –

Building Positive Peace: Reducing Poverty and Social Exclusion

> The top 20 percent of humanity now captures 86 percent of all income; the bottom 20 percent only 1.3 percent.... The North-South differential was about 30:1 in 1965 and is now 70:1 and rising.
> — Susan George in *Oxford Today*[1]

War and Other Poverty Drivers

MANY OF THE relief and development NGOs were established as their founders reacted to the impact of war and violence on civilians, especially children. The founders did not believe that children should be hurt by adult wars, or be the largest percentage of those crippled or made homeless by them. Today millions of financial supporters demonstrate their agreement as they send these NGOs their contributions. The founders of these organizations were also aware that wars deepen poverty just as poverty can be one of the contributory forces leading to violence. What they could not have foreseen is the impact of all that was to happen in the last decade of the twentieth century: financial crises, state collapse, and the opening up of the old Soviet Union. This chapter will discuss this changing context of poverty work—and how the NGOs are responding to it with projects, programs, and policy work.

NGO leaders and staff would prefer to be building positive peace rather than responding to conflicts. While, of course, NGO leaders and staff feel morally compelled by both need and circumstance to respond to civil wars, they would prefer to work upstream—to have prevented the outbreak of conflict in the first place. Leaders and staff are committed to reducing poverty and facilitating long-term sustainable development.

Poverty reduction is more frequently, and eloquently, their stated goal in mission statements, on their Web sites, in their annual reports, and in their advocacy and development education documents than is relief work. CARE USA, for example, emphasizes the goal of addressing the root causes of poverty, stating on their Web site: "CARE's goal is to help families find long term solutions to poverty. We also help communities prepare for and recover from emergencies.... We target our efforts at the household level, often combining different types of interventions for a holistic approach that addresses the root causes of poverty." NGO staff see extreme poverty as silent violence that corrodes the social contract. Unfortunately, however, there is often much more funding from official donors for short-term emergency relief and far less support for longer-term work on hunger, homelessness, and poverty.

Nor are wars the only "drivers," or causes, of poverty. Adverse terms of trade, ill-conceived public policies, financial crises, under-investment in health and education, and bad governance—all are contributing factors. Many also point to the adverse impact of geography and climate on initial conditions, noting that malaria, fevers, AIDS and HIV, and other rare viruses and tropical diseases flourish in many tropical countries, where poverty is most prevalent.[2]

Other factors in a globalizing world, in particular the ease with which large amounts of capital move rapidly across borders, coming in or leaving, at electronic speed, also cause people to become newly poor. Countries must pursue more open trade agreements to take advantage of opportunities and earn scarce foreign exchange—but they feel the impact of competitiveness with other countries also trying to attract capital. Moreover, their own lags in science and technology may keep some countries from being fully competitive. Governance also matters. Many countries, especially in Africa, need public attention to multiple factors affecting competitiveness—legal frameworks, judicial reform, as well as political competitiveness. Governance—or the lack of it—means in some cases inability to stop the ways in which terrorists raid rare natural resources (diamonds, other precious jewels, and so forth)—costing the country both increased violence and lost revenue.

Globalization and Changing Concepts of Poverty

The social and cultural impact of the ways the Internet shrinks spatial differences are as complicating as they are worthwhile. On the one hand, information is more available; on the other, different social mores enter into people's homes in ways that many find intrusive if not offensive. And the Internet assures that many more people than before are today aware of inequities and their own relative poverty.

As Simon Maxwell questioned years ago, "Does globalization now mean that we are all developing countries? Are there new comparisons or lessons to be drawn across geographical boundaries about the characteristics, causes and remedies of poverty and social exclusion? Does the rapid increase in poverty and social exclusion in the North signal a new convergence between North and South? Are there theories to hand which will expose connections between poverty and social exclusion in North and South?"[3] There is some—though not enough—research on these questions. Meanwhile, NGOs are experimenting and learning by doing. They have found that there is a more immediate dialogue between North and South now because of greater awareness of being increasingly interdependent.

Maxwell's first question—does globalization now mean that we are all developing countries—appears to be answered by current NGO work with a resounding "yes." In part this is because the conceptual thinking about poverty has also moved into new terrain. Definitions of development have changed markedly in the past fifteen years. Most notably, they have moved away from a narrow focus on economic growth to a wider set of commitments. Amartya Sen's work added capability as a necessary component in looking at poverty.[4] His recent book, *Development as Freedom*, further widens the boundaries of the field.[5] In our own earlier work, development was defined as increasing people's capacities in an interdependent world.[6] The World Bank's *World Development Report 2000: Attacking Poverty* analyzes poverty around three major components: capacity, empowerment, and security, singling these out as areas to be strengthened in any poverty-reducing approach.

Conceptualizations of poverty and techniques for measuring it have changed, as have policies, practices, and techniques for ameliorating it. The experience of the "transitional" countries (those of Central and Eastern Europe and of the former Soviet Union) have led to much new thinking, for example, about the interrelationship of poverty and institutional development. How we now think about poverty and what we have learned about effective ways to address it have changed in light of this new experience. Consultations with the poor have also clarified that far more than income poverty is impeding their progress. They experience powerlessness, ill being (bad health, loss of energy, declining access to assets), and social exclusion as both causal factors and conditions of their poverty.[7]

Thus there are both changes in the ways we think about poverty and in the kinds of programs and projects that need to be identified and implemented in order to reduce it. And of course the ways in which it is measured have changed—as income poverty is no longer the only measure. In this rapidly changing context, NGO leaders, their staffs, boards, and stakeholders find they must work differently. Figure 4.1 on the following page below depicts the changing conceptual and operational context for poverty-reducing work. Needed are different kinds of projects, different kinds of data, and different partners in order to meet

Figure 4.1. The Changing Context of Poverty Work for NGOs

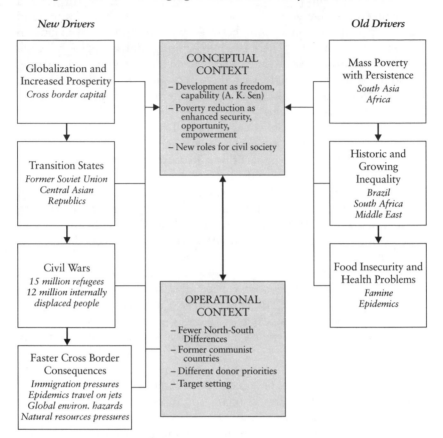

New Drivers

Old Drivers

Globalization and
Increased Prosperity
Cross border capital

Transition States
*Former Soviet Union
Central Asian
Republics*

Civil Wars
*15 million refugees
12 million internally
displaced people*

Faster Cross Border
Consequences
*Immigration pressures
Epidemics travel on jets
Global environ. hazards
Natural resources pressures*

CONCEPTUAL
CONTEXT
– Development as freedom,
  capability (A. K. Sen)
– Poverty reduction as
  enhanced security,
  opportunity,
  empowerment
– New roles for civil society

OPERATIONAL
CONTEXT
– Fewer North-South
  Differences
– Former communist
  countries
– Different donor priorities
– Target setting

Mass Poverty
with Persistence
*South Asia
Africa*

Historic and
Growing
Inequality
*Brazil
South Africa
Middle East*

Food Insecurity and
Health Problems
*Famine
Epidemics*

needs. In addition, NGOs are being asked to work in a wider array of countries with increased competition for their time and talents.

The striking fact is that all the new contributory drivers of the "new" poverty are *additional* to the older causes of poverty. New drivers include globalization and increased inequality, "transition" and its failures, civil wars, and faster travel across borders for both good and ill. In addition to fast-traveling capital—which can be for good or ill—there are new age viruses, growing international environmental problems (acid rain, global warming), and increased tension over scarce natural resources (water, energy, forest products).

Meanwhile the older causes of poverty remain: poor governance, weak resource management, dependency upon trade in low-priced commodities, low levels of productivity due in part to little investment in health and education, wholly inadequate infrastructure (transport, roads, telecommunications), weak fiscal policies (little resource genera-

Table 4.1. Total Number of People Living on Less than $1 Per Day (millions and percentage)

Region	1987		1998 (est.)	
	Number	*Share of Population*	*Number*	*Share of Population*
East Asia and the Pacific	417.5	26.6%	278.3	15.3%
(excluding China)	114.1	23.9%	65.1	11.3%
Eastern Europe Europe and Central Asia	1.1	0.2%	24.0	5.1%
Latin America and Caribbean	63.7	15.3%	78.2	15.6%
Middle East and North Africa	9.3	4.3%	5.5	1.9%
South Asia	474.4	44.9%	522.0	40.0%
Sub-Saharan Africa	217.2	46.6%	290.9	46.3%
Total	1,183.2	28.3%	1,198.9	24.0%

Source: Adapted from *World Development Report 2000/2001* (Washington D.C.: World Bank, 2001), 23.

tion), and inadequate banking sector performance. It does not help that donors move among fads, emphasizing one or another sectoral program, but rarely looking at the range of both macro and micro causes of traditional poverty and their linkages to one another.

The cumulative result of these new and the old drivers is that there are 1,198 billion people living in absolute income poverty measured as living on less than $1 a day. This number reflects an increase from the 1,183 billion living on a dollar a day in 1987 (adjusted for purchasing power parity). But the regional distribution of absolute income poverty varies. There has been significant reduction in the numbers of the absolute poor in East Asia and the Pacific. China's performance in poverty reduction is the most dramatic. Yet other regions—notably Africa, South Asia, and Latin America—show markedly less improvement. Table 4.1 provides an overview of overall performance in regard to poverty between 1987 and 1998.

These numbers tell but a small part of the income poverty story, however, since the cutoff point of living on less than $1 a day captures the most severe poverty. For example, that cutoff point would not include the homeless people in Northern industrial countries. One would need a cutoff point of at least $5 a day to put this into comparative prices and include those living in the most severe poverty in the United States. Most of the comparative studies—for example, that of Robin Marris—actually use a higher cutoff point when looking at the United States. (It is also worth noting that poverty studies now use some new, relatively awkward terms in order to distinguish between different kinds of poverty—for example, "income poverty" in contrast to "asset poverty.")

In *Ending Poverty,* Marris provides a table comparing First, Second, and Third World income poverty using, respectively, the measures of less than $1, $5, or $15 a day. Counting in this manner, he concludes that, of those living in income poverty, 28 percent are in the Third World; 20 percent in the Second World (the transition states); and 10 percent in the First World (the industrial states). Other comparative data, however, reveal that, on some critical dimensions—for example, life expectancy—some Americans are more disadvantaged than their counterparts who, while they live on considerably less, are able to enjoy a longer life. Sen provides an illuminating set of tables comparing life expectancy for African-American men and women to that in China and India. African-American men live shorter lives. Even when controlling for violence, they live shorter lives than men in China and India do. Other factors beyond the dangers of urban criminality are at work: inadequate employment opportunities, limited access to quality health care, poor nutrition, and greater stress all take their toll.

All of the different drivers of the currently changing context of poverty-reduction work were reflected in interviews with NGO leaders and staff. Their daily work choices are directly affected by the dynamic quality of the ongoing changes in concepts, measurement, and operational possibilities. The changing context of poverty-reduction work also has an impact on everything else that NGOs are doing: the kind and scale of support they need, their terms of engagement with partners, accountability processes, and determination to strengthen advocacy work.

Those made poor by the transitions in Central and Eastern Europe, Russia, and the Central Asian republics are adding to global poverty—while the persistent poverty long characteristic of South Asia, Africa, and Latin America remains. While globally the past decade may well be labeled the gilded age of the twentieth century in terms of the wealth accumulated by some, millions in Russia and the Central Asian republics have not shared in that growth. While they have gained politically, their life circumstances as measured by income, health, or life expectancy have not improved and in some cases have seriously deteriorated.

Moreover, there are serious poverty problems beyond the transition states. In Western Europe and in the United States, poverty problems are apparent at a glance in inner cities, in rural areas, and among all minorities. As Sen points out, the life expectancy of a young African-American man in one of America's inner cities is less than that of a young man in Bangladesh. The poverty on Native American reservations, in rural areas, in inner cities, in older suburbs in the dying industrial belt of the American Midwest remains persistent—so persistent that it is taken for granted. It is poverty woven deeply into the very institutional fabric of the country, taken to be part of the rules of the game. Over time, these poor become invisible; they are nowhere to be found in any national policy debate. The poverty problem festers in its intractability.

When Michael Harrington captured the nation's attention with his book *The Other America,* poverty was found to be serious in all these groups, and especially so among the elderly.[8] That has changed. Today the problem is poverty among the young, especially children. In the United States, 22 percent of the children under six years of age are growing up in poverty.[9] Those children live in inadequate housing, suffer poor health, poor schooling, and go to bed hungry. Their poverty is multigenerational and is self-replicating. Is this not a development problem? In important ways, all countries are today developing countries.

Policy issues matter in the reduction of poverty—often more than projects or programs. The amount spent on a sector often means little in terms of its results. The World Health Organization points out, for example, that the United States ranks thirty-seventh (while France ranks first) among all countries in terms of the health status of its people. Often a low ranking of this sort is symptomatic of underlying income inequality, but in fact the United States and France have strikingly similar income distributions.[10] The gap instead reflects policy differences in the two countries with regard to public health, access to health care, and policies about that access.

World Vision, in its *Annual Report* for 1999, lists poverty reduction as the first of ten most urgent issues for the new millennium. A contributing author writing in the magazine *World Vision Today* writes, "You and I are probably 150 times richer than the world's poorest 20 percent. Both biblical faith and long term self interest demand that we end this scandal of widespread poverty amidst escalating affluence." He goes on to point to the progress that has been made in addressing poverty. "Since 1970, the percentage of people in developing countries who are chronically malnourished has dropped from 35 percent to 20 percent. The situation is not hopeless."[11]

Both points are important—that inequality (relative poverty) is as important a concern as absolute poverty—and that some progress has been made in reducing absolute poverty. On the first point, it is worth noting that at the grassroots level, where these NGOs are working, people are often even more aware of inequalities than of absolute, measurable differences. Inequalities generate the most resentment—especially if they reinforce existing patterns of discrimination, or ethnic divisions in a society.

The greatest progress in reducing absolute poverty has in recent years been achieved in China and East Asia. (Because of the size of China's population, and the country's progress in reducing poverty, when calculations are made solely on the basis of aggregate population, the record for the globe looks better than when one looks country by country.) With World Bank help, a constant poverty line was devised for China. Research then demonstrated that, from 1970 forward through the 1980s, the total number of poor fell from 270 million to 100 million. There was more progress in the 1990s—as growth rates continued to rise—though inequality during this decade increased rapidly. Malaysia, Thailand, and Indonesia also managed to reduce their poverty numbers in the 1980s. In the 1990s, however, many of the East Asians who had just escaped poverty (not the Chinese) were pushed back into it during the decade's financial crises.

It is important to note that progress has been made, and not just in China and East Asia, since those outside the field of development often do not know that positive side of the story—or how much has been learned. For example, several African countries—Uganda, Ghana, and Botswana—have in the past several years reported economic growth as well as improvements in reducing poverty. The steady, difficult, quiet work of development decision-makers struggling with age-old problems has led to increases in life expectancy, lowering infant mortality, improving literacy, attacking infectious diseases, and expanding opportunities.

NGOs have innovated, and much has been learned. Microfinance projects can make credit available when it is well targeted for those ready to use it for productive work. Improved attention to birthing, as well as prenatal and postnatal care, leads to improvement in maternal mortality and infant mortality. Life expectancy in many countries has been improved due to advances in health services. Literacy has improved, with increasing numbers daily making their way into the information revolution. Hundreds of thousands of local nongovernmental organizations are growing in the larger number of countries that have become more open to citizens forming and participating in such organizations.

Precisely because of the quiet but steady progress, more official agencies—the World Bank, bilateral and multilateral donors, and the United Nations—are now talking about how much more could be done if adequate levels of development assistance were available. At one point, official donors talked about the possibility of halving the numbers of absolute poor (those living on a dollar a day) by 2015. They are now revising their estimates, as shortfalls in funding, lack of international commitment, and country-specific problems will make this goal recede to a more distant future. Nonetheless, increasing numbers of donors are presuming that an ever-larger percentage of their funding will flow through NGOs to come as close to this target as possible. On the other hand, many NGOs are trying to move away from reliance on donor contracts. Just how these disparities in means and goals will evolve remains unclear.

Nevertheless, all of the new and old causes of poverty are getting more attention today. The international NGOs have helped to get many of the issues on the public agenda while also working on them through partners, projects, and programs. Globalization, with its increased quantity and speed of cross-border movements of goods, services, and information, affects both the ways we think about poverty and the ways that it changes, grows, or could be relieved.

Each of these drivers of change has affected both the conceptual and the operational work of NGOs. While we cannot provide here a detailed discussion of all these issues, we will take a look at inequality, social exclusion, humanitarianism, and structural violence as the arenas in which NGOs have demonstrated their poverty policy and program concerns. We will then turn to a discussion of NGO responses.

Inequality and Social Exclusion

The two important and interrelated drivers of increased inequality and social exclusion have led not only to new approaches but also to new understanding that poverty must be addressed in both North and South. The increases in inequality within and between countries has been cited as a major problem by unlikely sources, for example, the IMF and *The Economist*—neither of which is noted for liberal inclinations. In a paper written for the IMF's *World Economic Outlook*, Nicholas Craft points to the startling growth in inequality as rich nations (and the rich within them) have grown richer while poor countries (and the poor within them) have grown more poor. "Income in Mozambique fell from $1,000 [per capita] a year in 1950 to $850 in 1990, while in America growth went from $10,000 [per capita] to $24,000 (all in 1990 prices)."[12]

The rapid increase in inequality and poverty is the fundamental problem of our times. According to the World Bank, the ratio between the average income of the world's richest 5 percent and the poorest 5 percent increased from 78:1 in 1993 to 123:1 in 1998. Inside the United States, in 1976, 1 percent of the population held just under 20 percent of the national household wealth. By 1999, that figure had doubled: 40 percent of U.S. national household wealth is in the hands of 1 percent of the population. These disparities are more extreme in the United States than in any other advanced industrial country—but they are growing in Europe too.

Consequently many NGOs have moved to increase their domestic work—with the poor and socially excluded in the countries within which they are based—while also continuing their work abroad. The concept of "social exclusion"—a relatively new term in the United States—warrants some clarification. This concept was first introduced in France by Rene Lenoir within the Chirac government in 1974. Lenoir wrote about those excluded from employment-based social security systems—including the disabled, suicidal people, the aged, abused children, and substance abusers. He argued that these represented about 10 percent of the population. New social programs were subsequently put into place to address the need for national solidarity. The concept spread across Europe, especially with the advent of European integration.

But social exclusion is defined differently by different authors. In general, the concept has been expanded to include minorities, especially when discrimination excludes them from full participation in the life and benefits of the community. Yet prejudice is not the only factor within a focus on social exclusion. There are those who are excluded from full economic and social participation for a variety of reasons—joblessness, racism, drugs, alcohol, disabilities, or religious or cultural differences.

An inherent question is how one delimits this concept, and how social exclusion relates to another new concept—"structural violence"— introduced in the literature on civil wars, especially in Peter Uvin's book, *Aiding Violence*.[13] We will return to the issue of structural violence below; here, however, it is worth noting because some NGOs, for example Oxfam America, have been thinking about their role in addressing social exclusion. Sometimes, especially when considering the impact of racism in the United States, these NGOs use the term social exclusion interchangeably with structural violence.

Some NGOs, most notably Oxfam GB and Save the Children UK, are moving away from separating their domestic and international operational work—pointing out that much is to be learned for project work as well as policy advocacy when merging programs. Moreover, their work feels more coherent with this integration.

An Oxfam spokesperson told us, for example, that it worked well to bring community organizers who had facilitated their microcredit program from Bangladesh to England to work with people in housing estates to help develop microcredit programs. While people were initially surprised, if not annoyed, doubting that people within a "developed" country needed help from someone from a "developing" country, Oxfam leaders simply responded why not? Why should anyone assume that we have more right to work in their country than they do to work in ours? Why assume that learning needs to happen only in one direction?

Proving their point, an exchange of views and perspectives was set up for the actual project participants and their Bangladeshi organizer. More innovative ideas emerged that proved entirely relevant. He pointed out how they could improve trash collection—and do it in a manner that was locally income-generating for entrepreneurial residents of the public housing units. The project participants in turn helped him to think about appropriate roles of the state. Although they did organize themselves to take over local trash collection as a way of improving income generation, they also queried whether it was wise in the long run to fill in for the role of the government rather than push the government to perform its responsibilities.

As already noted, in its *World Development Report 2000: Attacking Poverty*, the World Bank posits three major goals in poverty reduction: increasing opportunity, empowerment, and security. These goals are the major themes that will be used in guiding the Bank's operational work in the near future.[14] Opportunity, strengthening capacity, empowering people, and improving security are important and sought after by poor people. They have been featured for decades in NGO work. Yet one can argue that these are not the only factors affecting economic improvement for, and by, the poor. Furthermore, while *income* poverty is not the whole of the poverty story, it is a central part of it. In short, in its effort to move to newer terrain, the World Bank may have lost sight of some of its own important earlier contributions on the need for investments that improve productivity. Economic growth is driven by improved productivity (of labor and capital). Without that, there is too little to distribute or invest or trade in the first place.

That said, the more progressive approach of this *World Development Report* is to be welcomed. It is the case, however, that their approach stops short of a rights-based approach to poverty reduction. There are politically significant differences between arguing for more opportunity, security, and empowerment as goals in contrast to arguing that basic human needs are rights common to all people and recognizable as responsibilities by states. The *World Development Report* is written for Bank staff as well as for its wider audience. It directly influences projects, programs, and policy dialogue until the Bank's next *World Development Report*. Thus we can be sure that the debates about the appropriate role for the state were thoroughly vetted, and therefore necessarily cautious. In the Bank's approach, the role of the state remains limited to facilitating and enabling economic growth through open markets, providing basic infrastructure, adequate opportunities, and investments in health and education. In the rights-based approach, the state has further responsibilities—to ensure the inclusion of people who fall through social safety nets, and to widen access rules so that the disabled or disadvantaged are enabled. The locus of responsibility thus shifts away from the poor as petitioners to the state to prove its determination and capability to deliver socially inclusive policies. (Operationally, it is the difference between having a right to health care in contrast to having the right to work in order to buy health insurance.)

NGOs are contributing to the ongoing debates about these choices. They know they cannot do everything; that there is an important role for the state. That said, the issue is finding the operational niche to improve productivity, or to secure more effective poverty reduction, either in their projects or in their policy advocacy. They work to identify the places where they can make a difference and struggle to hit the balance between projects, programs, and policy advocacy to achieve the best ends. The problem is that they must do this when all roles—those of the state, those of the private sector, and those of the nonprofit sector—are all simultaneously shifting. As we see below, the humanitarian dimension adds to the ongoing debate on the place of the rights-based approach.

Humanitarianism and Rights-Based Approaches

The most rapidly shifting boundary is that between humanitarian work and development work. In the past, development agencies focused on problems of poverty reduction and economic growth, while human rights organizations focused on "witness" and providing voice for those adversely impacted by human rights abuses. When natural disasters occurred, the unit or section within the largely development-oriented NGO responded. Some of the older NGOs—especially ones that had their roots in postwar relief and recovery work, were natural sources of such work when man-made disasters struck again. As we saw in Chapter 3, that kind of relief work came to be called humanitarian assistance in the large number of man-made emergencies of the post–Cold War era.

With the increase in internal civil wars—often happening in part as a result of ethnic tensions—this humanitarian work entered a whole new era. Médecins Sans Frontières work exemplifies some of the best-known humanitarian work. MSF is also quick to point out that it is not a development but rather a humanitarian organization—a human rights group that works on relief and reconstruction with people whose human rights have been violated. Their intellectual roots are in the Enlightenment, and their commitments are to a secular and independent, rights-based approach.

Their domestic work focuses directly and immediately on working with the excluded (*les exclus*). Work on social exclusion blurs the boundary between NGOs that consider themselves to be in the development field, and those that consider themselves to be humanitarian organizations—human rights groups and refugee-focused organizations that work on relief and reconstruction. Yet outside observers of NGO programs who had not thought about such distinctions would not see a major difference between, on the one hand, Médecins Sans Frontières' work in building water towers in Indonesia or their work with street children in Egypt, and, on the other hand, the work of NOVIB (the Dutch Oxfam) on water supply in Kosovo, or that of Save the Children with street children in Latin America.

As a humanitarian organization, however, MSF believes in issues of access to basic services needed for basic human dignity as rights under a rule of law. This is in contrast to the language and its implications in the Anglo-American development tradition, where the concepts and language used are about equal opportunities, or moral imperatives to give back through charity. Arguing that there are rights—to health, education, and participation in social security programs—changes the discourse. It says that appeals for charity, or even equal opportunity, is not the first need; the first need is to secure state responsibilities. MSF is often concerned that development actors forget the distinctions between the roles of states and the roles of independent, nonprofit actors.

This difference in views became especially troubled as the international security system began using language to describe peacekeeping as "humanitarian action." Kosovo was a greatly complicating case, especially when NATO—a major military force—began justifying bombing as humanitarian action. MSF staff felt this was an appropriation of language to provide NATO cover for carrying out the antithesis of humanitarian goals: bombing people in order to enforce rights. Humanitarian NGOs, especially the European MSF members, wondered how to respond to this kind of militarism in the name of humanitarianism. They were not sure that they could continue to call themselves part of a humanitarian movement. They feared a turning point had been reached. The international system would now associate humanitarian action with the use of bombs and militarized forces to enforce human rights.

MSF's domestic projects are working with asylum seekers, AIDS victims, the disabled, and those who are socially excluded in order to help them secure their rights to health. Its central concept is *temoinage*—inadequately translatable as witness—it is more accurately about being in solidarity with those who are undergoing misery, helping where possible, and bearing witness to others about that suffering. To do this, independence is critically important. As a result, MSF Paris takes no funds from the French government in order to ensure its independent voice on these issues.

CARE Paris, one of the smaller national members of the CARE network, echoes this approach, reflecting its own French cultural context, as it also wants to increase its own advocacy and outreach to work with those marginalized and at risk within France. Like MSF, CARE Paris has to factor in another aspect of its context—that there is little French respect for volunteering to meet human needs. This is the public opinion side to the rights-based approach to social change. There is little public support for voluntarism, yet much support for the politics of refusal—for saying "no" to the state and insisting that it assume responsibilities. The downside of this is of course the fact that there is less of a tradition of direct private philanthropic giving to support volunteer work. On the other hand, the strong support for advocacy for social justice that resonates with the French social justice tradition means that direct mail appeals for support can be attractive to French citizens when they perceive that the NGO has a real and immediate social justice component.

The French concept of social exclusion has now spread far beyond France to become an integral part of the European Union's social policy. One reason for the greater salience of this concept in the integrating new Europe is the prevalence of diversity, and the high correlation between poverty and minority status. Another is that, as Amartya Sen points out, social welfare policy in Europe stands in contrast to that of the United States. European governments assume that the state has a responsibility to provide a social safety net; the United States believes that the role of the state comes in guaranteeing equal opportunities, not welfare.

In Europe, as in the United States, there are significant minorities. Often minorities are socially excluded, and often it is taken for granted that they both are, and are likely to remain, poor. (That assumption is somewhat less prevalent in the United States, as it is a country of immigrants.) Whether they are Roma (gypsies) in Eastern Europe, or North Africans in France, or Africans or Arabs in England, minority people are often highly represented in poverty counts. Thus there are major questions not just of inclusion in society, but of equity. The European Union and several European governments are now adopting policies to advance social inclusion and solidarity. These governments also tend to believe that these policies will also positively affect their future competitiveness as their labor force becomes healthier, more educated, less poor, and possibly more productive. It remains to be seen what impact, if any, this approach and its consequences will have on poverty policy, or approaches to productivity, in the United States.

Peter Bell, president of CARE USA, well known for his lifetime work on human rights, has been working to integrate a rights-based approach into CARE's operations. He says, "When we first tried to introduce a human rights perspective some colleagues expressed concern that we might be seeking to transform CARE into a hard edged advocacy organization. That is not what we have in mind. . . . I see our evolving approach to human rights as strengthening our work in humanitarian assistance and development cooperation." Following a thorough testing against country case experience, CARE USA now has rights-based guidelines for their work, which are enhancing operations.

Oxfam America also seized this concept and has held regional workshops on the implications of this concept for its work. Like its counterpart in Britain, Oxfam America, too, is exploring more integration between its international and domestic programming. One of the preliminary findings is the same as that learned internationally about empowerment: that increasing "voice" is directly relevant in the domestic context. Thus in this area too, we are finding that poverty is not only a North-South issue but a global one.

The historic problems of racism in the United States, and treatment of African-Americans as well as Native Americans—and the impoverishment that both minorities have experienced—should be analyzed through the lens of social exclusion.[15] Oxfam America is now taking the lead within the Oxfam family to give more attention to social exclusion in their work.

Minority status and poverty have long been highly correlated—and that has happened so often historically that it comes to be taken for granted by development historians. Moreover, following early work on inequality it came to be assumed that growing income inequality was inevitable during a period of economic growth. The first assumption is challenged by the concept of social exclusion. And the second concept is increasingly being challenged by econometric analysis that indicates the drag created for an economy when inequality is high.

In the past, economists argued that increases in inequality were inevitable—that they *had* to happen during periods of economic growth. Now, new empirical research indicates that presumption is often wrong. There are cases in which high rates of inequality slow down growth—and make it less sustainable. This is especially true, for example, when access to assets such as land is highly skewed. The World Bank's *World Development Report 2000* points out that: "these results [of the new studies] open the possibility that policies to improve the distribution of income and assets can have a double benefit—by increasing growth and by increasing the share of growth that accrues to poor people."[16] The significance of this finding for future NGO work on poverty and inequality is provocative—the research results show there is more room than previously thought to argue that national solidarity is not only good social policy—but is good for economic performance as well.

Relief, Postwar Poverty Reduction, and Structural Violence

Since the fall of the Berlin Wall, there have been scores of civil wars—all of them in poor countries. As these wars predominantly take place in poor countries and have even more devastating consequences for those who are most poor within those countries, their impact has been to deepen poverty for millions of people already living at the margin. Since much has been said about this in Chapter 3, our point here is to look at how poverty problems were exacerbated by these wars, and at the NGO programming and techniques put in place to cope with these problems.

The relief-to-rehabilitation-to-development continuum often referred to in NGO programming is described in Chapter 3. Acknowledging that there is little that is linear about relief, or rehabilitation, or development, the point is that the nature of the projects and programs to be put in place varies by where a place is in terms of this continuum. Most specifically, at the household or family level, choices have to be made about what is most needed and when. Even in times without civil war, poor people move in and out of poverty, go through crises, hungry seasons, and experience periods of improvement. Some move out of poverty altogether while others may fall back into poverty. Sometimes a "peace" that is kept in place only through top-down control—a peace brought about through force and control, which do not address underpinning tensions—leads to violent eruptions and the cycle of relief has to start again.

NGOs are innovating in this troubled terrain with all the different ways to create opportunities for change. Chastened by the Rwanda experience, they are also rethinking their roles when social exclusion turns into structural violence. Peter Uvin has characterized "structural violence" as the forces of exclusion, inequality, pauperization, racism, and oppression as these get entrenched and woven into the very interstices of politics, society, and governance within a country. Earlier we said that it is hard to draw the boundaries between social exclusion and structural violence. The differences are more a matter of the degree and the extent to which the exclusion is embedded so deeply that violence is a regularly recurring phenomenon. It is possible to think of there being a continuum running from social exclusion to structural violence where structural violence stands, for example, for use of the policing powers of the state to repress a group, or groups. South Africa's apartheid state was such a case.

Structural violence may be present in varying degrees of extremity in a great many countries where NGOs work. Certainly social exclusion is present in many countries. It is extremely hard for an NGO to take up the issue of structural violence in the very country of their largest members. For example, it is easier for Save the Children US, or World Vision, or Oxfam America to address structural violence in Burundi or East Timor than it is for it to address it in the United States. Yet many NGOs do address it at the project level—working in inner cities or with Native Americans. (In Chapter 5, we will turn to NGO advocacy work related to this issue.) Such projects may be brave—and they can cost an NGO financial support when its constituents feel more threatened by a minority in their own country than they do pointing to equivalent or comparable issues in another country. Note that donor agencies—bilateral or multilateral—can avoid addressing the challenging issue of structural violence, since, unlike NGOs, the World Bank, for example, does not work inside any Northern industrial country— nor do the IADB, the UNDP, or any of the official bilateral development agencies. This being so, it is the international NGOs that are the path breakers when they work as they do with Native Americans, with gypsies in Europe, with undocumented Algerians in France, or with Kurds in Turkey.

Reducing poverty and social exclusion (especially when it becomes structural violence) holds more promise for long-term sustainable development than do several other strategies. This is not to say that reducing poverty is a panacea for all the causes of violence. It is to say that reducing poverty and social exclusion—thereby assuring that poor people can become stakeholders in the places where they live and work—holds out more possibility for progress toward a more inherently peaceful world. It would also be a step toward affording increased opportunity for freedom and for human capabilities to reach their potential. Those processes in turn create more of an enabling environment for peace. Once they have more to lose than to gain from violence, people develop an interest in peace. Thus development is about giving peace a chance.

The countries that have erupted into violence in the wars since 1989 were all characterized by widespread poverty. That calls attention to the ways in which vulnerability increases tensions, and signals that deepening or worsening patterns can be identified. Writing about Rwanda, for example, Peter Uvin argues that development workers in the country did not look for, or heed, the signals that pointed to the coming genocide in the years preceding it. There were several aspects to their turning a blind eye. First, too little attention was paid to the ways in which the flows of benefits from projects were exacerbating underlying tensions. Looking at beneficiaries of projects to consider whether ethnic inequities were increasing—or perceived to be increasing—was not part of the project identification process. And then too, development specialists either were preoccupied with their own projects or oblivious of the overarching pattern to be found in, for example, rising violence—tending to see incidents as singular events and not as part of a pattern. Nor did they pay attention to increased military expenditures, increased localized chronic violence, and progressively polarized tensions between Hutus and Tutsis in the months before the full-scale genocide of 1994 took place. Moreover, when the flow of benefits from projects reinforced social divisions within the country, the development workers did not consider how they were adding to the problem.

Uvin's book, *Aiding Violence,* sent a chastening message to the development community—arguing cogently that structural violence is an institutional problem that demands attention, and that the development community, acquiescent in its silence, was complicit in it. Moreover, when the violence continued, their silence was increasingly problematical. Since new money arrived for these development professionals to provide humanitarian relief—and some food relief was used by terrorists posing as refugees—the problem deepened. Sometimes relief workers unknowingly engaged war criminals as local staff in camps without realizing that this fed into the re-imposition of terrorist authority over the camp's refugees.

Some NGOs, for example Médecins Sans Frontières, did pull out when they discovered abuses. Others, like CARE USA and CARE Canada, went through wrenching introspection about their roles and new needs (like better security from international authorities—hence their meeting with the Security Council). CARE Canada later concluded that either pulling out, or privatizing security, would be better than relying on the international community. CARE Canada's thoughtful study of three cases, detailed in *Mean Times,* is essential reading for anyone considering NGO roles in civil wars in poor countries.[17]

Mary Anderson, whose work with NGOs (including Save the Children and Oxfam America) in active humanitarianism is cited in Chapter 3, points to the roles that lead to building a more positive peace.

> When international aid agencies arrive in conflict zones to provide assistance to people affected by war, their programs often miss the [local capacities for peace making]. They design programs, make decisions, distribute goods, employ and deploy staffs in ways that ignore, and negate other realities—those on which past peace rested and future peace could be built. What additional good could be done by assistance that is provided in conflict areas if, while emergency needs were being met, local capacities for peace were also recognized, supported, encouraged and enlarged?
>
> The introduction of external resources into an environment where people are in conflict and where, very often, resources are scarce can increase tensions and suspicions among groups in two distinct ways. First, the resources brought by the aid agencies can be taxed, stolen, or diverted by warring parties to support their

efforts directly, or they can be manipulated by warring parties to enhance their power over civilian populations. Second the systems through which the resources are provided very often carry implicit ethical messages regarding power and violence. For example, when aid agencies negotiate with the leaders of armies to gain access to civilian populations, or when they hire armed guards to protect the goods they bring, they appear to accept as legitimate the right of arms to determine who gets access to food, medical care, and other humanitarian goods. It is difficult for aid agencies to meet human needs without playing into and reinforcing existing conflicts.[18]

The results of much of this introspection have led leaders and staff to think more about how they might work differently, what additional knowledge and skill-training they need, and what approaches hold more promise for effectiveness. They ask whether working more "upstream"—that is, well before an emergency erupts—and noticing whether and how much the flow of benefits from a project or program is overcoming structural violence, are among the answers. While there is an emerging consensus on these ideas, there are no easy answers.

There are several levels of work in undermining social tension and diminishing violence. First, of course, is more attention to prevention, conflict resolution, and mediation work. At another level, there is what Mary Anderson calls "finding the connectors," the possible connectors among people of different groups, factions, and warring parties. This is closely related to all that has been learned about local level listening in participatory development in order to learn as much as possible about underlying problem-solving capacities. Nurturing those capacities and not undermining them in a rush to "results" is part of the solution. At the very least, projects—as they have a flow of benefits to specific client groups—should be undertaken with an eye toward not exacerbating the tensions. Where possible, projects and the process of identifying them could more "pro-actively" help people communicate to avert triggering the violence that springs from misunderstanding and competing interests. Well-designed and thoughtfully implemented projects help participants acquire problem-solving and conflict-resolving skills.

It is also the case that such projects provide a positive example, or a safe space amidst the looming catastrophe. Oxfam America is working with Hutu and Tutsi war widows in Rwanda to help strengthen local organizational capacity for community healing. In the case of natural disasters, there are instances when projects demonstrating best practice provide important models. For example, World Vision can point to projects in Ethiopia that were effective at reforestation work in natural disaster areas, and when the drought of 2000 hit, these project areas served as oases for those fleeing the impact of the drought. A variety of approaches are being tried—including ways in which consultation processes matter for giving people voice to participatory strategies so that they gain real access to decision-making.

Poverty in Transition States

The absence of widespread violence does not, however, always mean that transitions are working well. The serious economic decline of many of the states formerly part of the Soviet Union is a case in point. While Westerners have had a period of unparalleled economic gain, Russia and the Central Asian republics have experienced record declines in GNP per capita and in life expectancy (a significant indicator of human well-being). Only some of the Eastern European countries have managed economic growth, notably the Czech Republic, Hungary, and East Germany. The increase in poverty in other transition countries, especially Russia, is so deep and widespread it is ominous. It remains to be seen what its implications are for future international stability. It is now widely acknowledged that Europe, the United States, and the Bretton Woods institutions—the International Monetary Fund and the World Bank—pushed a transition strategy that was too rapid and too ill-conceived.[19]

The UN Development Programme's Bureau for Europe and the Commonwealth of Independent States (CIS) points out that: "No region of the world has suffered such reversals in the 1990s as have the countries of the former Soviet Union and Eastern Europe. The number of poor has increased by over 150 million."[20] The Central Asian republics are not faring well either. Chechnya was a large-scale human catastrophe. Thus the transition states in general remain deeply mired in real problems of poverty and economic growth strategies. The older economic orthodoxy failed, and better approaches have yet to be devised.

NGOs responded to the challenge of working in the wholly different context presented by the transition from a command to a market economy. They have adjusted programs to include project work in these countries—ones that were closed previously, and hence were largely unknown to them during the Cold War. With the opening of a food aid program in Moscow, St. Petersburg, and other major cities in 1990, CARE was among the first of the NGOs to work in this region, with CARE Germany serving as the lead member. Médecins Sans Frontières had worked in Afghanistan since the 1970s and hence had knowledge of the Central Asian area that it could draw upon.

Poverty that comes after people have known some social and economic security carries challenges different from those in Third World countries with long histories of mass poverty. Anger and frustration run higher, and demands for improvement more intense, confronting outside advisors with more questioning and resistance. Technical advisors have had to learn anew what would and would not work. It can also be argued, however, that as a result, the general quality of technical assistance was improved in the harsh conditions of transitional economies. The IMF and the World Bank came under heavy criticism inside and outside the CIS for lacking the kinds of systemic, structural analysis that allowed for prescriptions more attuned to the institutional context and needs of these countries' polities and societies. Restructuring these economies with too little attention to institutional capacity—or lack of it—for a market process is now recognized as a serious mistake.[21]

NGOs have come under less fire than the Bretton Woods institutions, largely because NGOs are generally better listeners and have more experience with participatory approaches. They have been active in meeting several emergency needs as well as in strengthening local organizations to address what they can of local problems. But large-scale structural changes are not ones that NGOs are positioned to help with—such changes require leverage, access to conditionality, and systemic work that falls outside the purview of most NGOs. Even so, MSF has worked with the Ministry of Health in Kyrghizia to undertake a large institutional overhaul on their own as part of a health sector reform. MSF focused within that work on treatment of syphilis as well as on training in prevention and information activities.

The breakup of the command economy, and of the safety nets that had been in place, did open up the possibilities for growth—and there have been signs of real improvement recently. But inequality has greatly worsened, and poverty widened and deepened as the Russian economy came apart. All the economies linked closely to Russia—from Estonia to Tajikistan—felt the consequences as it disintegrated. One major study of the Russian economy says that national income in Russia declined 34 percent between 1989 and 1991—a decline comparable to the depression of the 1930s in the United States.[22] But the decline did not stop there. It continued for another 30 percent in 1992, and then 10 percent in 1993.

The Russian Statistical Office and the World Bank worked to construct a measure of poverty. They defined poverty as income that would allow for enough food consumption to maintain a normal body weight at an average level of activity. They estimated that 37 percent of the population was falling below this poverty level—and the problems were worse for children. Forty-seven percent of the children (under the age of fifteen) were living in poverty. Chief among the problems was the collapse of the health system, which led to a steep increase in morbidity with the reappearance of measles, whooping cough, tuberculosis, and syphilis. There was also a rapid increase in crime.

In the early 1990s, Azerbaijan experienced inflation of up to 2000 percent. Conflict with Armenia resulted in 700,000 displaced people. Oxfam began working in Azerbaijan in 1993 in response to the crisis—focusing initially on emergency water supply and sanitation, but also addressing longer-term needs when it became clear that people were not going to be able to go back to their homes. Oxfam's programs are clustered in five sectors: health and education, livelihoods, gender equity, and people's rights to have a say in their futures by strengthening local organizations.

Oxfam also is at work in Armenia. But after Armenia experienced a major earthquake, progress toward rehabilitation was far slower, as there were still 300,000 refugees from Azerbaijan living in Armenia. The Oxfam program in Armenia supports local disabled peoples' organizations and women's organizations working on health and gender issues. It is also involved in supporting small business, encouraging microcredit projects, and running sustainable health insurance schemes through community groups.

Tensions that had been made dormant under the control of the state in the old system resurfaced with a vengeance throughout the region, resulting in civil violence and war. MSF, following its humanitarian mission, worked in Chechnya where few other NGOs were present. It also works in Eastern Europe on poverty-related problems such as drug-resistant tuberculosis, as well as AIDS and the AIDS Standard Treatment Drugs. In recent years, MSF also has been working in Armenia, Azerbaijan, and Russia—with programs focusing on homelessness, and the lack of adequate health coverage (a problem exacerbated by the disintegration of the health system).

Members of the International Save the Children Alliance work in these same countries—Armenia, Azerbaijan, and Russia—as well as in Georgia, Kyrghizia, and Uzbekistan. The plight of the children in the circumstances of these countries has evoked a major response from supporters, especially from those members of the Alliance based in Western Europe and in the Nordic countries.

Children in Poverty

Of the 1.2 billion people who are the absolute poor, more than half—650 million—are children. That ratio holds equally true among internally displaced people, refugees, or those living on less than $2, or $5. While it has always been true that children account for the largest number of those who are the most poor, the past decade's civil wars and the AIDS epidemic have generated both child soldiers and child-headed households. This term—child-headed households—was not known before 1990. Despite the fact that the Convention on the Rights of the

Child is now agreed to by most countries (President Clinton signed this Convention; it has yet to be ratified, however, in the United States), children are suffering in ways not known before. Child soldiers are forced into fighting in many local wars. But this is only one of many egregious infractions of children's rights; others needing attention are widespread economic and sexual exploitation.

All of the NGOs discussed in this book have projects that reach children in need, but three of them—World Vision, Save the Children, and PLAN International—specifically make child welfare a central part of their work. Save the Children has made the Rights of the Child its major campaign since its founding. World Vision works through other faith-based local organizations to reach children in need through education, training, and health programs; its programs stretch around the globe as well as throughout the United States. PLAN International works through six priority programs that impact on child poverty and community development.

World Vision reaches children in orphanages in Romania, sends medical supplies to Mongolia, repairs schools in East Timor, and runs literacy training in India. It often runs centers for traumatized children—in Kosovo, Uganda, Rwanda, and Bosnia. These centers are especially focused on reaching child soldiers, mutilated children, and otherwise traumatized children. In the United States, World Vision works with street children and on the problems of homelessness, as well as those who are not in school. Since World Vision sponsors 1,290,000 children in over eighty-seven countries, it can and does keep its sponsors informed about the violence and poverty problems that children are experiencing. The literature and frequent mailings of these organizations are important sources of public education on the issue of child poverty.

Both Save the Children and PLAN International have worked to strengthen their focus on children in recent programming initiatives. Long ago, child sponsorship meant direct attention to the child and her or his family. That evolved into working to improve the community within which the child resided on the grounds that children's situations could not be addressed without attention to the context in which they were living. Gradually, in the 1970s, this approach became more separated from an immediate focus on children—in part because the needs were both wide and complex in most countries. But, for example, in 1996–97 Save the Children UK went through a strategic planning process and resolved to have a more explicit focus on children. They also simultaneously decided to have "One Program"—that is, to strive for "greater coherence and a clearer sense of overall direction across the program...[acting] as one program across the world." They also decided that this meant "improving the links between our overseas and

UK work that previously ran quite separately." Much of that led to their integrated approach to poverty reduction discussed above.

New Modalities of Poverty Work

Thus far we have looked at some of the NGO project work on challenging poverty problems. But NGOs have come to have a far wider repertoire of possible ways to impact on poverty beyond projects. For any given NGO intervention undertaken in response to a particular "driver," the first choice NGO senior managers confront is which of their various modalities to use and in what combination and sequence. Broadly, there are three major choices: policy change advocacy, setting program priorities, and identifying projects. In an overarching negative policy environment, projects swimming against that tide are of course most likely to encounter sustainability problems. But sometimes the policy environment is not at all clear, and a creative project, especially one with a participatory process, highlights new possibilities. So there are exceptions.

Within these choices of how, when, and whether to proceed, the options require something of a consultative process within the network family. On projects, sometimes there are clear comparative advantages; hence it is easy to decide to work through a particular member. Sometimes funds come to NGOs earmarked for a specific country—in those cases, most NGO families check out who is working there, and allocate those funds in furtherance of that work. But what to do, and how, and when, is a little different in the case of policy work. As we will see in more detail in the chapter on advocacy, policy choices that look one way carry different implications depending upon where one sits. For partners in countries with not very open governance (Vietnam, Laos), some policy positions taken by the network family could put them in an awkward spot. We will return to that issue in Chapter 7 below.

Poverty-Oriented Policy Work

Here, however, we want to point to the increased salience of NGO poverty-oriented policy work as it strengthens the reach of an NGO into the poverty problem. Campaigns on where major initiatives are needed are a combination of development education and advocacy. For example, Oxfam's education campaign, *Education Now: Break the Cycle of Poverty,* is an instance of an old problem getting new attention, especially in light of its implications for poverty reduction. Media stories followed its introduction, and supporters were targeted who had not thought about all the implications of the chronic neglect of illiteracy and the barriers to getting schooling. Both domestic and Third World projects resulted. In the United Kingdom this meant encouraging the provision of, or directly providing, night schools—as Oxfam had done abroad for working children (though in the United Kingdom they are generally for teenagers). All over the world, often children must work; doing so too often means having to forego schooling. Night schools are a major way to provide them with education. Their dialogues with children, with partners, and their experience inform their positions on this issue. In short, in desperately poor families, there are no alternatives. (Both civil wars and HIV/AIDS have added to the problem.) Hence total abolition of child labor is not enforceable. Better regulations are clearly needed in many countries. But above all, making it possible for children to get an education is critical for their own capabilities.

The MSF family network's first major campaign—Access to Essential Medicines—has far-reaching poverty-reducing implications. Poor people, by definition, cannot afford expensive medications, and for many of the most debilitating and life threatening diseases, better drugs are either not available (for example, for drug resistant malaria) as there is too little research and development, or they are available (for example, the tri-therapies for AIDS) but far beyond their means. The campaign involves pricing policies and patents of pharmaceutical companies—two complex arenas for action. The legal, financial, economic, and social implications surrounding research, development, patents, pricing, and trade are both country- and drug-specific. Thus this campaign has to be waged on many fronts simultaneously—first with public awareness of the issues in the powerful industrial countries, and with WTO, the World Bank, and WHO, then with almost endless negotiations on a drug-by-drug basis and a country-by-country basis. Large pharmaceutical companies can bring a lot of muscle to bear in smaller, poorer countries, arguing as the company will that, for example, more time to protect the patent on one drug is one aspect of getting a better price on others drugs such as those essential for AIDS victims. Each national legal framework is different; each deal the companies negotiate is different.

The Access to Essential Medicines campaign has already achieved high visibility in a very short time. The issues are reaching a mass audience fast because unlike landmines, for example, everyone in an industrial country has experienced at one time or another the problem of expensive medication. MSF doctors' work with those most in need of medical attention is thwarted because of the difficulties of treating, for example, tuberculosis or sleeping sickness. Older medicines are no longer as effective and come with more adverse side effects; new drugs, if they exist, are too expensive. MSF doctors confront thousands of patients in need of access to these medicines. The tri-therapies for AIDS in South Africa cost $1000 a month, if one has health insurance with prescription coverage. That price makes treatment impossible for thousands suffering with AIDS living on $5 a day. Several developing countries now have acquired the capacity to develop generic versions of "cutting-edge" medicines, but they encounter problems with the World Trade Organization's regulations as well as with the power of large pharmaceutical companies leveraging their patents. Needed are ways to make these essential medicines available—through either a tiered pricing system, or allowing a generic version to be produced locally. The implications of MSF's campaign for public awareness on this major policy problem are far-reaching. Some drug companies have already begun to respond. For example, in April 2001, South Africa won a major victory when some of the world's biggest pharmaceutical companies abandoned their legal battle to stop South Africa from importing the less expensive generic AIDS medicines. Some drug companies have lowered prices or have entered into programs for donating essential medicines. But much remains to be done given the impact of disease on poverty in poor countries.

The work that many NGOs, especially Oxfam, started and are continuing on the debt-relief initiative—a major poverty-reducing initiative—is another case in point. Getting parliamentary approval of monies that were pledged but not appropriated requires a degree of engagement with political processes that play out with contextual specificity. Oxfam has concentrated significant attention on debt forgiveness precisely because of the many ways that debt forgiveness could effectively break one of the most destructive components in the vicious circles experienced by poor countries.

Too few people realize how debt servicing impacts on heavily indebted countries—how it constrains governments from investing in health or education. The extent to which public opinion has shifted in favor of debt reduction is largely due to the work of Oxfam, Bread for the World, and other NGOs that helped put the issue on the public agenda. Some prominent political leaders now proclaim the importance of debt forgiveness, but that was not their position fifteen years ago, when the NGOs began their debt-forgiveness campaigns.

This section began by pointing to the need for consultations within network families when decisions are being taken upon modalities for poverty work, especially advocacy or policy work relating to poverty. While the amount of autonomy that many national members have to set their own programming or sectoral priorities is still wider, even this is changing. Having other members of the same NGO family or network working in the same country—and doing so with different programming priorities and different processes—can be confusing. For example, if Save the Children UK has an active program priority and guidance about consultations with young people wherever it works, and another Save the Children member working in the same country does not use that process, there is inevitable confusion among their constituents about what the organization's "brand" means.

Of all the network families examined, the one with the most integration of programming priorities across the family is PLAN International. With its focus on children, PLAN International has five major domains within which all members operate: growing up healthy, learning, habitat, livelihood, and building relationships. These in turn are governed by key principles: child centeredness, institutional learning, gender equity, environmental sustainability, empowerment and sustainability, and cooperation. PLAN International has also developed and is currently rolling out a network-wide performance monitoring via performance indicators that ensures being able to answer questions about results achieved. (We will discuss this in greater detail in Chapter 8, which focuses on accountability.)

Project Identification

The third part of the modality equation comes in projects. Projects are the sturdy vehicles on the ground that translate, or fail to translate, priorities into action. They need to be grounded in the larger context of program and sectoral priorities. Reminding ourselves of the interrelationships among policy advocacy, programming, and projects is key because all too often viewers of NGO activities look only at projects. If they see one or two projects that, for example, do not work or fail to reduce poverty, they jump to the conclusion that a particular NGO is not effective, omitting the rest of the picture. That approach fails to illuminate the poverty work underway. Figure 4.2 on the following page shows some of the relationships among policies, programs, and projects.

When NGO leaders consider approaches to new work—given the factors in the new poverty (transition, civil war, social exclusion)—they have to pick and choose the combinations of advocacy work and operational work that make the most sense. Fortunately, the Internet and e-mail greatly ease the consulting process across family networks, as well as with relevant partners and stakeholders.

Crosscutting the poverty operational puzzle are some major process issues close to the value core of these NGOs. Two examples are: (1) the emphasis on participatory development and its relationship to empowerment and civil society, and (2) working with, as well as through, partners. As Chapters 5 and 6 show, the varieties of partnerships—with local, community-based organizations, or with larger, well-established organizations, or with private for-profit partners—intersect with how NGO leaders think about these choices.

Process and Partners

In critical instances, the NGO leadership may work simultaneously on two or on all three of the modalities of advocating policy change, set-

Figure 4.2. Modalities of Poverty Work

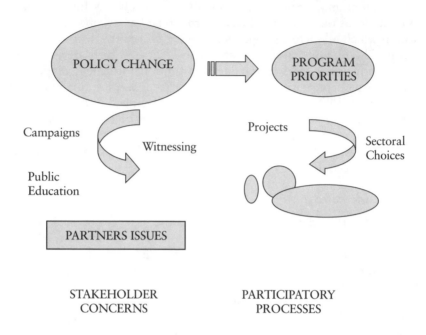

ting program priorities, or identifying projects. Consider the debt-relief campaign, for example: Oxfam worked for years on this campaign before official donors and other major political leaders finally took it up. Building up the case, negotiating its acceptance, winning over others, and talking and listening to a multitude of local partners about their particular needs was a part of the process. Simultaneously, Oxfam was gaining perspectives on what governments could—and as yet might not—do with the monies made available by debt relief. It worked in liaison with all kinds of partners both within developing countries and within strategically placed developed countries to further their goal of achieving debt reduction. Oxfam also worked with other national-level NGOs (for example, Bread for the World) on securing congressional or parliamentary support. That support was needed (and still is needed) in every Group of Seven (G-7) industrial country if the campaign is to succeed.

Only after more than a decade of work did the major heads of state pledge themselves to make available $1 billion in debt relief. But the campaign cannot—and will not—stop there, since debt reduction has yet to be fully funded or implemented. Monies pledged must be approved or appropriated in all the national legislatures, parliaments, and by the U.S. Congress. Only in the autumn of 2000 did the Congress appropriate funding that would make good on relief that had been promised more than a year before. Advocacy work in this arena has had to be ongoing for more than a decade. Moreover, given the scale of the debt problem for very poor countries, even $1 billion in relief will not address more than a fraction of their debt. As the first step in getting the relief is implemented, each country will have to come up with a Poverty Reduction Strategy Paper approved by the World Bank and IMF in order to qualify for such relief—the first step for getting the relief implemented. In many of these countries, Oxfam also has projects with partners, and continues to assist them in building capacity to monitor progress toward their countries' poverty-reduction plans. In short, all three modalities have been mobilized. Debt relief is not yet a reality. Getting there is a long, arduous process.

While the Oxfam Washington office works on the U.S. Congress and the IMF–World Bank front, Oxfam field staff work in the countries that are candidates for relief to monitor and learn about local events and perspectives. They watch what, for example, the Ugandan government is likely to do with the money released, and what role they (the local community-based NGO) might undertake to monitor compliance with the goals of the relief initiative. Those goals are that the money is to be used for human development—education and health or other sectoral work closely related to poverty reduction. (There is a concern that the money released might otherwise just be consumed, for example, by guns or military equipment.)

The local partners have major roles in monitoring, or at least observing, how the country's progress in poverty reduction is either coming along, or has stalled. That information also flows back through the network and helps inform choices made by other member Oxfams as they get questions from those considering the impact of debt relief. Among the many striking aspects of the systemic nature of this communication process are the opportunities it gives at every level for shared learning, especially about the most daunting problem: implementation. Rolling out goals and objectives into the far messier world of problem solving, attention to details, compromise, amendment, and perhaps movement backward but then forward again, are intrinsic to what must be done to actualize more pro-poor developmental governance.

Participatory Development and Poverty Reduction

One of the major contributions of NGOs to poverty reduction is their securing donors' acceptance of participatory development. In the early 1960s, when official development donors held sway over the size, scale, and content of development programming, little attention was given to two critical aspects: to poverty's being rooted in powerlessness, and to the inherent knowledge that poor people have their own needs and preferences. The only key to unlocking the impasse was by way of increasing the participation of those who were then called "beneficiaries" in both project identification and implementation.

There is no space to detail the long evolution of the participatory development movement except to say that much of it took root and grew originally in Asia—and especially in Asian action research organizations and NGOs.[23] The Gandhi tradition of a grassroots movement, coupled with an abiding commitment to decentralization, provided a fertile ground for creative work on participatory development. Over time, international NGOs, and others working in Asia, picked up the conceptual framework and practice and spread it westward. It was helped along by the civil rights movement in the United States, and later by the human rights movement. But NGOs were the ones who firmly established participation's role in the development process as they labored to get this focus into the Bretton Woods institutions.

NGOs have been instrumental in furthering the relationships between poverty reduction and participatory development, often providing handbooks and textbooks on how to organize and manage projects. Save the Children published *Toolkits,* which is widely used by practitioners in the field as well as scholars. Oxfam's three-volume handbook, *The Oxfam Handbook of Development and Relief,* discusses how to further participatory processes throughout the project process throughout the life of a project. The past decade has seen a flowering of projects devoted to the enhancement of civil society—a logical extension of participation into institutional development in order to have structures for voice in public policy determination.

Robert Chambers is among the leading authorities in this field and one of the most widely experienced experts in participatory development. His work starts with three major premises: first, that the poor best understand their own reality; second, that professionals all too often bring too much of their own top-down prescriptions without listening, and thereby get it wrong; third, that the causes of poverty are multiple and reinforcing. In his consultations with poor people, Robert Chambers drew from their stories and accounts a vicious circle of ill being (see Figure 4.3).[24]

The implications of participatory processes for planning, programming, and project identification are profound. They call for much more labor-intensive attention to consultations with poor people, recording their needs and assets, and engaging them actively in identifying what can, as well as should, be done. One of the implications of this work is that reducing poverty requires simultaneous interventions at several points. In other words, it is not enough to improve under-five-year-old immunization rates without attention to, for example, the rural water supply and nutrition education. Moreover, even that work needs

Figure 4.3. Web of Poverty's Disadvantages

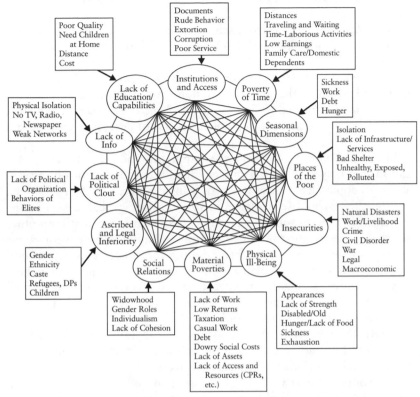

Source: Adapted with permission from drawing done by Robert Chambers and others as part of consultations with the poor.

to be done within the context of attention to the public health policy framework of the country in question.

A New Programming Approach: The Household Livelihood Security Index

CARE USA has developed one of the most innovative of the programming techniques that can be used along the relief-to-development continuum. Called the Household Livelihood Security Approach, it can also be refined through the construction of the Household Livelihood Index. The Household Livelihood Security Index has eight component measures, all directly focused on family well-being in developing countries.

This technique allows its users to look and learn through household-level interviews, observation, and rapid-appraisal methods how households are using their assets as well as when families are depleting their assets to emergency levels. Asset depletion, for example, occurs when they are eating their seed corn, or selling their draft animals, or withdrawing children from school to go to work. Household-level information then helps the NGO staff, preferably working with the community, to think through exactly what is most needed, who most needs it, and how best to meet those needs. This process allows for creative thinking about the complex and non-static needs of families—for a more demand-informed project planning. Projects can then be targeted. In short this technique is the complete reverse of designing projects and searching for where they are needed.

In relief situations, for example, rapid provisioning of water, sanitation, food, shelter, and emergency health care are critically needed to keep people alive. How much of which is needed when is refined through a household security analysis as the most critical needs become apparent. Immunizations, for example, may be more urgent than other health delivery to stop the spread of measles. In the rehabilitation stage, the focus may move to food provisioning for relocated refugees until they can get their crops planted. In development programming there may be a move to longer-term education and literacy programs, as well as to a monetized food program in order to keep incentives in place for resumed agricultural production.[25]

CARE, Mercy Corps, World Vision, and Oxfam have all used the Household Livelihood Index and its techniques in their programming. To get even more clarity on the constraints on family or community livelihood security, CARE has also gone on to experiment with a more detailed Household Livelihood Security Index that it pioneered in studies in Kenya, India, and Sri Lanka in 1995–97.

Closely related to CARE's household livelihood security analysis is Carolyn Moser's asset vulnerability assessment that points to the survival techniques used by people living at the margin when they head into crisis. Moser, writing about research in Ecuador, Zambia, Hungary, and the Philippines, explains how her researchers assessed labor, human capital, housing, household relations, and social capital as vulnerability increased.[26] Both this technique and the Household Livelihood Security Index afford opportunities to integrate qualitative and quantitative data, shedding much more light on the nature of poverty and more effective ways to address those needs.

Ethnology and Beyond

As in other chapters, we can now step back and ask some more probing questions about the ethnology of Northern NGO leaders' views about poverty reduction and its relationship to positive peace building. Can their views be supported by empirical data? What motivations may our respondents not have explicitly discussed? What nuances and details may have been known, but not explicitly discussed? What emerging trends or issues need further exploration?

Empirical Support

There is a great deal of material corroborating the leaders' views that the context in which poverty-reducing programs and policies must work has changed. The numbers on the increases in inequality have been getting attention outside of the work of the NGO leaders and their staff. Empirical analyses abound, and some of them are pointing to the ways that increased inequality can act as a brake on the rate of growth. There is a great deal of material on the transition states, on social exclusion, and on structural violence.

Underlying Motivations

It is worthwhile to consider again the underlying motivations of these leaders for their poverty work, and how they feel about the increased convergence of domestic and international work. Here we could observe variation among NGO families and within particular families. Invariably, some national members are more assertive about social reform than others. The most important difference in motivations among NGOs is that between NGOs that feel strongly about their secular foundation—notably Médecins Sans Frontières (but also CARE, PLAN International, and Oxfam) and World Vision, with its strongly faith-based nature. Yet what is striking is the depth of personal conviction that is equally strong in MSF and in World Vision—even though they are at opposite ends of the secular to faith-based continuum. The ways in which norms and integrity of purpose suffuse both organizations means they have as much in common as in contrast with one another. Both prize independence and, in practice, they are in some ways more alike than different—for example, both hire and staff with concern for their values. As World Vision moves toward undertaking more USAID contracts, it will be interesting to see whether, or how, this changes. MSF, on the other hand, is moving away from government contracting in order to further protect its independence.

Differences within family networks can be as wide as across all the different NGO families. For example, Save the Children (US) finds it has more in common with CARE USA, and less in common with Save the Children (Sweden). Their policy work as well as project and program preferences are influenced by where they are headquartered. This is, in large part, because many Save the Children national members have much longer histories than the other NGO families. Moreover, some rogue Save the Children groups are not members of the International

Save the Children Alliance, adding to the diversity of that network. The Alliance has made real progress on getting more shared views, but this is inevitably a slow process.

What was consistently impressive to us as outsiders, in visiting and interviewing, was the quality of staff motivation. This held true across as well as within network families. The passion was often palpable. It was intriguing that one could leave one NGO and doubt that such passion could be duplicated—only to encounter it again elsewhere. Telephone interviews—many of which were not anticipated by the staff and even came as interruptions—almost always met with real interest in the questions and a candid and worthwhile conversation about their work. The motivation of many NGO staff members—rooted in deeply held values—is inspiring to encounter. There is room for much more research about this factor and its impact upon organizational change and renewal strategies, as well as ways to avert "burn-out."

Details and Nuances

One point remains undiscussed that is more than a detail or nuance. There is more diversity among NGO leaders in the family networks about how much political access they need, or want, and how much distance they should keep, from governments. Leaders vary in their behavior and views about this issue. Some want to be, and to be seen as, totally professional—even more "corporate"—while others would choose not to use the word "corporate," but might opt for the term "professional." Still others such as MSF like the core concept of volunteerism, which to them means freedom from anything having to do with the state. Some NGO CEOs do meet with and provide advice to senior political leaders in the country where they are headquartered, while others who have political connections through past staff who have moved into highly visible political positions choose to avoid drawing upon those contacts.

One of the issues that warrants more research is the extent to which NGO leaders strive to address the underlying systemic causes of poverty versus continuing to work to relieve the symptoms of poverty. It is interesting that, although we could observe CEO choices, we could not discern the extent to which their choices affected their staff. Staff for the most part conveyed a sense of marching to their own internal drummers on issues about political change, role of the state, and the role of operations to affect long-term poverty reduction. Once again we came upon the strongly asserted lack of conformity and independence among NGO staff in contrast to staff in the corporate sector. Admirable as that may be, however, it surely makes the job of the manager more complicated.

Emerging Trends

At least two emerging trends bear watching in the future. The first is the move toward either more domestic work, and/or more integration between domestic and international work. Domestic work is inherently more controversial both for the NGO managers and for their stakeholders. There is less romance to be rushing off to Anacostia or Harlem. For many private contributors, there is less magic in sending a check for an inner-city program than there is for a village in Mozambique. It is easy to see that minority peoples in a foreign country should not be deprived of their rights. It is harder to confront the racist, or exploitative, behavior that exists at home. Often one remains silent to keep the peace with neighbors, saving outrage for condemning such behavior abroad. As NGOs increase their domestic poverty and social exclusion work, they will encounter more adverse criticism.

Second, precisely because progress has been made in the past four decades, there is more widespread acceptance of the argument that much further progress can happen with concerted effort. The international community, working through the OECD, the World Bank, and the UN system, has agreed upon the goal of reducing absolute poverty by half by the year 2015. These institutions already admit that meeting this goal might not be possible. But they will be turning to NGOs to help work toward that goal. Some donors are even under pressure from their legislatures, parliaments, or Congress to increase their contracting with NGOs to implement programs and projects (thereby cutting staff costs and taking advantage of the grassroots networks that NGOs often have). USAID, for example, anticipates having as much as 40 percent of its implementation done by NGOs. Some NGOs, on the other hand, are also increasingly concerned about becoming the instruments of donors.

It is not at all clear how this issue will get sorted out. Those NGOs determined to remain independent will have to find alternative sources of funding—probably through direct mail—in order to maintain their programs. Others will become more available for contracting work, but will thereby discover the costs to their independence. There will be all kinds of shifts and permutations between these two different positions in the years ahead.

What is clear is that the problem of global poverty will stay on the agenda for at least the next several decades. The needs that poverty gives rise to generate security implications: *not* addressing poverty means more conflict, more violence, more epidemics, and an increasingly fragile ecosystem. Poverty is no longer an ethical issue but an ethical issue with large security components. It affects the sustainability of global growth and well-being. This means that the stakes are higher and that other actors will get into the policy debates. The salience of poverty problems will do nothing but grow. The roles that NGOs have to play in this evolving story are only beginning.

We would like to extend our special thanks to Peter Bell, Damien Desjonquieres, Philippe Biberson, Bruce Mahin, Jean Herve-Bradol, Françoise Saulnier, David Bryer, Raymond Offenheiser, John Ruthrauff, Susan Holcombe, Martin McCann, John Greensmith, Charles MacCormack, Burkhard Gnaerig, Carolyn Miller, Gary Shaye, Ken Casey, John Reid, Ellen Stewart, John Healey, Tony Killick, David Lewis, Michael Lipton, Robert Chambers, Julie Fisher, Joan Nelson, Jacob Meerman, Ashok Gurung, and Shubham Chaudhuri for their contributions to the ideas in this chapter. We would also like to thank Ralph C. Bryant whose forthcoming book, Turbulent Waters: Cross Border Finance and International Governance, *led to useful discussions on the roles that are, or should be, played by international institutions in regard to global poverty. Finally, our special thanks go to Christina Kappaz who participated actively in the data collection and analysis and provided essential comments on successive drafts.*

Notes

1. Susan George, *Oxford Today* II, no. 3 (1999), Trinity Issue, 12. The same numbers originate in the UNDP, *Human Development Report 1999* (New York and Oxford: Oxford University Press, 1999), 3.

2. David Landes, *The Wealth and Poverty of Nations: Why Some Are So Rich and Some Are So Poor* (New York: W. W. Norton, 1998). Robin Marris echoes this point but goes on to more of the macroeconomic part of the problem in *Ending Poverty* (New York: Thames and Hudson, 1999).

3. Arjan de Haan and Simon Maxwell, "Editorial: Poverty and Social Exclusion in North and South," *IDS Bulletin* 29, no. 1 (Brighton, England, January 1998): 1.

4. See, for example, Amartya Sen, chapter 13, "Rights and Capabilities" in his book, *Resources, Values, and Development* (Cambridge, Mass.: Harvard University Press, 1984), 315–17.

5. Amartya Sen, *Development as Freedom* (New York: Alfred Knopf, 2000).

6. Coralie Bryant and Louise G. White, *Managing Development in the Third World* (Boulder, Colo.: Westview Press, 1982).

7. Deepa Narayan, Robert Chambers, Meera Kaul Shah and Patti Petesch, *Crying Out for Change: Voices of the Poor, II* (Oxford and New York: Published by Oxford University Press for the World Bank). See also the Web site carrying Robert Chambers's work on consultations with the poor: www.worldbank.org/poverty/wdr/poverty/conspoor.html.

8. Michael Harrington, *The Other America* (Baltimore: Penguin, 1960).

9. National Center for Children in Poverty, "Young Children in Poverty: A

Statistical Update, June 1999" (New York: Joseph L. Mailman School of Public Health, Columbia University, June 1999).

10. As of 1989, 42.1 percent of household income went to the top 20 percent of U.S. households; in France the equivalent figure was 41.9 percent. The bottom 20 percent received 5.6 percent of household income in both countries. See A. S. Bhalla and Frederic Lapeyre, *Poverty and Social Exclusion in a Global World* (New York: St. Martin's Press, 1999), 19.

11. Ron Sider, "A Livable Income," *World Vision Today* (Seattle: World Vision, Spring 2000), 4.

12. "A Century of Progress," Economics Focus, *Economist,* April 15, 2000, 86.

13. Peter Uvin, *Aiding Violence: The Development Enterprise in Rwanda* (West Hartford, Conn.: Kumarian Press, 1998).

14. World Bank, *Attacking Poverty* (New York: Published by Oxford University Press for the World Bank, 2000).

15. The debates on poverty and inequality in America have received more attention in the works of Sheldon Danziger and Peter Gottschalk, *America Unequal* (New York: Russell Sage Foundation; Cambridge, Mass.: Harvard University Press, 1995); Theda Skocpol, *The Missing Middle: Working Families and the Future of American Social Policy* (New York: W. W. Norton, 2000); Richard B. Freeman, *The New Inequality: Creating Solutions for Poor America* (Boston: Beacon Press, 1999); Frank Levy, *The New Dollars and Dream: American Incomes and Economic Change* (New York: Russell Sage Foundation, 1998).

16. World Bank, *Attacking Poverty,* 56.

17. Michael Bryans, Bruce D. Jones, and Janice Gross Stein, "Mean Times: Humanitarian Action in Complex Political Emergencies—Stark Choices, Cruel Dilemmas: Report of the NGOs in Complex Emergencies Project, Program on Conflict Management and Negotiation, Coming to Terms," paper circulated by the Centre for International Studies, University of Toronto (Toronto, January 1999), no. 3.

18. Mary B. Anderson, *Do No Harm: Supporting Local Capacities for Peace through Aid* (Cambridge, Mass.: Local Capacities for Peace Project, 1996), 4–5.

19. See Peter Nolan, *China's Rise, Russia's Fall* (London: Macmillan Press, 1995); also the Regional Bureau for Europe and the CIS, UNDP, *Poverty in Transition* (New York: UN Publications, 1998).

20. Regional Bureau for Europe and the CIS, UNDP, *Poverty in Transition,* 6.

21. See, for example, Shahid Javed Burki and Guillermo E. Perry, *Beyond the Washington Consensus: Institutions Matter* (Washington, D.C.: World Bank, 1998).

22. Nolan, *China's Rise, Russia's Fall: Politics, Economics and Planning in the Transition from Stalinism* (New York: St. Martin's Press, 1995), 17.

23. For example, there is literature within developing countries such as Walter Fernandes and Rajesh Tandon, *Participatory Research and Evaluation* (New Delhi: Indian Social Institute, 1968), and Yusuf Kassam and Kemal Mustafa, *Participatory Research: An Emerging Alternative Methodology in Social Science Research* (New Delhi: Society for Participatory Research in Asia, 1970).

Later, David Korten called attention to the work of the Management Institutes Working Group on Population and Social Development Management (these were institutes based in Latin America, Philippines, and Ahmedabad). See *Population and Social Development Management: A Challenge for Management Schools,* ed. Korten and Lander (Caracas: IESA, 1979). Much of this theory and practice was summarized in David Korten and R. Klauss, *People Centered Development* (West Hartford, Conn.: Kumarian Press, 1984).

24. Deepa Narayan, Robert Chambers, Meera Kaul Shah, and Patti Petesch, "Crying Out for Change: Voices of the Poor" (Poverty Group, PREM, World Bank, February 2000, photocopy). See also Robert Chambers, *Whose Reality Counts?* (Brighton, England: Institute of Development Studies, University of Sussex Press, 1997).

25. Marc Lindenberg, "Measuring Progress: Making the Household Livelihood Security Index Work," article under review at *World Development,* January 2001.

26. Caroline O. N. Moser, "The Asset Vulnerability Framework: Reassessing Urban Poverty Reduction Strategies," *World Development* 26, no. 1 (1998): 1–19.

– 5 –

Emerging Global Organizational Structures

AS WE SAW in earlier chapters, our key informants believed that the critical challenges during the last two decades have motivated them to begin transforming the organizational arrangements within their global families. These adjustments have been stimulated by: donor demand for greater accountability among affiliates; the opportunity to use new technology for coordinated global advocacy; the potential of economies of scale in recruiting, fundraising, and programming; and the need to maintain legitimacy of the organization across multiple countries. In addition, opportunities for worldwide organizational learning and greater impact also led to new experiments in organization across national boundaries.

The next two chapters focus on different aspects of emerging global structures. Chapter 5 looks primarily at the emerging worldwide organizational configurations inside multi-member NGO families like Save the Children, Oxfam, and CARE International as well as their attempts to form new alliances outside the family. Chapter 6 looks beyond these more loosely structured alliances to the effort to form even closer partnerships among NGOs as well as between NGOs and the private and public sector.

Looking inside the Family: A Typology of Global Structures

While there were many ways of characterizing organizational configurations within their NGO families, our informants found a fivefold classification focusing upon the level of central control of the mission and performance very useful.[1] This classification included:

- Separate independent organizations
- Independent organizations with weak umbrella coordination
- Confederations
- Federations
- Unitary, corporate organizations

This classification was based on a continuum of differences in rights and responsibilities of central units versus affiliates (see Table 5.1). At one end of the continuum, separate independent organizations shared a common name without surrendering any decision-making authority to an international headquarters. For example, in the early 1990s, organizations like Médecins Sans Frontières France as well as Belgium, or Save the Children US and UK had the same name, but each affiliate had its own strong board, fundraising, and programs, and each made completely autonomous decisions about its own actions. Cooperation took on an ad hoc, pragmatic basis without a formal central coordinating mechanism.

In the Weak Umbrella Model, independent organizations maintained virtual autonomy but established a weak coordinating mechanism to share information and facilitate cooperation. In the Confederation Model, strong members delegated some coordination, standard setting, and resource allocation duties to the central office. However, decisions from the center needed virtual unanimity. Most powers remained with the larger affiliates. In the Federated Model, the center had strong powers for standard setting and resource acquisition but affiliates had separate boards and implementation capacity. Finally, in the Unitary Model there is only one global organization with a single board and central headquarters, which makes resource acquisition, allocation, and program decisions. There are branch offices around the world, which are staffed by the central body and implement centrally taken decisions.

Family Self-Portraits

Our key informants used this continuum to locate their organizations' current global family structures as well as to describe structural changes over time. Virtually all noted that globalization put immense pressures upon their organizations to move toward more coordinated rather than purely decentralized or unitary models (see Figure 5.1 on p. 142). For example, both Save the Children and CARE were initiated as single member organizations with a unitary corporate structure but followed different evolutionary paths. CARE began as CARE USA in 1946, as did Save the Children UK in 1919. Separate independent Save the Children organizations developed in the 1970s, but without a central coordinating structure. By 1993, problems of maintaining standards and what some refer to as independent, "rogue" Save the Children organizations led to the decision to develop a weak umbrella coordinating mechanism. By 1997, a new effort was launched to form an even stronger confederation and to project a common "brand name" and quality standards. International Save the Children Alliance senior management now believes it is headed for a more federated model. In contrast, CARE USA moved from a unitary model to a confederation in the 1980s without

Table 5.1. Views of Alternative Models for Associational Structures as Expressed at NGO Presidents' Retreat I: Bellagio

INTERNATIONAL RELIEF AND DEVELOPMENT NGO SERVICE PROVIDERS

	Separate Independent Organizations & Coalitions	*Weak Umbrella Coordinating Mechanisms*	*Confederations*	*Federations*	*Unitary Corporate*
Locus of decision-making	Individual members	Individual members	Center has weak coordinating capacity with strong individual members	Center has stronger authority over system-wide decisions than members	Central
Who sets global norms	No one	Individual members	Members with central coordination	Central headquarters and board	Central headquarters and board
Central enforcement mechanisms	None	Weak moral suasion	Moral suasion and limited sanctions like expulsion	Stronger sanctions like withholding	Strong central enforcement and incentive system
Resource acquisition methods	At member level	At member level	Primarily at member level but some common acquisition	Primarily at member level but some common acquisition	Centrally and globally acquired
Resource allocation methods	At member level	At member level	Largely member level with some central allocation	Largely member level with even more central allocation	Central allocation
Common systems	None	None	A few *Primarily financial & programmatic quality*	More common systems	Common systems
Common name	No	Yes	Yes	Yes	Yes
Common logo	No	Sometimes	Sometimes	Often	Often
Franchising	No	No	Sometimes	Sometimes	Yes

Source: Adapted from Dennis R. Young, "Local Autonomy in a Franchise Age: Structural Change in National Voluntary Associations," *Nonprofit and Voluntary Sector Quarterly* 18, no. 2 (Summer 1989): 101–17.

Figure 5.1. Models of Northern Relief and Development NGO Structures

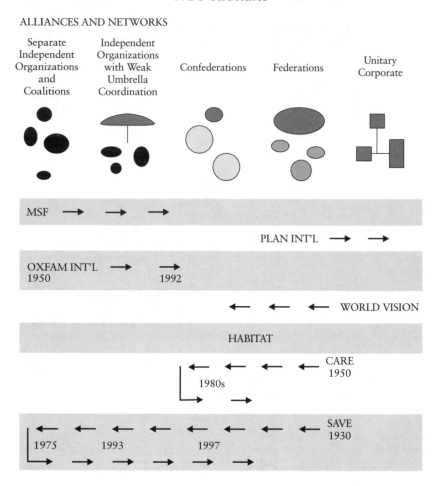

the development of totally independent member organizations. This was done as a conscious effort to keep common standards and to maintain a single, clear brand identity. CARE appears to be moving toward a slightly more federated model. Newer organizations like Médecins Sans Frontières report that they are moving from the separate independent organizational model toward the development of weak umbrella coordinating structures because of problems of overlap, duplicated services, and differences in member views about the identify of MSF. They are not sure what their future global organizational structure will look like but want to continue to maintain the flexibility of a movement and to limit their overall growth.

While the five organizational forms presented earlier were helpful as initial orienting points, our informants believed that the large Northern relief and development organizations were migrating toward three current dominant organizational forms: (1) competitive, independent national organizations with a weak umbrella-type coordinating structure, like Médecins Sans Frontières; (2) federations like PLAN International; and (3) confederations like CARE International. They identified the following strengths and weaknesses of the emerging dominant forms.

Competitive, Independent Organizations with a Weak Umbrella-Type Coordinating Structure

Particularly in emergency situations, competitive, independent national organizations benefit from flexibility, speed, and a strong national identity that provides solid fundraising capacity. Such organizations can move fast because they do not have to negotiate with other international coalition members before responding. They can project their own unique national image directly to their private and public donor community. Their national boards can guarantee relatively rapid action.

However, it is hard for competitive independent organizations with the same name and broad goals to provide the minimum coordination necessary without at least a weak umbrella-type coordinating structure. In an era of scarce resources, the appearance of four or five independent organizations delivering similar programs but with separate support and logistics functions may prove too costly for the world system. At the same time, the competition of organizations that bear the same name can waste time and confuse the public. In addition, without central norms, different organizations with the same name often provide very different levels of quality. In such a case, Gresham's Law can set in—the organization can become known for the quality of its weakest member. Brand identity becomes blurred. Finally, at a time when donors like the World Food Programme, UNHCR, or major bilaterals need to save resources, they have become reluctant to have relations with a plethora of organizations with the same name. Many have begun to prefer only one international organization to negotiate with. These forces combine to push the competitive independent organizations toward greater affiliation and cooperation through at least weak umbrella-like coordinating structures. Yet it is still difficult to develop and enforce common norms with such loose coordination.

International Federations

At the opposite end of the global organizational continuum is the international federation. Within such organizations, authority, power, and resource control are managed at a more central level, although the organization has a global delivery system. Headquarters makes many key decisions and has stronger control over resource allocation and the enforcement of norms.

One of the most important strengths of international federations is that they get economies of scale and efficiency through central support services such as finance, procurement, and human resources management. At the same time, they have strong global identity and scale because of the resources they can amass. The federated models can also respond rapidly to emergencies. They have the potential for strong global quality control due to their standardized systems and allocation procedures. Because they are often faith based, they have special ability to collect funds through a global church infrastructure.

However, the federated models can be overly rigid. They can stifle the creativity of their national chapters and block unique adaptations to national identity. Finally, few NGOs with their fiercely independent clientele and spirit can successfully find unifying principles other than religion that can bring members and chapters to surrender their authority to a central secretariat. Thus the federation form is stable but may not be one that many NGOs realistically can pursue.

Confederations

Confederations like CARE International, Oxfam International, or Save the Children fall in the middle of the continuum between the competitive, independent organizations with umbrella-type coordinating mechanisms and federations. In this model, strong, semi-independent subordinate units with autonomous national boards make key decisions and still have strong identity and authority. However, the confederation has an international secretariat to which members cede weak coordinating capacity and the right to set international standards. The survival of the organization depends upon the members' respect for a loose set of rules and a high level of self-control and discipline. The potential for conflict and non-enforcement is high. At best, members of the international confederation can sanction others or expel those who do not comply with the rules. However, the level of noncompliance would have to be extremely high to generate the kind of consensus that would result in such extreme measures. In such a system, it is hard to determine how members should work together in a developing-country setting. CARE International has developed the lead member system in which the confederation names an operational member to coordinate the activities of the others in a particular country. Non-lead members program resources through the lead member, which is responsible for line supervision of the country office and programs. Such systems may have combinations of operational members who directly supervise overseas programs, non-operational fundraising members, and hybrid members who raise funds and are operational as well.

The confederation model has several particular strengths. First, it blends members' ability to project their national identity within their own countries with a system of lead-member operational oversight and cooperation at the field level. Such a system has the potential to eliminate the problems of conflict that the competitive, independent NGOs have with each other in the field. Second, the confederation model with lead member operations also eliminates the problems of duplication of support systems, staff, and processes that the competitive, independent organizations do experience. Finally, in the absence of a unifying principle like religion, which permitted global federations to form, it may be as close as a non-religious multi-country organizational member group can come to coordination.

The confederation model has its weaknesses as well. First, since most power rests with the independent members, moral suasion is a weak tool to assure quality and support of rules. Thus, the levels of friction around normal noncompliance can be quite high. Second, since the confederation must name the lead member to coordinate work in new countries, there can be a lot of political infighting around the allocation of territory. Third, there can be tensions between members' needs to project their national identity for fundraising purposes and to show operational independence, and the need for the confederation to project one image. Fourth, as in the competitive, independent model, the performance and mistakes of the weakest member can determine the overall image of the organization. Finally, since confederations require more discussion and coordination before action, they can be slower in emergency response. On the other hand, however, the competitive, independent organizations and federations can be on the scene quite quickly, while the confederation members can spend days debating who should take the lead or coordinate an emergency response operation.

Collaboration and Growth within the Family

Emerging Northern Relief and Development Families

Our informants believe that there is no one best model. The history and key characteristics of major organizations like Save the Children, Oxfam, CARE, or Catholic Relief Services determine where they began and the limits of where they might go. For example, it would have been difficult for CARE International to start as a federation with a single global structure and a multi-country board, since its original members, particularly CARE USA, were unwilling to cede authority to an international body.

Regardless of their particular history and origins, all of the three major forms of organization are inherently unstable and will continue to evolve. For example, during the emergencies in Somalia, Rwanda, and Bosnia, between 1995 and 1997, many of the relief organizations faced problems of overlap and competition. As a result, some of the competitive independent organizations, including Save the Children and MSF, are beginning to form confederations similar to CARE International. Similarly, some confederations, for example CARE International, are increasingly experimenting with strengthened common systems and uniform structures. These experiments have not turned them into strong federations, but they have stronger rules and ties than the confederation structures initially permitted. For example, while CARE's independent national-member boards would be reluctant to cede overall authority to the CARE International board, the organization is beginning to experiment with structures like regional service and support hubs that could be supervised by one member or another. Most of the organizations are beginning to staff their country offices with citizens from those nations and to hire more multinational staff in their headquarters operations.

Both the federations and confederations are also beginning to experiment more with a mix of industrial-country and developing country affiliates and membership levels. A variety of membership types are beginning to emerge, such as: (1) donor members who raise funds in their nation but do not manage overseas programs; (2) recipient members who do not raise funds in their nation but are the site of programs; and (3) hybrid members who both raise funds for programs in their own and other countries and have programs within their countries. There are changes at the board level as well. Many organizations are beginning to globalize their board membership with citizens of all parts of the world. Some organizations are providing equal representation on the international board to all affiliates.

Emerging Southern NGO Families

Tracking the development of the emerging global NGO families with Southern roots is easily the topic of another book (not this one). But it is worth noting some of our respondents' initial impressions of the variety of forms emerging that global NGO families with Southern roots are taking. Our respondents believed there was an asymmetry in the development of global organizations with Northern as opposed to Southern or Eastern European origins. According to our Northern respondents, Northern organizations with a longer history appear to have developed multi-regional and multi-country members and programs more quickly than have their Southern and Eastern European counterparts. Strong globalizing operational, multi-region and multipurpose relief and development organizations with Southern roots appeared to our respondents to be harder to identify. Exceptions were organizations like Grameen Bank and CIVICUS, the World Alliance for Citizen Participation. For example, although Grameen Bank had its roots in microcredit activities in Bangladesh, today it promotes and operates microcredit programs in many other parts of the world, including the United States.[2] It also has spin-off operations like Grameen Phone, which helps rural women set up village cell phone operations and use information technology, and Grameen Foundation, which raises funds in the United States and Europe. CIVICUS is one of the few global organizations with largely Southern membership but a worldwide structure.[3] Its purpose is to develop a global network of organizations whose members promote the development of civil society.

According to our respondents, it was more common to find Southern organizations working in one or more Southern countries, or having umbrella networks in a single region. These families focus most frequently on single-issue areas like women's rights, microcredit, or activities like policy studies or advocacy. One example is ALOP, the Asociación Latinoamericano de Organizaciones de Promoción.[4] Its mission is to support policy analysis and advocacy about issues of trade and development in Latin America. ALOP has strong, independent national members who have unique advocacy agendas for their own countries. They also have a regional board with a one-country, one-vote system and a coordinating secretariat whose purpose is to help share information and coordinate advocacy and policy study agendas. ALOP's structure most closely resembles the model of strong, independent organizations with a loose umbrella coordinating structure. Another example is El Taller, an emerging African network of women's rights organizations, whose governance structure is most similar to that of ALOP.[5]

The evolutionary process will be both slow and bumpy within the organizational families with Northern—as well as Southern or Eastern European—origins. Examples already exist of new affiliates collapsing due to lack of sustainable resources or lack of strong local community support. Conflicts regularly occur over differences in perceptions of standards and enforcement between old and new members. Some Northern boards and affiliates have viewed globalization and power sharing with real reluctance. Southerners have feared co-optation and have looked for more indigenous solutions. A better understanding will be needed about what the comparative advantages of Northern, Southern, and Eastern European affiliates within the family are in order to build new roles for the future. In addition, all the organizations have struggled to learn how to maintain commitment and passion both within their own organizations and with younger people. As they have gotten larger and their problems more complex and/or dangerous, they have increasingly emphasized professionalism and fundraising relative to voluntarism. Yet volunteerism, not check writing, formed the core of much of the passion and commitment they generated. The problem of establishing this link and sustaining commitment has haunted all the organizations.

Regardless of the type of evolving global organizational structure, the new multi-member organizations experience and must resolve generic tensions within their families. These tensions include: (1) deriving common principles, (2) reaching agreement about who can use the brand name and under what circumstances, (3) engaging in fundraising in another member's home country, (4) deciding when members can approach media and engage in advocacy in another member's home country, (5) coordinating multi-member operational work in a country where programs are offered, and (6) developing common systems and structures. The agendas of most international multi-member meetings include discussion of these topics.

Reaching Out: Loose Alliances beyond the Family

The maintenance—"care and feeding"—of the growing internal affiliate structure of most modern NGO families involves intensive and time-consuming management. These activities are so all-consuming that leaders rarely have time to think about extensive broader cooperation outside their immediate organizational family. They described their cooperation with other organizations as occasional and sporadic rather than systematic and purposeful.

However, most of our organizational informants believed that they *must* reach beyond their own immediate affiliates to create global networks of relief and development organizations in the new millennium. Such networks hold the promise of even greater impact on global poverty alleviation, refugee relief, and conflict mitigation, as well as of maintaining their organization's legitimacy in the developing world. Our informants see five kinds of emerging inter-organizational cooperation: (1) ad hoc single issue collaboration, (2) participation in existing global coordinating committees, (3) the creation of new coordinating committees and working groups, (4) new issue-based advocacy, operations, or learning networks, and (5) participation in longer-term, broader-based global movements.

It is useful to cite examples of some of these emerging activities. A constructive case of single-issue ad hoc collaboration was the decision by the presidents of Oxfam, Save the Children, CARE, and Médecins Sans Frontières to provide a special briefing session to the UN Security Council in New York on the Sudan conflict.[6] Each president felt the problem was sufficiently grave to warrant an exceptional effort in col-laboration. Many organizations have recently decided to increase their global cooperation by becoming members of existing coordinating bod-ies like the World Bank NGO consultative group, InterAction (the U.S. umbrella coordinating body for relief and development NGOs), and the International Council of Voluntary Agencies (ICVA), which serves as the European umbrella coordinating body for relief and develop-ment NGOs. New groups like the Sphere project (a working group for development of standards in humanitarian response), or SCHR, the Geneva-based Steering Committee on Humanitarian Response, which includes Canadian, European, and U.S. organizations, have been formed to respond to new needs for global coordination. These groups often help organizations share training courses, engage in joint analytic stud-ies, advocacy activities, and joint learning exercises. They sometimes also select one or two joint special initiatives each year.

Advocacy, learning, and program delivery networks are some of the strongest emerging forms of global organization. Such networks are loose alliances of independent organizations to accomplish a specific purpose through a virtual technology-based organizational structure. These new networks use the latest Internet and information technolo-gies to accomplish global objectives. They coordinate internal activities through list serves, chat rooms, satellite phones, e-mail, and video con-ferencing. This permits them to quickly harmonize advocacy agendas and coordinate lobbying efforts in, for example, Washington, Ottawa, London, Paris, Geneva, and Tokyo simultaneously. They use well-developed Web sites, real time Web streaming of speeches and events, e-mail, and other methods to reach potential supporters. Examples of successful recent network efforts are the Nobel Prize–winning inter-national campaign to ban landmines, the worldwide protest efforts organized around the Seattle WTO meetings in December 1999, and the Jubilee 2000 debt relief campaign. Learning networks are also developed to share best practice within and among organizations. For example, the World Bank developed content-based global learning networks for areas like public health, microcredit, and agriculture. CARE International de-veloped similar networks. Finally, there are recent attempts to form more broad-based social movements that combine organizations from around the world that may want to work on human rights, women's rights, basic economic rights, or environmental issues. (See Table 5.2 on the following page for examples of NGO collaboration.)

There is a great deal of experimentation with global coalitions that include both international and national NGOs. Such coalitions can be formed around common global policy advocacy or around project co-operation. An example of such a coalition is the collaboration of CARE, World Wildlife Federation, Nature Conservancy, and many Ecuado-

Table 5.2. Examples of Successful Northern NGO Collaboration

DEVELOPMENT PROGRAMS

- Girls Education Skills Development (*Save / PLAN / World Vision / CCF*)
- Joint Water / Sanitation Training (*Oxfam, MSF*)

ADVOCACY ACTIVITIES

- Rwanda Security Council Briefing (*MSF, Oxfam / CARE / ICRC*)
- Global Financial Crisis (*World Vision, Oxfam, NOVIB*)
- Family Planning (*CARE / Save*)
- Campaign to Ban Landmines (*Most Participating Organizations*)
- Bangladesh Garment Workers Rights (*Save / Oxfam*)

SYSTEMS

- Program Evaluation Software (*LANn / Oxfam*)

RELIEF OPERATIONAL ACTIONS

- Camp-based Coordination Meetings (*CARE / Save / MSF Oxfam / World Vision*)
- Withdrawal from Baidoa Unless Community Security Is Assured (*CARE / World Vision / Oxfam*)

FUND RAISING

- Joint Fund Raising Initiative— ACT (*Lutheran World Relief and Ecumenical Groups*)
- DEC (*Many UK Groups*)

STANDARDS AND TRAINING

- Sphere Project Relief (SCHR and Members)
- Operational Monitoring Project (*PLAN / NOVIB / Oxfam*)

rian organizations in an environmental resource management project called SUBIR. CARE also helped form, and currently participates in, an umbrella organization of microenterprise-lending NGOs in Peru.

In some cases, for example, Northern-based organizations are starting up and building Southern affiliates as well as forming alliances with existing Southern organizations outside their current family. For example, Northern microcredit groups and Southern groups like Grameen Bank were beginning to establish operational programs in each others' countries and were examining the potential for alliances. In the case of World Vision, a unique process of devolving central authority to affiliates while keeping a coherent mission was taking place. In still other cases, unaffiliated Northern and Southern organizations simply competed in each other's geographic space. (See Figure 5.2 for examples of emerging NGO structures in global space that include both expanding the family and alliances with other families.)

Participants reviewed examples of successful cooperation and felt that they had the following common foundations. All produced real value added as perceived by those who collaborated. They were based on enlightened self-interest. They used pre-agreed frameworks, which were comfortable to all participants. They believed that cooperation did

Figure 5.2. Emerging Global Structures

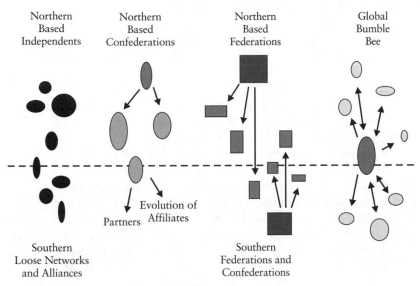

Northern Based Independents   Northern Based Confederations   Northern Based Federations   Global Bumble Bee

Partners Evolution of Affiliates

Southern Loose Networks and Alliances   Southern Federations and Confederations

not make sense when it was formalistic, when it resulted in the lowest common low-quality denominator, and when there was no reciprocity.

Reconfiguring the Family and Reaching Out to Others: The Case of Oxfam International

While it may be easy to identify the potential foundations for global co-operation, the actual success of new arrangements will require a great deal of practical experimentation and dialogue about where the synergy may be and when it makes little sense to collaborate. One of the most interesting works in progress is the Oxfam International dialogue with an informal group of six globalizing organizations with Southern origins: El Taller, IBASE, Third World Net, ALOP, ADAB, and an organization that might soon become Oxfam India. The purpose of the dialogue is to learn from each other about when global alliances for poverty alleviation and advocacy might be useful and when it might make less sense to form alliances. For example, the six Southern organizational participants at the June 2000 Oxfam meeting said they would have found collaboration useful in the following activities (in descending order of importance): gathering global information, mapping, managing the international part of global or regional advocacy campaigns (like the banana negotiations between the Central American countries, Ecuador, and the European Union), and common work on global economic and social rights, capacity building, and special studies. They were not interested in Northern organizations taking a lead role in advocacy or operational programs within their borders.

They also discussed the roles they hoped Oxfam International would play should they have an alliance with them in the future. They hoped Oxfam might take the lead in changing the Northern institutions and perspectives through advocacy in Northern countries, and where they had special expertise. They hoped Oxfam might accompany them (not lead) in full international advocacy campaigns, and in the international dimension of regional campaigns. They expected Oxfam to take a low profile where national or regional issues were at stake and to do nothing where it had little expertise to add to their local or regional strategy.

The challenge of globalization presents an inescapable reality. No organization interested in relief and development can be successful alone. The scale of problems is too large; the issues are too overwhelming, and the structural pressures are too debilitating. For organizations committed to the ideal of genuinely global human improvement and mutual obligation, the imperative to develop global approaches is unavoidable. These very ideals remind them that they need to work harder not only to cooperate in their own spheres but also to find ways to link with their allies in the developing world and devise global governance and organizational structures consistent with their ideals and political realities. This realization has led many organizations to seek even closer relationships with organizations outside the family. Many call these new relationships partnerships—the topic of the next chapter.

Ethnology and Beyond

Empirical Support

There is clear evidence that the organizations studied in this book are deeply involved in both discussions and actions to adapt the structures of their global families. There is the greatest degree of change in the relationships within each of the immediate organizational families as well as experimentation with new alliances and network relationships outside the family. Our respondents exhibited a high degree of awareness of their own experiments and those of other Northern relief and development organizations. However, they have less knowledge and awareness of the forms of emerging Southern networks, or with developments of this kind in Eastern Europe or in the now independent states of the former Soviet Union. It is interesting to note that while Southern global and regional networks are developing, there is less mapping, research, and documentation of the emerging forms. This can and should be a major area of important new research. Finally, since they are so new, there is still little systematic research available on emerging global and virtual networks like Jubilee 2000 or the campaign to ban landmines. This poses another interesting challenge and a promising new research agenda for scholars and practitioners alike.

Additional Explanations

In addition to clear motivations for adapting global family structure—such as efficiency, brand clarity, and economies of scale—one cannot help suggesting that there may be a healthy fear of bankruptcy and obsolescence on the part of the leadership and stakeholders of the Northern relief and development organizations. We also cannot discount the leadership's desire to continue to play a dominant role in decision-making and program formulation on a global level. We cannot help asking whether this drive for survival and dominance in decision-making will not make genuine alliances and partnerships difficult to develop.

Missing Details

One of the most interesting elements missing from many of the discussions with our respondents is the lack of focus on asset-based models of cooperation as opposed to intense interest in competitive models. Viewing other NGOs outside the family as potential competitors can lead to structures and to resource use that might be sub-optimal for global poverty alleviation. It is well worth thinking about cooperation models and aspects of resource sharing. How might cooperative, asset-based models lead to even greater impact in saving lives and improving human development?

Another missing element in the discussion of global structures was awareness and study of the potential of new "virtual networks" maintained by Internet contact versus established organizations. The danger of not exploring the full potential of virtual organizations could be obsolescence for existing NGOs. New virtual organizations could turn out to be less expensive than maintaining full-time staff and facilities all over the world—the current practice of the large existing NGOs. Virtual organizations' use of global information technology could also make them more nimble and more efficient in advocacy and in some elements of operations than existing organizations.

The group did not focus in any detail on the potential of global networks and movements and their own role as part of such movements. Some of the new, looser movements and networks—for example, the Direct Action Network that helped mobilize the WTO protests in Seattle in 1999—have an emotional appeal for the young that cannot be found in the traditional relief and development organizations. Just how the traditional organizations will remain relevant in the new world of movement politics is an important issue.

Finally, as part of the focus on competition, the Northern organization families are heavily focused on establishing and projecting brand identity. This approach could well get in the way of the kind of programmatic flexibility and the learning-process approaches so necessary to exceptional work in grassroots poverty alleviation.

Emerging Issues

It is hard to predict the future, but we believe that the Northern organizations interested in global emergency response and poverty alleviation will probably have to broaden their menu of global structural options to include the potential of networks, virtual organizations, and asset-based models for cooperation. Only the broadest thinking will lead to even more effective strategies. They will have to think even more experimentally about relationships with organizations outside their own families and about creative new relations with the public and private sectors. Our next chapter will look more deeply into the specific opportunities and dilemmas of such partnerships.

Notes

1. Bryan Hudson and Wolfgang Bielefeld, "Structures of Multinational Nonprofit Organizations," *Nonprofit Management and Leadership* 8, no. 1 (Fall 1997): 31–49. See also Kleith Provan, "The Federation as an Interorganizational Linkage Network," *Academy of Management Review 1983* 8, no. 1 (1983): 79–89. See also R. L. Warrent, "The Interorganizational Field as a Focus of Investigation," *Administrative Science Quarterly* (1967): 396–419. And also Dennis R. Young, "Local Autonomy in a Franchise Age: Structural Change in National Voluntary Associations," *Nonprofit and Voluntary Sector Quarterly* 18, no. 2 (Summer 1989): 101–17.

2. Alex Counts, president of the Grameen Foundation in the United States, interview by Marc Lindenberg, Seattle, Wash., June 10, 2000.

3. See CIVICUS, *Civil Society in the New Millennium* (West Hartford, Conn.: Kumarian Press, 1999); also interview with Kumi Naidoo, president of Civicus, by Marc Lindenberg, Seattle, Wash., June 10, 2000.

4. Manuel Chiriboga, executive secretary of ALOP, interview by Marc Lindenberg, Montreal, June 2000.

5. Mary Okumu, president of El Taller, interview by Marc Lindenberg, Montreal, June 2000.

6. NGO Briefing on Sudan to the UN Security Council, New York, October 1998.

– 6 –

The Promise of
New Inter-Organizational
and Inter-Sectoral Partnerships

SINCE THE END of World War II, there have been dramatic changes in interaction styles both between Northern relief and development organizations and local communities, and among nonprofit-, public-, and private-sector actors. In the immediate postwar period, relief and development organizations viewed communities and local organizations in devastated areas as program "recipients" in need of immediate support. They provided food, clothing, and shelter directly to war-torn communities. The worldwide delivery mechanism was often a simple, standard product like the CARE package.

Over the years, the staff of these relief and development organizations learned that their programs helped solve some very immediate problems of survival but did not contribute to building resilient individuals, families, or communities. Direct program delivery often made "recipients" feel helpless, dependent, and sometimes resentful. Furthermore, the concept of "one size fits all" programs did not work effectively across cultures. As a result, many organizations focus today on "participatory" programs in which communities and outside organizations jointly identify problems and potential solutions, and work together in implementation. They employ what is called a "learning-process approach" based on experimentation, joint evaluation, and program adjustment.[1] Today, organizations all over the world are exploring what they call "new forms of partnership," based on mutually compatible skill sets and shared decision-making.

Since 1945, the tone of public, private, and nonprofit relations has also changed. It has moved from suspicion and distance to greater openness and increased experimentation with multi-sectoral partnerships. After the defeat of Germany and Japan, the world was quickly divided into two power blocs based on different ideological conceptions of the appropriate roles of the state, private, and nonprofit sectors.[2] In the communist world, the strong "provider state" assumed the functions

155

of private production and civil society and its nonprofit organizations. The political party, the state, and civil society were fused into one entity. The development of an independent nonprofit as well as a private sector was viewed as a threat to the power of the state. In contrast, in the free-market world, the private sector continued to produce goods and services where prices could be set, goods were consumable, and supply and demand could be well identified. The role of the state was to help provide public goods (like defense, social welfare transfers, electricity, and water) that are not easily produced by the private sector. Nonprofit and voluntary organizations, for example church and community groups, were often formed for common purposes other than profit making.

Within the free-market, capitalist world, there were various conceptions of the appropriate role of the state. In Europe, the social welfare state played a large role in income redistribution and expanded social services. In the United States, a smaller public sector regulated the private sector, provided some public goods, and made limited social transfers from wealthier to poorer groups. The growth of the nonprofit sector was encouraged through favorable tax legislation. It sometimes filled roles normally associated with the more active welfare states in Europe. While there were differences in the sectoral roles within the capitalist world, public, private, and nonprofit organizations viewed each other less with the fear prevalent in the communist world, but more with suspicion and naiveté.

After the collapse of the Soviet Union in the late 1980s, the role of the producer state and planned economy and even that of the European social welfare state fell out of favor. The size of the state shrank as citizens were unwilling to pay taxes to maintain it. Many public organizations were privatized and, as noted earlier, the role of the nonprofit sector grew. People from all sectors began to recognize that large unmet global social needs and insufficient worldwide resources might make it necessary to experiment with new forms of public, private, and nonprofit relationships. Many of these new experiments took place in the 1990s.

This chapter explores two broad themes: the forms of emerging relations between organizations in the relief and development community in general, as well as the new forms of partnership emerging among relief and development nonprofits and private-sector organizations more specifically. We have placed particular emphasis on this latter theme, which has received far less attention from students of the international NGO sector than many other subjects.[3] The chapter focuses on the key concepts, as well as the "drivers" and the dilemmas inherent in the new organizational relationships; on the experimental responses the NGO community is employing in its new organizational and sectoral relationships; and, as in every other chapter, on ethnology.

Concepts

While the concept of a social contract was initially used to discuss the relations between citizens and the state, it also provides a useful way to discuss the exchange relationships between nonprofits and other organizations. For those in the nonprofit community, the idea of a social contract is appealing because it moves symbolically beyond the realm of a legally binding contract to a relationship that is morally binding in the broadest sense. It carries with it deeper obligations based on mutual respect. The idea of a social contract, traceable to the sophists of Greece,[4] appears later in the works of medieval writers as well as those of renaissance theorists.[5] But its most widely known development comes from the eighteenth-century writings of Jean-Jacques Rousseau.[6] For the purposes of this chapter, a social contract implies a set of explicit rights, responsibilities, and mutual expectations that members of each legally constituted organization have of its partner.

Although there are many kinds of social contracts based on a full continuum of equal versus less equal relationships,[7] one of the most useful ways to categorize this continuum in the nonprofit sector is Karen Casper's "partnership arch"[8] (see Figure 6.1 on the following page). Casper classifies possible exchange relationships along two dimensions. The first dimension is the degree of active service delivery (which she calls "hands on" as opposed to "hands off"). The second dimension is equivalence and nonequivalence—or the degree to which the relationship between the organizations is equal or unequal.

For Casper, the foundation of partnership is equivalence and mutuality through a well-understood, shared view of balanced rights and responsibilities. Thus a genuine partnership implies a balanced social contract. However, as one can see from the partnership arch, there are a whole variety of relationships that organizations might have. For example, at the base of the left side of the arch, direct delivery of services implies a highly interventionist style, in which one organization delivers goods and services to a population without help from partners. Casper calls this an "inequivalent, hands on" relationship. At the base of the right side of the arch is the "inequivalent, hands off" style that Casper classified as a direct donation or grant. In return for such a grant, the donor organization has a legally binding set of requirements that it expects another organization to achieve. Along the right side of the arch, the organizations involved already have capacity. One can contract with the other for delivery, or they can form partnerships with each other to provide some of the services. Along the left side of the arch, one organization is assumed to have capacity while the other does not. The idea is for the organization with capacity to help the other build its capacity. In a true partnership, each organization has valued capacities that

Figure 6.1. The Partnership Arch

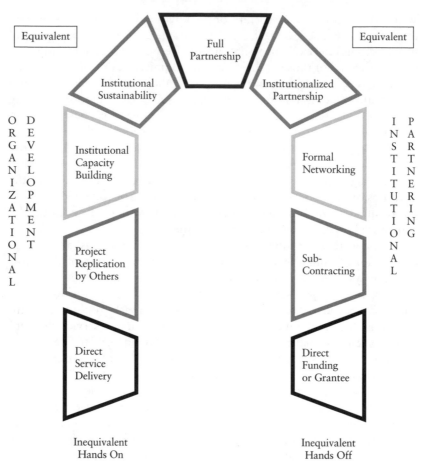

Equivalent

Full
Partnership

Equivalent

Institutional
Sustainability

Institutionalized
Partnership

O R G A N I Z A T I O N A L
D E V E L O P M E N T

I N S T I T U T I O N A L
P A R T N E R I N G

Institutional
Capacity
Building

Formal
Networking

Project
Replication
by Others

Sub-
Contracting

Direct
Service
Delivery

Direct
Funding
or Grantee

Inequivalent
Hands On

Inequivalent
Hands Off

Source: Karen Casper, "Gateway to Partnering and Institutional Strengthening," *Program in Touch,* CARE, Atlanta, vol. 2, 1996.

the other may lack. A partnership is based on the use of the special capacities of each organization to add greater value than either could on its own.

As useful as Casper's conceptual framework is, we have found even more variations in the ways that senior managers use the term "partnership" in actual practice. Some managers use the term to reflect only on relationships of other Northern NGOs to local associations in developing countries, and for agencies that provide services within projects, or financial support. They also use it to describe a host of entities such as associations, foundations, businesses, churches, subgroups of donor agencies, other Northern NGOs, sojourners in campaigns, networks of

Southern NGOs, and alliances. Moreover, the strength of relationship in such partnerships varies greatly in intensity, salience, and meaning for the resulting work. At one end of the range, it may mean nothing more than a public relations term, or a mutually supportive posture. At the other extreme, it may mean full-scale reciprocity in critical decision-making. It is useful to remember this caveat when reading much that is written about partnerships.

It is also helpful to remember that there have been many critiques, for example, of North-South NGO partnerships.[9] Such partnerships have often been fraught with well documented, operational as well as political and social tensions. Often the argument is made that there is a moral imperative for greater reciprocity in partnering relationships. While this is fundamentally correct, it is also important to remember that if an NGO claims to have four hundred or more "partners," there is no way that all of these relationships can possibly reflect an ideal reciprocity. The issues of locus of decision-making, quality control, and financial support have a dynamic and constantly evolving character for each Northern member of any of the NGO families discussed in this book. In this chapter, we first turn to the "drivers," and then focus at greater length on one of the most complex and compelling issues—NGO corporate partnering.

Drivers and Dilemmas

Changing Organizational Relationships

When asked why they were currently highly motivated to seek new partnerships based on mutuality and equality with organizations outside their own immediate family, our Northern relief and development respondents frequently mentioned five forces:

1. Accumulated organizational learning about sustainable development

2. Growing strength, size, and expertise of the non-Northern nonprofit sector

3. Scarcity of global resources

4. Donor trends

5. Opportunities offered by the new global information technology

Through almost a half-century of learning, many of the Northern relief and development organizations believe that there is a relationship between community and local organizational participation and project sustainability and impact.[10] In addition, they report that the growing, highly competent non-Northern relief and development NGO sector is impossible to ignore. Partnerships with local organizations not only save resources but also permit greater cultural relevance and adaptation in program design and implementation.

At the same time, our respondents feared obsolescence if they did not cultivate such alliances. They report that donors increasingly insisted that local partners take the lead in their own countries. They indicate that fashion and ideology in northern industrial countries also place a premium on partnerships. The ease of facilitating partnerships and networks with new global information technology is also a strong incentive. For example, many respondents mentioned the role of technology in the Nobel Prize–winning International Campaign to Ban Landmines as a driving force in permitting a successful worldwide advocacy network to develop. Finally, all of these forces combine with increased competition for scarce global resources to create an environment conducive to new partnerships.

Changing Sectoral Relationships

Traditionally, deep mutual suspicion among governmental, private-sector, and nonprofit organizations limited the prospects for partnerships. On the one hand, many NGOs were formed to help mobilize community-based responses due to the failure of government. At the same time, in many countries, independent NGOs have become the target of governments that view them as threats to their own base of power. In other countries, states have attempted to use NGOs as pawns in power struggles or to serve their own ends. As a result, NGO staff have sometimes suffered physical attacks, imprisonment, and human rights abuses—none of which led to sympathy for the state. On the other hand, some NGOs traditionally viewed private-sector organizations with profit-making objectives as an enemy of community social well-being and a source of exploitation of cheap labor. Many NGOs were organized specifically in response to what they perceived to be private-sector abuses.

The weakening and collapse of the state in the 1980s and 1990s has been a major "driver" for the search for new inter-sectoral relations. But it has also created new dilemmas for the NGO sector. Should NGOs try to function as a substitute for the state and provide basic health services, teachers, schools, water, or sanitation? Ironically, without a state to actually provide services or security, NGOs face the task of how to rebuild communities alone—without safety and security. Organizations that provide on-the-ground relief and development programs often face special conflicts with the state when they identify what they perceive to be human rights abuses. If operational NGOs advocate against the abuses, they can endanger their access to the country and people who need help, as well as place their own field staff and local partners at risk.

These new contradictions make it hard to know whether to cooperate with or confront governments.

The weakened role of the public sector in the last two decades has been accompanied by an expansion of the private sector—another driver of new partnerships. Economic globalization produced new wealth and employment in some places and left many corporations with additional resources that might potentially be donated to the NGOs. Whole new sectors of wealth, often based on global enterprises, have emerged without a tradition of giving or a vision of public commitment. The opportunities for cooperation have increased substantially.

These factors as well as the creation of new private wealth have also created new dilemmas for the NGO community. On the one hand, NGOs face contradictions as they search for new relations with the private sector. For example, many are involved in strong fundraising efforts to attract corporate donations or form innovative partnerships. On the other hand, NGOs question whether they should take donations from companies they perceive to be socially irresponsible. New innovations in both cooperation and providing countervailing pressure are unfolding. Some NGOs are embarking on global advocacy campaigns for corporate codes of conduct in the Third World. Others are working with new funders to educate them to the possibilities of fighting global poverty. Ironically, many of those with new wealth are resolutely anti-statist and more inclined to work with the NGO sector. As a result, new partnerships between corporations and NGOs are being developed in various communities around the world. NGO leaders experience the tensions generated between the opportunities and risks of collaborative versus contentious relations with the corporate sector.

Our respondents felt that the dilemmas of new organizational and sectoral relations leave them with four important, unanswered questions. First, when does it make sense to cooperate with the corporate and public sector, and when might it be necessary to provide contravening pressure? Second, should criteria be developed about corporate conduct to help NGOs make more informed choices? Third, when partnerships do make sense, what are some of the most innovative models? Fourth, when countervailing pressure is necessary, what examples of successful NGO initiatives might provide tips on how to proceed? A look at actual practice sheds light on at least partial answers to these questions.

New Directions in Organizational Partnerships

When our respondents were asked to describe their overall program portfolios in the context of the partnership arch, their most frequently reported modalities were still overwhelmingly direct delivery, followed by institutional capacity building, networking, and limited subcontracting. Many programs featured both direct delivery and institutional capacity building. Most respondents predicted that, within the next decade, their portfolios would have higher capacity building, networking, and partnership components and less direct program delivery.

As our respondents develop relationships with new organizations outside their family, some of the options they employ are: mergers with existing organizations, the transformation of inside organizations into affiliates with their own national boards and sources of funds, the formation of entirely new partners, loose alliances with independent organizations, network membership, and negotiated partnerships with independent organizations. Most are currently members of organizational networks and loose, ad hoc alliances.

Since most respondents told us that their future partnership strategies are still in the process of formulation, it is hard to generalize about the preferred modalities. CARE USA, for example, has continued to experiment with a variety of organizational transformation models without selecting a dominant style to guide its broad strategy. Thus, it transferred its entire program in Costa Rica (largely a microenterprise portfolio) to local organizations. In Thailand, it worked to convert the local CARE USA office into an independent affiliate with a national board which has stewardship responsibility for strong local fundraising and program delivery. In the Dominican Republic, it simply withdrew the CARE program in the belief that local organizations provided the same services equally well.

Figure 6.2 shows provides a glimpse of the organizational evolution strategy emerging at Oxfam International, as discussed at its May 2000 board retreat in Montreal, Canada. Oxfam International members favor a search for strong and compatible partners among existing, independent organizations, as well as network relations as opposed to mergers, the creation of new organizations, or the transformation of its own local affiliates.

New Directions in Engagement with the Private Sector

In June 2000, our respondents were asked to characterize their current and future plans for private-sector partnerships[11] and the collaboration styles they currently employ.[12] Characterizations of these styles, as initially developed by James Austin at the Harvard Business School, range along a continuum that our respondents broadened to include suspicion, interaction, philanthropic, transactional, and integrative.[13] One of our organizational respondents, Médecins Sans Frontières, used the term "engagement" as well. (MSF encounters thorny issues in its relationship with pharmaceutical companies; on the one hand, it seeks to

**Figure 6.2. Changing Public, Private, and NGO Relations:
Collaboration or Counter Pressure**

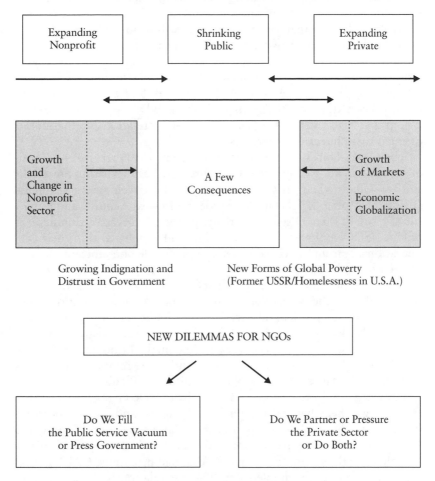

engage them in dialogue, and on the other, it needs to help mobilize public criticism of these companies as part of its advocacy work—for example, about drug pricing.) All NGOs face this conundrum—for example, when they learn through local Southern NGO partners about what they consider to be unfair labor practices or human rights problems. Many of World Vision's relationships could, for example, be depicted as "constructive private engagement," which sometimes takes the preferred form of off-the-record dialogue with top executives.

What we learned from our respondents was that so far the number of their experimental inter-sectoral partnerships was very low. Moreover, they reported, along the above-described spectrum, most of their existing inter-sectoral relationships fell into the part of the range characterized by suspicion at worst and philanthropy at best. Despite this, our respondents believe that by the end of the next decade, more extensive transactional and integrative partnerships will be in evidence.

It should be noted, however, that the paucity of extensive, new inter-sectoral collaboration that our respondents reported masks the highly innovative and exciting experimentation currently under way in some NGOs—for example CARE USA, Oxfam GB, and Save the Children USA. The CARE-Starbucks partnership is a good place to begin, because it helps perceive several phases in a decade-long relationship that in this case led to an integrative partnership.

The CARE-Starbucks relationship began in 1991, when Peter Blomquist, the CARE Northwest Office Director, began visiting Starbucks staff to interest them in CARE programs and development seminars. During this period, Starbucks President Howard Schultz and Senior Vice President Dave Olsen had already pursued innovative employment practices like employee stock ownership and benefits within their U.S. operations. Starbucks needed to remain profitable and efficient but also wanted to find ways to develop what it hoped would be new policies for social responsibility throughout its global operations. Profitability continued to be the cornerstone of the Starbucks mission, but the company did not see profits and social responsibility as antithetical ideas. Both Starbucks's officers and Blomquist were well aware that Starbucks bought coffee from producers in Guatemala, Ethiopia, and Kenya, where CARE had development projects, and where infant mortality was high, life expectancy low, and living conditions difficult.

Both organizations searched creatively for a convergence of interest to move them beyond the purely interactive and communications stage.[14] The first relationship was a philanthropic one. During the 1992 Christmas season, Starbucks provided a special sampler of coffees for sale from three countries where CARE had programs. CARE got $2 from the sale of each sampler. By 1994, the relationship became more transactional. Starbucks directly donated resources to CARE projects in water and sanitation and microcredit for regions where Starbucks bought coffee, and CARE staff helped Starbucks leaders understand more about the developing world and labor practices. In the late 1990s the CARE-Starbucks relationship moved from the transactional stage to a more integrative one. CARE staff were offered opportunities for training and sabbaticals in Starbucks corporate units such as human resources and marketing. Starbucks staff participated more frequently in CARE development seminars, volunteered their time in fundraising and other CARE activities, and began to serve on board committees. Finally, Starbucks began to seek advice on overseas codes of conduct and labor practices. In June 2000, Starbucks took the unusual step as an industry leader to offer the sale of "fair-trade" coffee in its stores. Fair-trade coffee is coffee purchased from producers whose labor practices are certified as meeting fair labor standards. While it would be hard to demonstrate causality between the evolving CARE-Starbucks relationship and the Starbucks fair-trade coffee decision, Dave Olsen, the Starbucks vice president who played an instrumental role in this decision, attributes many of his new insights about social responsibility in business to his decade-long involvement with CARE.[15]

Oxfam GB's Director, David Bryer, provided a fascinating overview of an evolving comprehensive strategy marked by real complexity and multiple corporate relationships.[16] The Oxfam corporate engagement strategy includes three strategic dimensions: funding and cooperation, policy dialogue with joint standard setting and monitoring, and pressure tactics. Bryer defines funding and cooperative relationships as ones in which Oxfam and its corporate partners had similar, long-term values and goals about the development process—not unlike the decade-long relationship between CARE and Starbucks. Oxfam GB has such relationships with both Northern Foods and the Cooperative Bank, two U.K. corporations. The Quaker origins of the ownership and management of Northern Foods make for a compatible value fit with Oxfam's mission, staff, and directors. This has allowed Oxfam family members to feel comfortable receiving program funds and Northern Foods players to feel comfortable donating them. The value fit is sufficiently close for the Northern Foods Board to be willing to support Oxfam advocacy work. When Oxfam GB engages in policy dialogue, the second dimension of its strategy, neither they nor the corporations involved are under any illusions that their values or basic objectives are highly compatible; their commitment was to engage in civil discussion about issues of common concern.

Bryer cited the examples of ongoing dialogue with Levi Strauss about labor standards and with British Petroleum about its impact on development and living conditions as a major extractive industry producer. He believes that the dialogue efforts exceeded the initial expectations of both groups and led to constructive joint action. In the case of Levi Strauss the result was joint design and participation in "the ethical trading initiative"—in which labor standards for overseas workers were discussed and defined. Then Oxfam and Levi Strauss began a joint labor-monitoring program. Discussions with British Petroleum had resulted in a broader definition of issues in the role of extractive industries in development and social responsibility. Finally, Bryer notes that outright pressure, media advocacy, witnessing, and demonstrations—the third prong of the strategy—are sometimes necessary when Oxfam believes that particular corporate practices need to be brought to the public's attention. He cited, for example, recent efforts to raise public awareness about the relationship between the world diamond trade, the arms trade, and the support of warring groups in Angola, Sierra Leone, and other African countries. In this campaign, Oxfam's objective was to sensitize the public to the link between the diamond trade and human suffering. In particular it looks at how diamond revenues are used in arms sales and the perpetuation of conflict.

Bryer believes that it is indeed possible to maintain cooperative relations, dialogue, and pressure relationships in an integrated private-sector strategy, and that it is constructive to do so. Such a strategy, however, is not without its problems. Bryer noted, for example, the case of one member of Oxfam International working for a cooperative relationship while another was involved in pressure tactics with the same corporation. Bryer's three lessons for managing constructive corporate engagement were: (1) be very clear about your purpose and objectives and those of your partners, (2) be transparent about these objectives and watch out for being co-opted, and (3) use multiple approaches where possible and maximize impact and learning.

Like Oxfam, Save the Children USA also has a systemic outreach strategy for its alliances with the private sector. Charles MacCormack, SAVE's president, also described an innovative, three-pronged, strategy.[17] In the first prong, capacity building, Save the Children works closely with a wide range of companies that provide pro bono services. Andersen Consulting helped Save the Children with strategic planning. The Boston Consulting Group assisted with studies to improve SAVE's efficiency and effectiveness. Johnson & Johnson made management training available to Save the Children employees without charge. Corporate staff from all three organizations expressed satisfaction at contributing their skills to activity they considered to be of great social value. The corporations involved reinforced their image of social leadership, and SAVE staff gained skills, knowledge, and improved systems and practices as a result of the relationship.

MacCormack called the second strategic dimension a marketing, merchandising, and visibility relationship. He cited the examples of Save the Children "realities" (silk ties made by Celanta) and the US Air–donated frequent flyer miles program. In each case, a company contributed its own sales and marketing with support from Save the Children.

Finally, MacCormack described closer transactional relationships with organizations like T. J. Maxx and Denny's. For example, T. J. Maxx had its own special employee program for child sponsorship, which gave its staff a sense of direct program involvement. SAVE benefited through receipt of new resources for its children's programs around the world. And, through the support of Denny's restaurants and their patrons (through menu items, coin collections, and sponsorship of one thousand children), Save the Children has been able to expand service

Figure 6.3. New Innovative Private Sector Relations: Case Studies

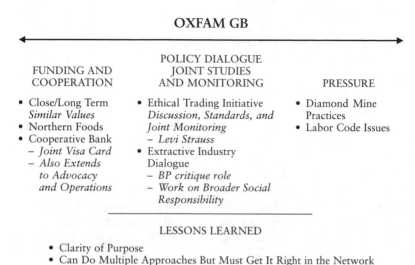

OXFAM GB

FUNDING AND COOPERATION	POLICY DIALOGUE JOINT STUDIES AND MONITORING	PRESSURE

• Close/Long Term *Similar Values*
 • Northern Foods
 • Cooperative Bank
   – *Joint Visa Card*
   – *Also Extends*
     to Advocacy
     and Operations
	• Ethical Trading Initiative *Discussion, Standards, and Joint Monitoring*
	   – *Levi Strauss*
	 • Extractive Industry Dialogue
	   – *BP critique role*
	   – *Work on Broader Social Responsibility*
		• Diamond Mine Practices
		 • Labor Code Issues

LESSONS LEARNED

- Clarity of Purpose
- Can Do Multiple Approaches But Must Get It Right in the Network
- Watch Out for Co-optation

SAVE US

CAPACITY BUILDING	MARKETING MERCHANDISING VISIBILITY	CLOSER TRANSACTIONS
• Andersen Consulting *Pro Bono* • Boston Consulting Group *Planning* • Johnson & Johnson *Training*	• SAVE Ties Celanta • US Air Miles	• Priceline.com *Employee/child sponsorship* • T. J. Maxx *General Purpose Support* • Denny's

INTERESTING INNOVATION

- Internationalizing National Partnerships
- Amex

delivery to U.S. children in over 250 communities. Figure 6.3 provides an overview of the Oxfam GB and Save the Children USA approaches.

Regardless of the level of their experimentation with new sectoral relations, our respondents noted a set of new tensions and opportunities generated by the promise of partnerships. On the opportunities side, they noted the importance of getting beyond the typical stereotypes of the nonprofit community as a group of "naive idealists" and of the corporate sector as "concerned only with profits." They saw the real importance of mutual trust and understanding of the complexity of the world of each sector. They cited the tremendous reservoir of good will that they had begun to experience among employees who wanted to volunteer their time and shareholders who wanted to think broadly about social responsibility. They saw the potential for integrating new ideas of social responsibility into overall corporate accountability. The opportunities for mixed strategies of both philanthropy and advocacy needed further exploration. Based on the Oxfam, CARE, and Save the Children examples, it became clear that it was possible to manage a complex, multi-dimensional set of relationships with many private-sector organizations simultaneously.

The respondents were, however, also highly aware of some inevitable tensions in managing their relations with the private sector. Among these tensions were: the trade-off between social goals and profitability, the contradiction of overlapping governance, the style differences between corporate and nonprofit cultures, the difficulty of managing relationships that include both advocacy and operations, and the problem of not being able to manage a large number of complex, private, and nonprofit partnership relations because of the limitations of time and money.

Finally, our respondents reaffirmed that the foundations of any new organizational or sectoral partnerships had to be based on clarity of purpose on the part of each group, transparency in sharing each group's goals and interests, trust building, and a real commitment to invest in a long-term relationship. Our respondents found Austin's criteria for successful new strategic alliances useful for development of both new organizational partnerships as well as cross-sectoral relationships.[18] These criteria include: (1) connection with purpose and people, (2) clarity of purpose, (3) congruence of mission strategy and values, (4) creation of value, (5) communication between partners, (6) continual learning, and (7) commitment to a long-term relationship.

Ethnology and Beyond

Empirical Support

The respondents believe that major environmental changes made the exploration of new organizational and sectoral partnerships an imperative. There is ample material to confirm that resources for the NGO community are more scarce than previously, that there are more healthy and strong non-Northern nonprofit organizations with which partnerships can be formed, and that donor pressures and tastes are moving in the direction of partnerships with non-Northern organizations. They also note that, to date, there has been more discussion than actual transformation of organizational and inter-sectoral relations. It is also easy to confirm their perception of the slow pace of change, since many of the organizations studied in this book are only in the initial process of discussing and defining new strategies and carrying out experiments. Their board minutes, strategy papers, and other documents confirm this.

Motivations for New Partnerships

The respondents did a systematic job of identifying the underlying "drivers" for new partnerships and sectoral relations. Although they have mentioned fear of their own organizations' obsolescence should they not develop new relationships, they may not have acknowledged the full weight that this driver deserves. Other observers of the sector strongly argue that the motivation behind partnerships is not so much enlightened self-interest as pure survival since NGOs will not be able to carry out their work in the future without such partnerships.[19] Our informants also probably underplay the extent to which Northern organizations can learn from non-Northern partners, or the extent to which real, long-term sustainability of development activity and humanitarian action may be predicated on strong local organizations.

Underexplored Areas

Several areas of the new drive for partnerships did not receive detailed attention. First, why, in spite of the strong pressure for new partnerships and inter-sectoral relations, is progress in the sector so slow? Why are the respondent organizations undertaking only their very initial experiments and strategic readjustments after almost a decade of discussion? Second, why is so little attention devoted to emerging "virtual" organizations and loose global networks as opposed to more traditional partnerships?

While it is hard to provide definitive answers, it is possible to speculate. Perhaps the slow pace of organizational strategies for new partnerships and sectoral experiments is partially due to the intense pace of normal operations work in the relief and development community. Perhaps the idea of new work styles is sufficiently threatening to existing staff that it is hard to get their support. In fact, there may be passive or, more likely, very active resistance. What if, for example, many Northern organizations no longer worked operationally in non-Northern countries, but instead worked only through Southern partners? Would that not mean cutbacks in Northern staff? Would it not require that Northern staff learn new skill sets? Another possible reason for the slow pace of change might be that most of the Northern NGOs have little discretionary money for their operations. Money and time to experiment with new partnerships must be found somewhere, and most organizations simply do not have it. Finally, employee fear and resistance to change is a well-documented phenomenon in organizations generally.

Perhaps top NGO leadership could play an even more proactive role in explaining why such changes might be important and in managing change.

The lack of attention to experiments with networks and virtual organizations may well be attributable to the same earlier-mentioned forces that keep the overall pace of change slow. One might add the more general lack of understanding or comfort that many people have regarding the use of new information technology in the workplace.

Emerging Issues

Perhaps more so than in the case of other areas discussed in this book it is important for us, as sympathetic participant observers of the Northern relief and development sector, to voice two concerns about the slow pace of change. There are serious risks to not moving more aggressively with new experiments in organizational alliances, partnerships, and sectoral relations. There are serious risks to not understanding and experimenting with the potential of new information technology-based network alliances for operations, advocacy, communications, global learning, and fundraising. Case studies from other fields should serve as a source of concern. For example, IBM's success with the mainframe computer contributed to its inability to see the new opportunities of laptops, palm pilots, and the Internet. IBM's failure to respond proactively to these new technologies almost led to its demise. The Northern relief and development sector needs to move much more quickly and proactively to explore the potential of new partnerships and sectoral relationships if it plans to stay at the cutting edge of relief and development work.

Notes

1. Derick Brinkerhoff and Marcus Ingle, "Integrating Blueprint and Process: a Structured Flexibility Approach to Development Management," *Public Administration and Development* 5 (1989): 145–56. Samuel Paul, *The Strategic Management of Development Programs: Guidelines for Program Action* (Geneva: International Labor Organization, 1983), and David Korten, "Community Organization and Rural Development: A Learning Process Approach," *Public Administration Review* (1980): 480–511.

2. Marc Lindenberg, *The Human Development Race: Improving the Quality of Life in Developing Countries* (San Francisco: ICS Press, 1993), 67–70.

3. For a few of the most recent publications on this topic, see Jem Bendell, *Terms of Endearment: Business, NGOs and Sustainable Development* (Sheffield, England: Greenleaf Publishing and New Academy of Business, 2000), and James Austin, *The Collaboration Challenge* (San Francisco: Jossey-Bass, 2000). For interesting material on the dilemmas of NGO and public sector relations, see *Too Close for Comfort: NGOs States and Donors,* ed. Michael Edwards and David Hulme (London: Earthscan Press, 1996), and Julie Fisher,

Nongovernments: NGOs and the Political Development of the Third World (West Hartford, Conn.: Kumarian Press, 1998).

4. See Plato, *The Republic;* the Greek text, vol II, with notes and essays by the late B. Jowett and Lewis Campbell (Oxford: Clarendon Press, 1894).

5. J. W. Gough, *The Social Contract: A Critical Study of Its Development* (Westport, Conn.: Greenwood Press, 1978).

6. Jean-Jacques Rousseau, *The Social Contract and Other Discourses* (London: Everyman Publishers, 1913).

7. See, for example, James Austin, *The Collaboration Challenge* (San Francisco: Jossey-Bass, 2000); *Making A Difference: NGOs and Development in a Changing World,* ed. Michael Edwards and David Hulme (London: Earthscan Press, 1992); Fisher, *Nongovernments;* Alan Fowler, *Striking a Balance* (London: Earthscan Press, 1997), particularly chapters 5 and 8.

8. Karen Casper, "Gateway to Partnering and Institutional Strength" (Atlanta, Ga.: Program in Touch, CARE, 1996), vol. 2.

9. See for example David Brown, "Private Voluntary Organizations and Development Partnerships," in *Social Development: A New Role for the Organizational Sciences,* ed. Pradip N. Khandwalla (Newbury Park, Calif.: Sage, 1988), 71–78; Alan Fowler, "Building Partnerships between Northern and Southern NGOs: Issues for the 1990s," *Development in Practice,* vol. 1 (1): 5–18. See also "Globalization and Northern NGOs: The Challenge of Relief and Development in A Changing Context," *Nonprofit and Voluntary Sector Quarterly* 28, no. 4 (Supplement 1999); as well as "Special Issue: NGO Futures Beyond Aid," *Third World Quarterly* 21, no. 4 (August 2000).

10. Brinkerhoff and Ingle, "Integrating Blueprint and Process"; Paul, *The Strategic Management of Development Programs;* and Korten "Community Organization and Rural Development."

11. NGO Leaders' Conference at the Daniel J. Evans School of Public Affairs, University of Washington, Seattle, June 9–11, 2000.

12. They found Austin's categories of philanthropic, transactional, and integrative most useful in discussing styles of interaction and added two others—suspicion/animosity and simple interaction—to the continuum. See Jim Austin, *The Collaboration Challenge,* particularly chapter 2.

13. Our NGO respondents added two categories, which they called suspicion and interaction, to Austin's three categories of philanthropy, transactional, and integrative. Suspicion and animosity simply imply sufficient distrust to enter into a relationship. Interaction is the exploratory stage where there are conversations and initial contact. Philanthropy implies simply providing money for projects. Transactional activity might involve a whole set of exchange relationships beyond funds. Finally, an integrative relationship implies a closer set of shared values, high trust, and complex activities in which each organization more deeply impacts the other's behaviors, values, and mission.

14. Dave Olsen, Peter Blomquist, and Kevin Henry, interview by Marc Lindenberg, Seattle, June 9, 2000. Also live case presentation by Dave Olsen of Starbucks, Peter Blomquist of Global Partners, and Kevin Henry of CARE in the session on partnerships offered by Jim Austin at the NGO Leaders' Conference at the Evans School of Public Affairs, University of Washington, Seattle, 9–

11 June 2000. Austin's book, *The Collaboration Challenge,* also has a detailed description of the evolution of the CARE-Starbucks relationship.

15. Dave Olsen, senior vice president of Starbucks, interview by Marc Lindenberg, Seattle, June 9, 2000.

16. David Bryer, president of Oxfam GB, June 10, 2000.

17. Charles MacCormack, president of Save the Children US, interview by Marc Lindenberg, Seattle, June 2000.

18. Austin, *The Collaboration Challenge,* chapter 8.

19. See *Making A Difference,* ed. Edwards and Hulme; and Fowler, "Building Partnerships between Northern and Southern NGOs."

The Evolving Role of Advocacy*

R ECENT YEARS have seen a marked growth in the visibility and mobilization of NGOs around policy issues. From the Earth Summit
in Rio in 1992 to the first-ever meeting of NGOs with the UN Security Council in 1997 to the convergence of NGOs on the meetings
of the World Trade Organization and World Bank in 1999 and 2000,
NGOs have been carving a niche for themselves at the policy table.
NGO leadership in the successful global campaigns for debt relief and a
ban on landmines demonstrated that the NGO community knows how
to effectively augment operational experience with sophisticated policy
analysis and negotiation skills and how to utilize new technology to get
its message out to the public.

These activities reflect a change in the role of international development and relief NGOs. Historically, these NGOs focused primarily,
if not exclusively, on service delivery rather than advocacy. Advocacy
work entails moving beyond implementing programs to help those in
need, to actually taking up and defending the causes of others and
speaking out to the public on another's behalf. In our analysis of NGO
advocacy, we further define the term to refer specifically to speaking
out for policy change and action that will address the root causes of
problems confronted in development and relief work, and not simply
speaking out to alert people of a problem in order to raise funds to support operational work. For international relief and development NGOs,
advocacy includes the full range of activities (outreach, direct lobbying,
education, and research) they undertake in order to raise awareness and
contribute to public dialogue on issues at stake on any given relief or
development problem.

Most of the NGOs in our study did not include advocacy in their
original mandates, as they were established in response to wars or natural disasters and developed operational programs to meet the needs
of people affected by those crises. There are some notable exceptions—
Oxfam always combined operational work with advocacy and a focus
on addressing the structural causes of poverty, Médecins Sans Frontières

---

*This chapter was written by Christina Kappaz.

(MSF) incorporated witnessing into its humanitarian work, and Save the Children from its inception worked toward international protection for the rights of children. Even in these cases, however, the role of advocacy has been evolving with the changing political environment and the opening of new avenues for affecting policies.

Although the general trend among NGOs has been toward increased advocacy, the extent of involvement varies. As each NGO considers its own role in these efforts, it must address a series of new challenges as well as opportunities. While we have alluded to some of their advocacy work, especially in Chapters 3 and 4, in this chapter we will explore more specifically the role that advocacy plays within the organizations themselves. We first review the factors that have been driving advocacy among the international NGOs headquartered in industrialized countries, then examine the way these factors have resulted in different responses and approaches among the NGOs in our study, highlight the way in which coordinated advocacy has been effective in select cases, and, finally, examine the key challenges that advocacy poses for the organizations.

Factors Driving Advocacy Work

Many of the "drivers" identified in Chapter 1 that instigated reflection and change within the NGO community also impacted on NGO advocacy. The rapid growth of NGOs since the 1980s and the increasing role in delivering official development assistance has contributed to the growth in size and sophistication of many NGOs and positioned them to speak out on policy issues. While the exact combination of external and internal drivers varies within each national member, there are some commonalities. External factors include the changed global policy framework, the persistence of poverty and the increased number of complex emergencies, re-examination of Northern NGO competitive advantage, and the emergence of new global communication technology. At the same time, internal forces within NGOs emerge—in large part derived from frustration with the slow pace that project work entails and the increased acknowledgment that policies are part of the problem of persistent poverty. The horrifying experiences of field staff in complex emergencies also pushed staff to become involved in the political context that was influencing their ability to carry out humanitarian work.

Global Policy Framework

The global policy framework has changed over the last two decades, in part because of NGO voices, and those changes facilitated a stronger advocacy role for NGOs. As discussed in preceding chapters, NGOs have become integrated into the official development arena, and, more important, into policy dialogue. They participated in the definition of new policy agendas, as demonstrated by their influential role in the 1992 Rio Conference on Environment and Development and the 1995 Beijing Women's Conference.[1] Moreover, the development community as a whole moved to work on programs and policies rather than just projects, and this influenced NGOs to also become involved in policy work. The number of formal vehicles for NGO/government consultation has grown steadily since the 1970s. NGOs can have access to policymakers through official NGO consultative status with various UN agencies and participation on NGO working groups at the World Bank and other donor organizations. Even those NGOs who did not actively participate in the process of forging these partnerships can now more easily take their place at the discussion table.

Persistence of Poverty and Increase in Complex Human Emergencies

The persistence of extreme poverty as well as the emergence of new types of poverty have contributed to the push for NGOs to broaden their scope beyond alleviating suffering to working more directly on attacking the root causes of that suffering. In the 1990s, the rapidity with which international financial capital flows could wash out of countries demonstrated the dark side of globalization. In the debates over markets versus states, few had expected that financial markets would begin failing as they did in the late 1990s. Not only were markets not delivering on the generation of wealth, but in some countries there were newly impoverished people—even in those countries whose policies had apparently been effective and who had been acclaimed as doing "the right things." The scale of modern global problems as well as the perception that the forces behind them transcend traditional political boundaries and jurisdictions has led many NGOs to explore a more active stance toward advocacy.

The changing context of relief work that emerged with the end of the Cold War also influenced the new move toward advocacy. NGOs have found it more difficult to carry out operations without becoming involved in the policy matters that directly affect their work. When caught in the middle of conflict and often manipulated by warring factions, NGOs find it hard to remain impartial. Furthermore, the changing political arena and the co-opting of the term "humanitarian" by military forces has increasingly blurred the line between the humanitarian and political character of NGOs.

In addition, the new kinds of emergencies pushed NGOs to think about proactively building peace. Oxfam GB's Cut Conflict Campaign demonstrates this new thinking. This campaign goes beyond working on alleviating suffering of people in crisis and undertakes advocacy to

resolve conflicts. Oxfam has commissioned a number of studies and research initiatives into the causes of conflict, its resolution, and initiatives
that can be undertaken to reduce conflict, and where it cannot easily be
resolved, to mitigate its effects. CARE is also dedicated to this issue
and has been active in both training staff in conflict mediation and in
lobbying, particularly the U.S. government, on policies that would foster long-term peace, especially in Sudan and the Great Lakes region of
Africa. World Vision is also interested in expanding its advocacy efforts
to focus on upstream peace building and is exploring effective ways of
working in this area.

NGO Effectiveness and Comparative Advantage

The increase in NGO advocacy work has come in part as a reaction to
the increased scrutiny by donors and academics of NGO effectiveness
that accompanied the growth of the NGO sector and the increased role
of NGOs in delivering official development assistance. Careful studies
were undertaken in the early 1990s of the work of NGOs, particularly those with roots in Europe and the United States that operate
programs throughout the world. The results of some of these studies
"cast doubt on many of the cherished assumptions about NGO comparative advantage—closeness to poor people, cost-effectiveness, high
levels of innovation and flexibility, and so forth."[2] Growing concern for
the effectiveness and accountability of NGOs raises questions among
donors and NGOs themselves as to whether NGOs are really working
to solve underlying problems, or are serving as "Band-Aids" in their
increasing work as contractors for many of the same donors whose economic agendas contribute to the poverty they are trying to alleviate. As
one NGO staff member suggested, NGOs are at risk of becoming mere
"ladles in the global soup kitchen."[3]

While some critics have raised concerns about the ability of NGOs
to deliver effective services, others note that many of the problems
are related to the development context as a whole and the difficulty
in achieving development objectives without addressing the underlying
structural problems in society that perpetuate circumstances of poverty
and social exclusion. As Peter Uvin argues, the nature of development is
called into question if working toward development objectives does not
help a society to eliminate the social exclusion, persistent poverty, and
powerlessness that create structural violence.[4] Repeatedly implementing development projects that improve specific aspects of people's lives
such as farming methods, or access to clean water, will not contribute
to long-term human development if those projects are done within a
context where other forces persist that limit people's access to opportunities and capabilities. Addressing these overarching issues requires not
only changes in operational work but also changes in policies and trade

regimes. A. Fowler and K. Biekart echo this argument when stating that "through [their] existing development and relief projects on the ground [NGOs] are not going to be catalysts and forces for poverty alleviation, inclusion and social justice in the New World order."[5]

At the same time that the effectiveness of large international NGOs has come under question, local NGOs throughout Africa, Latin America, Asia, and the former Soviet Union have grown in number and strength, thus raising additional questions about the appropriate role of NGOs based outside the countries where development work is taking place. As discussed in Chapter 6, local NGOs are increasing their ability to design and implement development projects in their own countries, and even to directly access international donor funding to do so. In addition to leading NGOs based in donor countries to develop more local partnerships, the emergence of a strong NGO sector throughout the developing world has also contributed to a re-examination of the comparative strengths and appropriate role of "Northern" NGOs. Although "Southern" NGOs have an important role to play in international advocacy, a certain comparative advantage for global advocacy work can be argued to exist among Northern NGOs due to their proximity to donors, organizational sophistication, and availability of resources to direct toward advocacy efforts.

Global Communications Technology

While other external factors push NGOs toward greater advocacy, the emergence and spread of electronic global communications open the door for new types of advocacy. The sharing of information has become easier, and the urgency to apply experiences from one region to another has increased. New technology allows us to see the cause and effect of events occurring around the globe, highlighting the impact of actions taken by the industrialized world upon the suffering of people elsewhere. Rapid communications make coordinated lobbying efforts and global campaigns easier and more effective. Private "intranet" communications allow for the internal management of global campaigns coordinated among many members of an NGO family or a global coalition of NGOs. The external Internet, meanwhile, allows for the dissemination of campaign information to a wide audience.

The Internet has dramatically changed not only the speed and the cost at which an organization can spread a message around the globe but also the very nature of the information and the responses that it elicits. Through the Internet, campaigns can provide catchy slogans with pictures and even videos or audio clips to capture people's attention to an issue. And unlike other forms of media, the Internet allows organizations—at low cost—to combine catchy messages with the provision of extensive additional information on the issue and links for easy reference and for taking immediate action. People can therefore respond to an issue as they read about it. Many NGO Web sites have user-friendly forms that help interested visitors sign on to petitions or send letters to political leaders in support of specific issues. Furthermore, e-mail provides a means of immediately updating interested supporters on the issues they care about. With the tremendous increase in Internet use, especially among youth, "cyber activism" has re-ignited activism in industrialized countries. Numerous listservs and Web sites such as netaction.org and organizenow.net have been established specifically for advocacy and social activism. The large turnout and concerted advocacy efforts that surrounded the protests at the World Trade Organization in 1999 and the World Bank meetings in 2000 resulted from the active use of the Internet as an organizing tool.

The adoption of effective technology by NGOs has been facilitated by technology-specific assistance from donors, new nonprofit organizations specializing in technology, and private technology businesses. The use of the Internet for communication and social movements has been a prominent theme from the early days of the World Wide Web. One of the leading multimedia applications that allows for the streaming of video and audio over the Internet, RealPlayer, was actually created by a company named Progressive Network that was established by a former Microsoft employee with a specific focus on nonprofit organizations. That organization has since expanded, but it maintains a division, RealImpact, that is dedicated to assisting nonprofit organizations to effectively use media to achieve their objectives, particularly in the area of advocacy. In addition to creating public service announcements that can be broadcast over the Internet, RealImpact technology specialists help NGOs track visits to their sites, maintain databases of people who respond to public service announcements distributed over the Web, and assist an organization in targeting effective campaigns that reach global audiences in a timely manner.[6] This is but one example of the types of technology services that have emerged over the past five years to enhance the ability of NGOs to utilize new communications technologies.

Internal Driving Forces

As external factors were encouraging NGOs to take a more active role in advocacy, other forces within the organizations themselves were moving in the same direction. One factor driving change was the growing frustration among staff that they were not making significant strides toward achieving broader objectives. With the persistence of poverty and increasing income gaps, there has been a growing realization within NGOs that field operations alone will not solve the underlying problems of poverty—especially in those places where the overarching policies undermine the context in which their projects are functioning. As stated by directors of Oxfam GB, many NGOs "have come to the view that in such a world their traditional (and still crucial) activities, such as development and emergency relief work, are unlikely in themselves to produce sustained improvements in the lives of impoverished people."[7]

The breadth of field experience and maturity of the organizations also has led to a growing sense that they have important insights to contribute to policy debates. Particularly in complex human emergencies, NGOs have more accurate insight into realities in the field than most policymakers. Many NGO staff members feel that their unique experience across cultures and countries with the structural causes of war and poverty gives them powerful incentives to advocate on these issues. These forces have been complimented by the increased professionalism of NGO staff that has had a transformative effect on the entire sector over the last ten to twenty years.

The role of NGOs in the new types of complex, man-made emergencies also has created internal pressures for the organizations to become involved in advocacy as staff have been exposed daily to horrific and life-threatening situations that have compelled them to speak out about the atrocities and injustices they have witnessed. The very nature of the conflicts in many cases has necessitated that NGOs advocate for policy changes or intervention, as their ability to provide humanitarian assistance has been jeopardized.

Selecting and Negotiating Advocacy Choices

Our interlocutors, when discussing their decision-making in regard to advocacy, pointed out the array of different factors and players they have to consider, as well as the range of modalities among which they have to choose. Advocacy work can take many forms, ranging from being highly visible to being very low profile, and from requiring extensive in-house resources to calling for little additional investment. As NGO leaders choose between approaches, they must navigate existing interests and priorities of their organizations. Specific modalities and approaches to advocacy are explored in greater detail below; here we examine the range of factors that influence advocacy choices and illustrate how they have played out in three cases.

As depicted in Figure 7.1 on the following page, various factors and interests of key players interact to influence choices taken by senior NGO management on advocacy strategies. One must consider how the mission and organizational culture support advocacy and how advocacy is perceived by the board, donors, staff, and other stakeholders. The internal expertise of the organization and its partners may lend itself to certain advocacy approaches rather than others and may require a change in staff skill-mix in order to build advocacy capacity.

Figure 7.1. Factors and Players Affecting Choice
of Advocacy Priorities

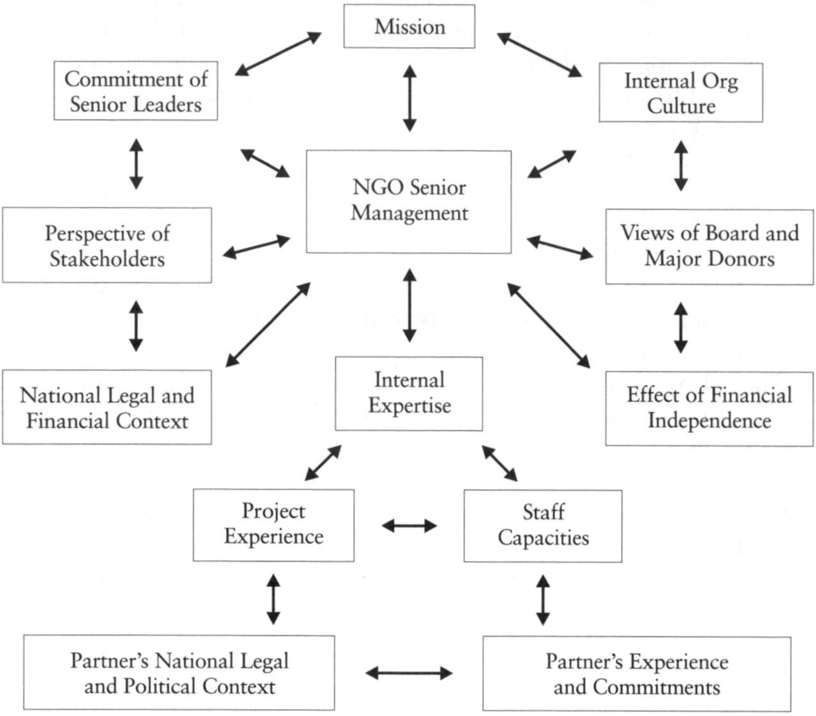

The legal and political context of both the NGOs' home countries and the countries where they operate must also be considered. Since most Northern NGOs work with partners—and advocacy work might directly affect local partners in developing countries—advocacy choices depend on the political context of local partners. Lisa Jordan and Peter Van Tujil point out the amount of negotiating that happens between the Northern NGOs in Europe or the United States and their Southern partners in deciding among priorities for an advocacy campaign.[8]

The emphasis of an organization on advocacy work is reflected in its mission statement and principal objectives. Some organizations' mission statements charge them with fundamental social transformation while others focus on relief of suffering. As some NGOs have moved toward more advocacy work, they have changed their mission statements accordingly. Advocacy is today included explicitly in the mission statements of Oxfam, Save the Children, MSF, and CARE.

In addition to its mission, each organization's unique history and programmatic approach influence the internal organizational culture and the way in which advocacy is integrated into existing operations. Choices on advocacy modalities often lead to a dynamic process in which approaches to both advocacy and operations evolve in light of work in each area. One of the interesting developments is the way that advocacy work leads to reconceptualization of an NGO's work. For example, as NGOs became more outspoken advocates of human rights, and as they became more aware of the European work on social exclusion, approaches to poverty reduction moved from a focus on services and capacities to one of a focus on proper rights to inclusion—that is, to a rights-based approach to poverty reduction (as discussed in Chapter 4). While it is quick to assert that it is a humanitarian and not a development organization, MSF has active projects on social exclusion. Other NGOs are also now thinking through programs and projects using a rights-based approach. CARE is in the process of adopting a rights-based approach, making integration of rights into CARE's work one of three objectives in the 2001 Strategic Plan. The focus on rights provides a new dimension to CARE's operational work on household livelihood security and also affirms the need for CARE to be an active advocate for social justice and global responsibility.[9]

Internal expertise and comparative strengths of an organization and its partners is another factor influencing advocacy approaches. For example, PLAN's hesitation on becoming involved in advocacy is not due to a lack of interest in or support for advocacy activities, but rather a concern that advocacy is outside the comparative advantage of PLAN. While PLAN is committed to promoting awareness and sharing its experiences with policymakers, it is currently leaving direct lobbying efforts to other organizations. Other NGOs are addressing similar concerns on internal capacity by forging partnerships and leveraging existing expertise. World Vision has an office dedicated to advocacy but takes advantage of existing resources for research on policy issues rather than duplicating efforts by extensively building up those capacities within World Vision.

The perspective of stakeholders toward advocacy work is another key determinant of advocacy choices. In many instances, a process of education is required to explain what advocacy entails and to break through old stereotypes. Political alliances and preferences of the boards and other stakeholders play an important role, and the nationality of donors can have a significant impact. Although attitudes are evolving, generally speaking, U.S. donors tend to prefer an emphasis on service-delivery rather than political activism; European donors accept and in some cases expect development and relief NGOs to be active in advocacy. In France, the political culture is such that being seen to be active in advocacy is important in order to raise private contributions. CARE France sees increase in advocacy as important to the financial bottom line.

The potential for donors to influence advocacy positions or react negatively to advocacy work leads some NGOs to consider the extent of their financial independence in making advocacy choices. Situations vary among NGOs. Some limit the receipt of government resources. Oxfam America accepts no financial resources from the U.S. government. It maintains that "as an organization that does not receive U.S. government funding for its development programs, Oxfam is able to project a strong and independent voice that draws on lessons learned from years of experience and that reflects the needs and priorities of the people it works with at the grassroots level."[10] Oxfam GB also strives to limit the influence of its donors and has been actively increasing private individual donations. In 2000, approximately half a million people in the United Kingdom gave monthly to Oxfam, and this number is growing.[11] At MSF, government funds cannot account for more than 40 percent of contributions—and in most cases they are well below this maximum limit.

Having a variety of corporate partnerships sometimes improves financial independence from donors. CARE has done this effectively with many corporate sponsors, such as Starbucks and Barnes & Noble. But some consider that such corporate partnerships can also impede independence. As Chapter 6 has shown, NGOs do not undertake any of these partnerships without a great deal of upstream thinking, preparation, and negotiation. They have much to lose if allied with what later emerges as a corporation with unfair labor or bad environmental practices. Often, in fact, some of their most useful advocacy happens well out of the spotlight of public attention as senior leaders of, for example, World Vision, engage the senior managers of a corporation with what World Vision has learned about unfair labor practices in a given country. In other instances, an NGO may take on a tailored approach, kept quite commercial, but of some mutual benefit—such as Save the Children neckties, which are manufactured by regular businesses but carry children's designs and the Save the Children logo. In short, corporate partners may help improve financial independence, easing the way forward for more advocacy work. But they also carry a risk if labor practices, trade issues, or patent policies of those partners are subsequently found to be offensive.

The Evolution of Advocacy Choices in Three NGOs

All of these factors play out differently in each NGO. Here we turn to highlighting how these factors have affected the particular advocacy choices of three NGOs. Both CARE and World Vision have increased their advocacy efforts significantly over the past five years. The evolution process in each illustrates the different ways in which the factors and players we have discussed play out in the process of negotiating advocacy choices. MSF provides another useful illustration: depicting how a unique organizational culture and mission influence a distinctive approach to advocacy.

CARE has undertaken some advocacy work over the last twenty years, but until the mid-1990s this work was very limited. As one of the United States' oldest and most prominent relief organizations, CARE has always played an important role in raising awareness among the U.S. public. CARE established a two-person advocacy office in Washington, D.C., in the early 1980s, but its work was limited primarily to lobbying the U.S. Congress on funding for foreign aid. By the mid-1990s, however, staff and senior management within CARE began thinking about expanding advocacy work. A major impetus for change was the commitment of CARE's new president, Peter Bell, who took office in 1995, with a vision for expanding CARE's role and leveraging the organization's expertise and stature as a spokesperson on policy issues. A core group of staff members supported the idea, but the expansion of advocacy required enlisting CARE's board of directors as well as staff, particularly in the country offices, about advocacy. CARE has a fifty-year history of operating primarily as a relief organization and had in the past focused its attention on the quality of its operational work rather than on expanding into new areas such as advocacy. Eventually, the incorporation of more advocacy work led to changing the organization's vision and mission statement.

When the process began, many people within the CARE community had a skeptical view of advocacy and misperceptions of what it meant for the organization to become more politically active. Some board members were uncomfortable with advocacy. There was concern that CARE might lose its operational focus and become a think tank on policy issues or that advocacy at CARE might primarily be about embarrassing policymakers. In 1996, a new director was appointed to CARE's policy and advocacy department who, together with the president, undertook a two-year process of educating board members and staff on how advocacy could advance CARE's mission. The increased acceptance of advocacy among CARE's many stakeholders occurred as the result of a combination of factors that converged between 1996 and 1998. As senior managers and policy staff were defining a broader vision for advocacy at CARE, the campaign to ban landmines was gaining international attention. The landmine issue was directly relevant to at least fifteen CARE country offices, and the existence of a global campaign made it easy for CARE to build up its advocacy work around this issue. This time period was also marked by growing concern among senior managers that the U.S. government would impose numerous restrictions on family planning programs overseas. The turning point for the CARE board came with the October 1998 meeting at the UN Security

Council, where CARE and three other NGOs spoke on the humanitarian crisis in Sudan and the need to advance toward a just peace. This in fact marked the second time that CARE managers spoke to the Security Council, but with the difference that, in 1998 (unlike the first time in 1997, when the meeting took place with little advance notice), CARE staff had about six weeks to prepare, allowing time to bring more board members and staff into the process.

All of these factors had an impact on the advocacy choices taken by CARE. The skepticism and caution of some board members and other stakeholders meant that advocacy work had to build up gradually at CARE and that the organization is selective about the issues with which it has become involved. The dedication and leadership of the president was a key factor moving the process forward. CARE's emphasis on operational work continues to play out in its advocacy approach. Its policy analysis capacity is small and draws heavily on field experience. It is less involved in issues like debt relief and fair trade where it is more difficult to draw a direct link to operational work. But the interplay among these factors is dynamic, and CARE's advocacy continues to grow as these factors evolve. As of December 2000, CARE's staff dedicated to advocacy had grown to eleven members, and it is expected to increase to fifteen in the near future. The integration of advocacy was a goal of the organization's strategic plans for fiscal years 1997–2001. CARE is investing in training and support for its country offices so that they can become more actively involved in advocacy. The number of country offices with strategic plans specifying increased advocacy doubled to fifteen in 2000.

World Vision has experienced a similar evolution in advocacy over the last five years, but the growth has been slower than at CARE as World Vision has negotiated its way through its own set of internal dynamics. The impetus for increased advocacy at World Vision came not from senior management but from staff members—specifically, from those working in the office of public policy and government relations in Washington, D.C. This office was opened in 1985 with a focus on assisting World Vision to access U.S. government funding. But by the early 1990s, the office's manager had begun to be involved in advocacy on specific public policies. Staff demonstrated the effectiveness that World Vision could have through advocacy to the organization's president and senior management, who gave their approval to the concept and joined with key staff in the difficult process of bringing the organization's constituents on board. World Vision's supporters are primarily conservative evangelical Christians who are very committed to fighting poverty, but who tend to be very suspicious of the government and skeptical of any perceived political work on the part of World Vision.

Within this context, World Vision staff undertook an active process of educating their stakeholders and crafting policy stances in ways that make sense to their constituents. For example, the language of child "rights," although widely used in most of the world, is uncomfortable for many World Vision supporters in the U.S., who perceive child rights to imply a decline in rights of parents and thus an erosion of the family. World Vision therefore refers to child "protection" in its work and is preparing a paper for its supporters clarifying the issue of rights. World Vision staff have had to respond to a general concern that the provision of policy advice to government officials is beyond World Vision's expertise. The process of building consensus within the World Vision community has focused on demonstrating that World Vision's extensive expertise in the field provides the organization with invaluable insights that are important to policymakers. A key part of this process has been cultivating donors within the World Vision community. Like members of Congress in the past, supporters have been invited to the field to gain a better understanding of World Vision's work and the issues involved.

The results of this process of bringing stakeholders on board are increasingly apparent. In 1999, World Vision staff still used terms like "promotion of social justice" and avoided the word "advocacy," but by 2000, the Web site had a section explicitly on advocacy. The policy and government relations staff who work on advocacy has grown to four full-time professionals and will soon be adding two more. World Vision's approach has been to leverage partnerships and provide support to campaigns run primarily by other NGOs. This avoids duplication of effort and also provides a buffer from criticism by working collaboratively with others. Moreover, much of World Vision's advocacy work has been low profile in style. The organization is steadily increasing its own policy analysis work and expects to launch a campaign of its own in the future. In the United States, World Vision has been particularly active on the HIPC debt relief initiative and is giving increasing attention to geopolitical issues such as Colombia, Sierra Leone, and the Democratic People's Republic of Korea (North Korea).

A very different set of cultural attitudes and perceptions about advocacy influence the approach taken by MSF. Work on advocacy at MSF grows out of its concept of *temoinage* and its mission: "Our definition of advocacy is being present among the victims to bear witness and speak out about their plight in order to improve their basic living conditions and to protect their fundamental human rights. Advocacy and witnessing are integral to our humanitarian mission."[12] This concept of witnessing, which has a particular connotation in the French term *temoinage* that does not translate perfectly into English, has primarily been associated with an awareness-raising function and speaking out on behalf of the victims. Yet drawing a line around advocacy by limiting involvement to awareness-raising is difficult, since any attempt to publicize abuses inherently also calls (that is, lobbies) for specific change. For example, MSF itself stated that, on the issue of banning landmines, "MSF staff intend to be present at the conferences in Brussels, Oslo, and Ottawa to share field experience of the impact of landmines with government negotiators, . . . and to demand a ban on mines for humanitarian reasons."[13]

Nevertheless, MSF views its role in direct lobbying cautiously. As stated in the MSF paper prepared for the Bellagio meeting, "[MSF] should increase our capacity to raise decision makers' awareness while avoiding politicisation and instrumentalisation of humanitarian action."[14] MSF explicitly distinguishes its own role of bearing witness and providing testimony from that of human rights organizations that specifically conduct lobbying against human rights abuses. MSF's position on advocacy is influenced by its vehement adherence to political neutrality and independence. The four elements of the MSF mission statement include assertions that MSF "observes neutrality and impartiality" and that MSF volunteers "maintain complete independence from all political, economic and religious powers."[15] MSF advocacy efforts are therefore selective and very careful not to pull the organization into political stances but to embark from an independent perspective.

In select instances where the role of bearing witness requires specific policy and legislative change, MSF does actively advocate for those changes. As discussed in Chapter 4, MSF is currently pursuing a global campaign to insist on access by the poor to essential medicines. This campaign has involved active lobbying and protests regarding specific policies under consideration by the World Trade Organization. The organization also advocates for specific legislative changes within donor countries. In France, for example, MSF's lobbying efforts played an important role in the 1999 passage of a health care bill that is expected to provide free and direct access to health care to almost 6 million disadvantaged people in France.[16]

Comparative Approaches to Advocacy

As NGOs weigh the implications of the various factors described above, they select from a variety of modalities and choose the extent of their involvement in each. NGOs attempt to influence successive levels of change by focusing on a variety of key groups ranging from decision-makers, to key leadership in a spectrum of organizations, to the general grassroots public. Advocacy involves not only direct lobbying of legislatures but also a process of education and tools that inform policy choices. Products include analyses and papers, speeches, newspaper articles, selected media products, books, and mobilization efforts like demonstrations. Advocacy may be directed to change or introduce specific legislation; or to influence special or more general opinion, attitudes, and behavior. These activities fall along a continuum from passive to direct engagement—from having consultative status with international organizations; to broadly defined development education and public awareness campaigns; to very focused lobbying on specific legislation at international, national, or even local levels. The extent to which each of the NGOs in this study engages in these activities along the continuum is explored in this section and summarized in Table 7.1 on pp. 188–89.

Consultative Status

At the international level, official vehicles in the form of consultative groups have been established to facilitate NGO participation in policy discussion at UN bodies and the Bretton Woods institutions (the International Monetary Fund and the World Bank). This represents one of the more limited means of engagement in advocacy work. Although this form of participation does not constitute a direct role in decision-making, the process of information sharing and public dissemination of NGO positions through these consultative groups can be important. Consultative bodies provide a means for NGOs to remain informed of ongoing policy dialogues and to present their experience and policy perspectives. In addition, participation in these committee meetings can build relationships with other NGOs as well as lend credibility to their advocacy work. For example, consultative status at the UN Economic and Social Council (ECOSOC) allows NGOs to receive provisional agendas, add items to the agenda, submit written statements, and make oral presentations at ECOSOC meetings. The increase in NGO activity in this area is illustrated by the dramatic growth in NGOs registered with ECOSOC, where about half of the 2000 NGOs that now have consultative status have gained it since 1995. Most of our interlocutors were active with ECOSOC earlier: Oxfam GB since 1973; Oxfam America, 1993; CARE International, 1991; Save the Children Alliance, 1993; World Vision, 1985; and PLAN, 1981. NGOs can leverage participation in these committees for press coverage. It is also possible to use these committees as a vehicle for low-profile policy discussions. While PLAN does not explicitly engage in advocacy, it is on the NGO working group at UNICEF, on the roster of NGOs at ECOSOC, and works with UNESCO.

Development Education and Humanitarian Awareness

Raising public awareness is one major avenue of advocacy work for several organizations. It is an important tool for educating their constituents as well as for building a broader base of public support for

Table 7.1.
Summary of Comparative Approaches to Advocacy

		Oxfam	CARE
Limited Activity	Consultative status at UN	Yes. SCHR, ECOSOC.	Yes. SCHR, ECOSOC.
	Education, Public Awareness Campaigns	Yes. Extensive program seen as core to mission. Provide curricula and teaching materials. Provide campaign toolkits.	Yes. Active program but not core activity. Frequent press releases. Op-ed articles. Produce public service announcements and educational newsletter.
	Research and Policy Papers	Yes. Large research program supports advocacy campaigns. Substantial research conducted by staff. Frequent policy papers and books.	Yes. Small program. Use external researchers, but building staff capacity. Produce mainly short analytical pieces. Papers based on field experience more than independent research.
	Lobby for Global Policies and Legislation	Yes. Extensive and broad-reaching lobbying on global issues. Current campaigns: education for all, cut conflict, fair trade, debt relief.	Yes. Previously limited but grown significantly since 1995. Work on select issues: landmines, Great Lakes, Sudan, North Korea, foreign aid budget.
	Lobby Donor Governments on Domestic Issues	Yes, but limited. More extensive in G.B. than U.S.	No.
	Advocacy Departments or Staff	Yes. OI office of 4 in D.C. (to add 2 in Brussels, 2 in Geneva, 1 in New York). G.B. advocacy staff: 17 in HQ and 8 in regions, plus 44 globally campaigning.	Yes. CARE USA has 11 (soon to be 15) staff total between D.C., Atlanta, New York, and country office.
Extensive Activity			

Table 7.1 (continued).
Summary of Comparative Approaches to Advocacy

PLAN	World Vision	Save the Children	MSF
Yes. ECOSOC.	Yes. ECOSOC.	Yes. SCHR, ECOSOC.	Yes. SCHR, ECOSOC
Yes. Active program aimed at direct donors, not general public. Issue press releases. Educational newsletter.	Yes. Active program aimed at direct donors, not general public. Issue press releases. Education through church ministry.	Yes. Extensive program in Europe especially U.K. but limited in U.S. All do press releases, op-ed articles. U.K. provides lesson plans to schools and campaign toolkits.	Yes. Extensive program. Awareness raising through witnessing is core to mission. Issue press releases. Generate media attention.
No in-house research or publications. Provide links to useful resources including research institutes.	Yes. Small program. Several policy papers. In U.S., 4 papers from 1996 to 1999. In U.K., 29 publications from 1994 to 1999.	Yes. Medium to large research program. Many papers and books, mostly published by Sweden and U.K. U.S. issues State of World's Mothers.	Yes. Medium to large research program. Research foundations. Primarily serves to inform operations but also advocacy. Many policy papers.
No direct lobbying. Some low-profile information sharing with policymakers.	Yes. New, small but growing program. Issues: Child protection, debt relief, landmines, North Korea, Sudan, Colombia.	Yes, but extent varies among members. Extensive program in U.K. smaller in U.S. U.K. active on child soldiers, child labor. U.S. campaign for mothers (reproductive health, education).	Yes, but limited to very select issues: Essential medicines, landmines, international criminal court. More work on awareness-raising not lobbying.
No.	No. Except very occasional, e.g., welfare reform in 1996.	Yes. Limited in U.K. and very limited in U.S.	Yes. Limited. Work on social inclusion and specific health care legislation in France.
No.	Yes. WVUS has D.C. office with 4 staff. U.K. has 4, WVI has 7.	Yes. Save U.K. has staff in London, New York, and Brussels.	Yes. Liaison offices for UN and large donors in New York and Geneva plus staff in Brussels.

policy change. All of the organizations contribute in some degree to public awareness and education on issues of relief and development. While development education can be a limited means of involvement in advocacy for some NGOs, it can be a much more extensive tool for those organizations that have active advocacy programs. As one example, PLAN, through mailings to its extensive network of private contributors, promotes a keen appreciation of the magnitude of child poverty. Other NGOs go a step further, working to educate not only on the scope of poverty but also on its causes and possible solutions. Some also use public outreach to mobilize citizens to participate in advocacy activities.

Oxfam has maintained education and dissemination of information as an essential component of its advocacy. Underlying Oxfam's work is a belief that educating youth to be concerned global citizens is an important step to achieving sustainable change. For Oxfam America, a key focus is education of young people about the root causes of hunger and the systemic challenges to development; the organization sponsors an annual Hunger Awareness Week and Oxfam Fast for a World Harvest on college and high school campuses throughout the country. Oxfam GB and Save the Children UK have two of the most extensive public education and awareness programs in our study. Both actively encourage citizens to become informed on issues and get involved in advocacy. At Oxfam GB people can sign up to receive a Campaigner Kit that includes subscription to a quarterly campaign magazine, campaigning guidelines, and other tools. In addition, Oxfam GB provides teaching materials for primary and secondary schools that fit into curriculum guidelines in Great Britain. Save the Children UK's program also provides lesson plans to schools and includes active outreach to youth of all ages as well as campaign kits to facilitate citizen activism.

Policy Research

The capacity to carry out substantial research in-house varies in each organization. Most NGOs base their policy work primarily on direct operational experience, but some, particularly Oxfam and Save the Children, have developed substantial expertise in economic and political policy analysis. Oxfam has the largest research capacity, most notably in Great Britain. MSF affiliates have several research foundations, such as the international Foundation MSF, the Belgian Epicenter, and Dutch Healthnet. These MSF research foundations are primarily dedicated to applied research that contributes to operational work, but they also influence advocacy positions. For example, the medical research of MSF's foundations supports the organization's advocacy work on access by the poor to essential medicines.

On the one hand, sophisticated policy analysis from within NGOs strengthens their ability to negotiate tough policy issues. But on the other hand, the development of such capacity in some ways changes the nature of an NGO's focus. Some therefore prefer to maintain an emphasis on operational work and draw on policy research from other sources to complement the policy positions they derive from experience in the field. World Vision and CARE are both slowly building up their research capacities but intend to keep these relatively small. According to CARE's advocacy and policy director, "CARE's mantra is to be sure that advocacy comes from operational work."[17]

Lobbying on International Policies

The focal point of advocacy work for international development and relief NGOs has been lobbying for specific policies affecting global issues. In some cases this includes advocacy related to program areas they have been working on for years, such as education, health care, or family planning. In a growing number of instances, however, global advocacy is taking on new policy issues emerging as important to other program work, such as banning landmines, relieving the debt burden of poor countries, and addressing geopolitical strategies affecting the poor in countries such as Colombia and Sudan. This advocacy involves direct lobbying of international governing bodies or international financial institutions, and also the lobbying of donor countries. Most NGOs are active in this regard and use their position and reputation to raise awareness domestically on key global issues.

Lobbying work is often supported by large publicized campaigns that rally public support around a cause. While many participate in coalitions around global campaigns, some NGOs—as they increase their level of engagement in advocacy—manage their own campaigns on specific issues of relevance to their organizations. Unlike the more coordinated efforts discussed below, these campaigns tend to be managed more centrally by one NGO or a family of NGOs even while encouraging the participation of a broad coalition of NGOs. MSF's first global campaign, Access to Essential Medicines, challenges drug-pricing schemes that limit accessibility for poor communities. This campaign has received significant press coverage and drawn strong public support. The issue draws the attention of people around the world, as it has relevance for both domestic and international policies and it is easy to relate to its goals.

Other issues, such as Oxfam's EducationNow campaign, have also captured media attention but do not draw in the public in the same way as issues like medicines and AIDS. The campaign literature recognizes this fact and urges the public to pay attention to the urgency of the scourge of illiteracy, even though "the education crisis in developing countries does not excite media attention or stir the world's most powerful nations to action" in the same way that wars, natural disasters, and epidemics do.[18] EducationNow represents one of the first campaigns initiated jointly by all members of the Oxfam family and illustrates the process of coordinating forces within a network for a common issue. The campaign is based on substantial research and makes concrete policy recommendations specifying financial commitments required from various countries to reach an investment goal of an additional $8 billion per annum over ten years to finance universal primary education in all developing countries within the next decade.

Lobbying on Domestic Policies in Donor Countries

Most of the NGOs that engage in advocacy do so primarily on international issues rather than on domestic issues that affect the condition of the poor in industrial countries. Even Oxfam America, which has strong roots in advocacy, focuses its efforts on lobbying the U.S. government on issues affecting developing countries and does very little work on domestic U.S. issues. Save the Children US also concentrates its advocacy efforts for children's rights on the International Convention on the Rights of the Child and is not very involved in the lobbying efforts of other U.S. NGOs such as the Children's Defense Fund or Child Welfare League, which lobby specifically on U.S. issues. The notable exceptions are Oxfam GB and Save the Children UK, which have active advocacy programs concerned with domestic issues in Great Britain.

A number of factors may contribute to the limited involvement of international relief and development NGOs on advocacy related to domestic issues. One significant constraint is the legal limitations for charities engaging in domestic political lobbying. In the United States, an NGO with tax-exempt status cannot dedicate more than 25 percent of its revenue to advocacy, but strict Internal Revenue Service rules and discussions of tightening those restrictions influence NGOs to play it safe and dedicate minimal resources to domestic lobbying efforts. National regulations exempt NGOs from accounting for their international advocacy work.[19] In Great Britain, Oxfam came under scrutiny for its political actions and in 1995 a new set of guidelines was issued clarifying the parameters within which nonprofit organizations can lobby. Other factors influencing lobbying decisions could include the specialization of many development NGOs on international issues and a concern for alienating donors within home countries when attention is turned to domestic issues. It is also interesting to note that the space for NGO advocacy within the global policy framework does not exist in the same way on a national level. NGOs face many more institutionalized barriers and resistance from well-established pressure groups in developed countries than they do when working with weaker institutional structures at an international level.

Lobbying on Domestic Policies in Developing Countries

The emphasis on advocacy for international issues raises the question of advocacy by Northern NGOs at the domestic level within developing countries. Advocacy directed at domestic governments is important to ensure sustainability of reforms and to address specific local issues affecting projects. Field-staff members of most NGOs are often engaged in advocacy in either direct or indirect ways as they maneuver through local bureaucracies and politics in the process of implementing projects. Although PLAN is hesitant about advocacy work, its local staff members often walk the halls of local council leaders advocating for specific policy changes related to their projects or the communities where they work. CARE also encourages advocacy by its country offices and has designated an advocacy staff member to provide training and support services for advocacy work by country offices. Oxfam GB emphasizes the importance of advocacy within developing countries and thus spreads its advocacy staff throughout its field offices. Oxfam GB has eight advocacy staff housed in various regional offices and most of its forty-four campaigning staff, who are responsible for mobilizing public action at a local level, are also located throughout the regional offices. While these staff support Oxfam's global campaigns, they are also positioned to work specifically on domestic issues within the countries where they are working. CARE's approach is to have local staff take on much of the advocacy of local governments, but headquarters staff will sometimes also participate, and on occasion the president of CARE meets directly with government leaders in other countries. For example, in September 2000, Peter Bell and CARE's country director in San Salvador met with business leaders and the president of El Salvador to advocate for specific changes in policies on water conservation and distribution.[20]

While local staff of Northern NGOs do some of this work, much advocacy of governments in developing countries is done by Southern NGOs. A key challenge of lobbying local governments is operationalizing the links between local realities and global policy formulation in ways that optimize voices of local partners in and through their advocacy work.[21] Effective advocacy should draw strong links between micro and macro perspectives, and good partnerships are important for achieving this. Local policies can grow from micro positions to having a macro impact. In many cases, operations at the local level require lobbying local governments to gain support for specific programs or to institute policy changes affecting local communities. By strengthening local advocacy organizations, it becomes more feasible to "leap-frog" over local elite and to create a more vibrant civil society that can exert influence on the government.[22] In the case of the debt relief program in Uganda, local community groups have a strong role in pushing the program and maintaining pressure on the government to hold it accountable for the reforms agreed under the Heavily Indebted Poor Country (HIPC) initiative. Oxfam considers its work to build local constituencies in Zambia and Uganda essential for the success of debt relief in those countries. Those local groups will be able to pressure their governments to stay the course with reforms and ensure that money saved from debt relief is invested in health and education. PLAN provides another example: it has been working in the Philippines in coalition with domestic NGOs on a project entitled Expanding Children's Participation in Social Reform that supports the participation of child leaders in the Children's National Sectoral Assembly, where children have a chance to voice policy concerns and lobby for their interests.

In some cases, political sensitivity or insecurity makes it difficult to lobby developing countries directly. This is particularly the case where human rights abuses are occurring. In those instances, there may be an important role for international organizations that can bring international-community pressure to bear on governments without facing the same risks as domestic groups. In general, however, there continues to be some debate over the appropriate role of Northern versus Southern NGOs in lobbying Southern governments. Some argue that Northern NGOs should provide training and tools to facilitate lobbying by local groups and only become directly involved when political restrictions inhibit local advocacy efforts. One Zimbabwean organization that promotes advocacy networks among Southern NGOs cautions that alliances with Northern NGOs can lead to reliance on external advocacy agendas, generate conflicts from donor pressures, and create competition of indigenous networks with externally initiated networks.[23] According to Oxfam America, Southern organizations need to manage more advocacy in their own countries, while Oxfam America itself needs to recognize its comparative advantage and increase advocacy at a global level.[24]

Staff Dedicated to Advocacy

Effective advocacy work requires significant resources, depending on the approach and extent of involvement. Even when drawing primarily on existing operations staff, substantial advocacy work requires a distinct set of skills. Staff is needed to monitor policies and represent the organization's positions before policy makers. Establishing news credibility, providing reliable information, and engaging the interest of journalists who cover relief and development topics can be time-consuming and, as noted by Oxfam America, a full-time press person makes a big difference. Press coverage is important; it helps supporters see that the NGO is taken seriously on its positions. An increasing number of NGOs have dedicated staff or advocacy departments. Others, such as Save the Children US, have added the task on to other activities of operations staff or senior managers. The amount of dedicated advocacy staff varies among NGOs, reflecting differing levels of activity. At one extreme, Oxfam GB has almost 70 advocacy staff throughout the world, including seventeen at the headquarters office in England. On the other hand, CARE USA currently has eleven advocacy staff and World Vision US has four.

For many NGOs, staffing can become complex and stretch capacity. Advocacy efforts require attention to policymakers in many cities around the globe, most notably in Washington for the multilateral development banks and the U.S. government, in New York and in Geneva for UN agencies, and in Brussels for the European Union. This is in addition to offices lobbying the government in an NGO's home country. As a result, many NGO families coordinate resources for advocacy staff. For example, various Oxfam country offices share resources through the Oxfam International advocacy offices; there are currently four Oxfam International staff in Washington, D.C., and commitments have been made to add another two in Geneva, two in Brussels, and one in New York. Members of the Save the Children Alliance are also contributing resources to coordinate advocacy efforts at various offices around the globe. In cases where the international coordinating bodies of NGO families do not yet have the resources to build up advocacy staff, individual members often provide initial support. This was the case with CARE, where CARE USA is financing a multilateral liaison staff position in New York for CARE International, with the understanding that CARE International will take on the financing of that position after two years.

Coordination in Advocacy Efforts

Given the scope and complexity of most issues of concern to international relief and development NGOs, coordination of advocacy efforts has emerged as an effective—and in most cases a necessary—means of affecting global policies. Numerous aspects of globalization are making such coordination efforts easier and opening the possibility for inclusive coordination with partners everywhere. Save the Children even suggests that the future could entail NGOs pushing for the development of a "People's Parliament for Global Affairs."[25] New communication technology, combined with increased interactions among senior managers and advocacy staff of different NGOs, has resulted in much more frequent communication. Now, for example, when CARE USA and Save the Children US are presented with a petition or letter for endorsement, their presidents are much more likely to pick up the telephone and discuss their organizations' respective positions than would have been the case five years ago.

The emphasis on international advocacy has partly contributed to the centralization and coordination of advocacy among affiliates of the same NGO family. For example, Oxfam International coordinates the advocacy efforts of the various affiliated Oxfams on an agreed agenda. These issues have included debt relief, landmines, peace, and reconstruction in the Great Lakes region of Africa, and education. In addition to the work of Oxfam International, the individual Oxfams independently pursue these issues with their donor countries along with their own agendas. Oxfam International determines policy priorities for the advocacy agenda through a process of consultations between the director of advocacy and designated teams comprised of executive directors from the affiliate Oxfam organizations.[26] CARE International recently approved general guidelines for advocacy by all members and created a twelve-member working group to develop a common policy advocacy agenda. Coordination efforts vary depending on a variety of factors. For example, Save the Children is an older organization with a longer history of independence among members as well as varying perspectives on advocacy. At CARE and World Vision, not all members within the NGO family have the same commitment to advocacy.

Coordination occurs both within NGO families and among a wide range of NGOs based in both industrialized and developing countries. This requires a complex set of negotiations around the common positions and respective roles of participating NGOs. Although most global advocacy campaigns strive to work within a framework of equality and global justice, the power dynamics between rich and poor often play themselves out in the campaign itself. On this point, Jordan and Van Tujil argue that NGOs need to exercise political responsibility in their transnational advocacy campaigns, meaning "a commitment to embrace not only goals in a campaign but to conduct the campaign with democratic principles."[27] NGOs must struggle with these issues as they move forward on global campaigns. But at the same time, some shifts in power dynamics are beginning to occur. Networks of Southern NGOs have been growing in size and sophistication. The role of Southern NGOs in global campaigns before the 1990s was limited to providing project information to campaigns that were designed and managed by Northern-based organizations.[28] Over the past ten years, the voices of Southern NGOs have gained prominence in recent debates, particularly in the calls for the closing of the World Bank and the IMF—often in contradiction to the position of many large Northern-based NGOs that favor reform rather than closure.

Three cases, presented below, illustrate successful elements of co-ordinated advocacy efforts: meetings of NGOs with the UN Security

Council regarding the new, complex human emergencies, the international campaign to ban landmines, and the debt-relief initiative under HIPC.

Security Council Consultation with Humanitarian NGOs

On February 12, 1997, the UN Security Council held its first meeting ever with NGOs—marking a dramatic change in the role of international NGOs and giving new legitimacy to the idea that NGO operational experience has direct relevance for policy decisions. Four organizations presented their experience and recommendations regarding complex human emergencies: CARE, Oxfam, MSF, and the International Committee of the Red Cross (ICRC). The Security Council acted informally and according to a newly devised arrangement known as the "Somavia formula" named after Ambassador Juan Somavia of Chile, a strong advocate for NGOs at the Council. This formula enabled NGOs with an active participation in conflict areas to brief the Council.[29] The meeting was mobilized by the UN Office for Complex Humanitarian Affairs (OCHA) and the International Council of Voluntary Agencies (ICVA). An advocacy network for NGOs, ICVA represents eighty members including CARE International, MSF International, World Vision International, and InterAction (the American Council for Voluntary International Action, which in turn includes among its members CARE USA, Save the Children US, Oxfam America, and World Vision US).

Despite little opportunity for coordination prior to the meeting, the positions expressed by the NGOs all converged. This demonstrated the extent to which NGOs have common experiences and served to break down some of the established stereotypes related to the difficulty of reaching consensus on advocacy positions. The NGO delegations consisted of several field staff members who had spent considerable time in conflict situations in Africa. Security Council members knew relatively little about the situation on the ground that aid workers were confronting on a daily basis. As a result of the success of this meeting, the Security Council has increased its consultations with NGOs. In October 1998, another meeting was held with the humanitarian NGOs, this time to speak specifically about the crisis in Sudan. Coordination efforts among Northern NGOs continued to grow since the initial meeting. In anticipation of the October 1998 meeting, a paper was published jointly by Save the Children, CARE, and Oxfam.

The February 1997 meeting is part of a complex set of changes that have impacted the role of NGOs and the workings of the United Nations. Institutional change has been slow but has been taking place. Interactions have continued to grow after that momentous meeting, and the process of NGO consultation has become institutionalized within the UN system. Four new committee mechanisms have been established under the Office for Complex Humanitarian Affairs (OCHA), including the NGO Steering Committee for Humanitarian Response (SCHR). The NGO working group is chaired by a senior UN official, who ensures cross learning between the Security Council and the NGOs. Under these mechanisms, an early-warning system has been developed, and SCHR manages a project known as Sphere, which drafted a humanitarian charter that identified standards and best practices in the delivery of services to disaster victims.

Most significant, the issues raised by the NGOs at that meeting have increasingly become part of the mainstream thinking on complex emergencies. Issues that were raised by NGOs included the need for safe access for humanitarian workers, separation of belligerents from civilian populations, recognition of the rights of internally displaced people as well as refugees, and a demand for governments to take on their responsibility for preventing as well as mitigating conflicts. One of the critical issues emphasized by NGOs that is now being adopted by the Security Council is the insistence on policies based on "responsible sovereignty." This concept, pioneered by Francis Deng, implies that a government's claims to national sovereignty as a wall against external intervention are no longer acceptable if a government is being predatory and violent toward its citizens. As noted in Chapter 3, many of the issues raised by the NGO community became central in ongoing debates on the development of an appropriate framework for humanitarian response.

Campaign to Ban Landmines

In December 1997, 122 countries signed the "Convention on the Prohibition of the Use, Stockpiling, Production and Transfer of Anti-Personnel Mines and on their Destruction." This act was the culmination of years of coordinated lobbying efforts by hundreds of NGOs from around the world. Relief and development organizations that had witnessed the horrifying effects of landmines—which kill or maim an estimated 26,000 people per year—began publicizing the issue in the 1980s. Six international NGOs came together in 1992 to form the International Campaign to Ban Landmines (ICBL), with the intention of combining their strengths and providing a flexible network for organizations sharing a common goal. The network grew rapidly and today is comprised of 1,100 organizations in sixty countries. CARE, Save the Children, World Vision, MSF, and Oxfam are all active members of the campaign.

The effort entailed a wide range of advocacy strategies that included massive media and education campaigns, dissemination of research findings, and direct lobbying to international bodies and national governments. Although supported by hundreds of local NGOs, this campaign was primarily led by NGOs based in donor countries. The campaign demonstrated many of the comparative advantages of large global NGOs in affecting international laws. Northern NGOs had access to policymakers and the ability to leverage resources for media campaigns. In addition, their existing networks of donors and other constituents provided an audience for the campaign and helped build widespread support for the initiative. The success of this campaign may also be related to its particular character as a single issue around which global consensus from civil society was readily attained. As stated by MSF, "the International Campaign to Ban Landmines ... is an excellent example of where denunciation can be effective without compromise of field activities. This sort of campaigning is focussed on a single issue, of concern to many countries, and not on a specific state authority or government."[30]

The Nobel Peace Prize was awarded to ICBL and its coordinator, Jody Williams, in October 1997, giving additional legitimacy and support to coordinated global advocacy efforts. By September 1998, forty countries had ratified the treaty, thereby making it international law, and as of December 2000, the treaty had been ratified by 109 countries and signed by 139.[31] Measurable signs of improvement have already been reported. As of August 2000, the number of mine victims in high-risk places such as Afghanistan, Cambodia, and Mozambique had decreased significantly; more than 22 million stockpiled anti-personnel mines were destroyed; more than 168 million square meters of land were de-mined; and production dropped dramatically from fifty-four to sixteen known producers.[32] Although success has been significant, the work of the campaign is not yet over. Fifty-four countries including the United States, China, and Russia refuse to sign the treaty or stop landmine production. A staggering 250 million mines remain in stock. The work of removing mines is still an overwhelming task, and the campaign continues to pressure governments to invest increasing resources into de-mining activities.

In the United States, CARE, SAVE, Oxfam, and World Vision have continued to actively press the government to ratify the treaty and to increase de-mining investments. Each of these organizations has been writing letters to the president, promoting the issue through media campaigns, op-ed articles, and information bulletins. In addition, CARE produced compelling public-service announcements, and Save the Children (jointly with UNICEF) published the report, "The Impact of Conflict on Children in Afghanistan." Although the United States refuses to comply with the treaty, some progress has been made. The United States expanded its de-mining program with an increase in funding from $68 million to $77 million in FY1998, and in May 1999, President Clinton made a promise that the United States would sign the treaty by 2006. The NGO community continues its lobbying efforts to urge the United States to sign the treaty immediately.

Debt Relief

The adoption of the debt relief program for Heavily Indebted Poor Countries (HIPC) is an excellent example of both effective NGO advocacy on a highly technical and politically charged issue and also of complementary roles of Northern and Southern NGOs. This movement was initiated and fueled much more by the South than was the campaign to ban landmines. Southern NGOs, especially those associated with political and social movements, had been voicing concern about the debt in their countries since the debt crisis first hit in the early 1980s. Protests grew as structural adjustment programs of the 1980s and 1990s exacerbated conditions for the poorer segments of society without relieving the debt burden. While Southern NGOs played an active role and organized themselves into networks around this issue, it was the large Northern NGOs that helped push the issue onto the agenda of donor governments and international financial institutions.

Specific calls to cancel debt by the year 2000 gained strength in the early 1990s. In 1990, the All African Council of Churches called for a Year of Jubilee to cancel Africa's debts. In 1994, three British activists joined forces to promote the Jubilee 2000 campaign in the United Kingdom. By April 1996, the Jubilee 2000 campaign in the United Kingdom was launched by three major Christian aid agencies and the World Development Movement. Jubilee 2000 became a global network of organizations working to achieve debt relief for poor countries by the beginning of the new millennium. While their full goal was not achieved, significant steps in debt relief have been made, in large part thanks to the successful lobbying efforts of NGOs.

The success of the debt relief campaign can be attributed to a combination of highly technical policy research and high-level lobbying together with global grassroots mobilization of public support for the issue. Campaign organizers used technology to reach out to the public and keep interested participants up to date. In June 1999, the debt campaign achieved a record with the largest Internet chat to date. When the rock star Bono of the group U2 went online to chat with the public about debt relief, 2 million people signed on to read what he had to say on the subject. Technology was used effectively for communication throughout the campaign, including a live Webcast of events as they unfolded at the summit of the Group of 8 industrial nations in Okinawa in July 2000.

A key element of this campaign was the technical research and policy analysis that allowed the NGOs to debate the issue within the framework and language of the financial institutions. Instead of focusing solely on social conditions of the poor in highly indebted countries, NGO advocates conducted economic analyses that demonstrated the financial inviolability of the debt burden within poor countries. Advocates made a clear link between debt and human development. As a result of those efforts, debt relief is not only being undertaken but also being linked to specific expenditures in social services, especially health and education. NGOs were proactive throughout the process in recommending specific policy options to address concerns of governments and banks. Oxfam, World Vision, Bread for the World, and others issued numerous policy papers and made submissions to the official HIPC review process of the World Bank and the IMF.

The creditors were soon willing to provide some form of debt relief, but the NGO campaign remained active at every step of the process, pushing for and gaining improvements along the way. NGOs worked closely with the financial institutions and also lobbied OECD (Organization for Economic Co-operation and Development) governments for bilateral debt relief and support of multilateral initiatives. For example, in October of 1998, the IMF explicitly stated that it would not review or modify HIPC, but by November of the same year IMF had changed its position and agreed to a 1999 HIPC review. The change in the IMF's position was due in large part to pressure from donor governments, particularly Germany and the United Kingdom, which had been exposed to extensive lobbying and education regarding debt relief from NGOs. In the United States, coordinated efforts by Oxfam and Bread for the World capitalized on the relative strengths of each organization. Bread for the World's research presented persuasive economic arguments, while Oxfam's Washington office's connections within the U.S. Congress facilitated the dissemination of those arguments to key policymakers.

Those efforts paid off in September 1999, when President Clinton announced that the United States would cancel 100 percent of the debt owed it by the world's poorest countries, provided that the money was spent on basic human needs. In a statement that reflected the tremendous shift in official policy regarding debt, President Clinton said that debt cancellation was a "moral and economic imperative at this moment of global consensus."[33] The United Kingdom followed suit, announcing in February 2000 that it would forgive 100 percent of its debt to twenty-six countries once they complied with HIPC guidelines, and in December 2000, the United Kingdom increased the number to forty-one countries. In October 2000, the U.S. Congress approved $435 million to finance the multilateral debt relief initiative.

Despite these successes, the campaign is far from over. Fifty-two of the world's poorest countries are $376 billion in debt.[34] The HIPC process is cumbersome and inadequate to provide sufficient relief for the

poorest countries. Actual debt forgiveness is delayed by the requirements that must be met in order for a country to fully comply with the
HIPC program. As the Jubilee year came to a close, participating NGOs
formed a new campaign, Drop the Debt, that will continue to push for
more comprehensive debt relief and a redirection of funds to health care
and education.

Challenges

We have seen that advocacy presents many opportunities to relief
and development NGOs. Yet advocacy within a primarily operational
organization has its own set of challenges. These are coupled with
challenges that emerge from the complexity of being Northern-based
organizations advocating on issues that affect people in other parts of
the world. Advocacy in operational organizations has been found to
be effective when it is based on direct field experience, speaks from
common experience, provides good examples about real people, and is
supported by sound analysis. Developing this combination of positive
elements requires NGOs to overcome a number of challenges, and in
some cases specific risks.

Unlike organizations dedicated mainly to advocacy, operational relief and development NGOs must always consider the impact of their
advocacy work on staff on the ground. The lives of field staff and program recipients can be put in jeopardy when the central organization
takes strong public advocacy positions. The issue becomes complicated,
since a decision not to advocate against certain policies or abuses in a
country where an NGO has staff does not necessarily protect those staff
members from the repercussions of other advocacy work. For example,
MSF volunteers were held captive in December 1999 in Sierra Leone by
the Revolutionary United Front (RUF), which is protesting against the
international community's work on disarmament and demobilization.
MSF's press release on the issue insists that MSF "has absolutely no im-
plication in this process [of disarmament] and requests the immediate
release of the volunteers." As international humanitarian aid workers,
MSF or other NGO staff can be targets regardless of their organizations'
direct involvement on any given issue.

Nevertheless, direct association with one organization or another in
terms of policy positions undoubtedly heightens security implications.
The risks to local NGOs is even greater, and thus continue to suggest
that there is a particular role for international NGOs in advocacy work
in cases where security concerns limit the ability of local groups to act.
In her study on Southern NGOs, Julie Fisher found that, in general, advocacy "is not usually relevant to repressive contexts, unless the issue
of security has first been confronted directly."[35] In order to address this

issue, many Northern-based NGOs take direction from their local country directors for final decisions on whether or not to pursue a particular advocacy path.

In some cases, advocacy work could result in the dismissal of operational staff from a country whose policies are under attack by the NGO. This was the case for several organizations working in Sudan. When World Vision and CARE took a leading role in advocating against the U.S. government policy of giving food aid to Sudanese rebels, the *New York Times* cited the work of both groups, thus giving international coverage even to work that had been relatively low-profile. As a result, the rebels evicted the relief workers of both NGOs from Sudan. NGOs face a challenge of balancing the conviction to speak out on policy issues and human rights abuses (which may lead to eviction) with the commitment to fulfill a mission of providing relief. The choice is a difficult one, since pulling out of an emergency situation would mean leaving innocent civilians behind without assistance. MSF is clear on its policy to pull out when necessary: "In extreme conditions where a situation cannot be improved by these means [humanitarian assistance and silent diplomacy], MSF will make the decision to withdraw its presence and speak out and attract international attention, believing that it is better to do so than to stay and support the systems which cause the suffering in the first place."[36]

Another key challenge to NGOs when undertaking advocacy is determining when to favor a policy of engagement and when to choose one of confrontation. Each organization has to determine the stance it feels most comfortable with. Oxfam has found a balanced approach that mixes the two, and usually engages actors before confronting them, to be most effective.[37] Related to this is the challenge of working with private corporations. In today's global marketplace, private business has an ever-increasing role, and the importance of influencing its policies and leveraging its resources is important for advocacy efforts. NGOs must find effective means of engaging corporations and benefiting from partnerships while still maintaining sufficient independence to lobby against those corporations when necessary. Several NGOs have developed policies on corporate advocacy, defining guidelines for occasions when public criticism is warranted and those when behind-the-scenes discussions and negotiations can be more effective.

International NGO advocacy is well served by global coordination, yet the process of building common positions among affiliate members or other organizations can be daunting. The time involved in consensus building might make the ultimate position irrelevant if its timelines were lost or the final results might be bland, watered-down positions. Northern NGOs also face the challenge of speaking for others. Without actually sounding out the views of local program recipients or local organizations, Northern groups might inaccurately present those view-points. Furthermore, immediate short-term needs of local communities may lead those communities to prioritize a different advocacy agenda or to support a different policy stance than would international NGOs, which are often focused on long-term change for poor communities. The issue of child labor is an excellent example of this tension. While both international and local NGOs may likely agree on the need to eliminate child labor in the long term, local groups may oppose the work of some international groups to immediately ban all child labor since in doing so, many poor families would find their incomes eroded. Save the Children UK chose to base their position on child labor on the views of their constituents within poor communities and therefore advocates for better working conditions as well as other policy changes that would reduce the need for families to depend on income from child labor.

NGOs are also faced with a complex interplay between advocacy and accountability, as they must strive to maintain legitimacy and uphold reputations. On the one hand, advocacy work can bolster credibility and enhance accountability, since it can demonstrate a commitment to addressing the structural causes of poverty and conflict. However, at the same time, the sensitive nature of advocacy and the resources required to do it well could alienate key constituents. In coordinated advocacy efforts, managing the complexity and nuances of issues can be very difficult. Often the need for simple, clear views with examples of real people may tend to simplify the complex nature of the issues involved. In addition, there is a danger that poor or incomplete analysis can destroy the advocacy organization's credibility.

As already mentioned, the additional funds and the changing skill mix required of development and relief organizations to conduct advocacy present an important challenge. Not only does advocacy in general require a different set of strengths than effective program operation, but the issues involved in addressing the root causes of poverty and conflict require very specific technical skills—on economics, tax policy, and political processes, just to name a few. Rigorous and objective research is essential to support legitimate advocacy positions, but this requires a very particular expertise. This might suggest specialization of organizations and division of labor between advocacy and operations, but that could jeopardize the beneficial link between the two. Development NGOs may need to increasingly operate in two different worlds within the same organizational framework and manage an effective synergy and learning between the two. Advocacy requires investment in staff resources and infrastructure. This has particular implications for organizations that depend on contracts and public funds. All organizations that want to dedicate increased revenue to advocacy will need support from their donors to divert resources from service delivery to advocacy.

Ethnology and Beyond

As in other chapters, we now return to our ethnology set of questions: Can the views of our interlocutors be supported by empirical data? What motivations may our respondents not have explicitly discussed? What nuances and details may the leaders have known, but not explicitly discussed? What emerging trends need further exploration?

Empirical Data

Since advocacy work within many of these organizations is relatively new and has evolved into a very dynamic process, there is not a lot of empirical data available on the extent of activity within NGOs. Nevertheless, research does confirm the general trends discussed by our interlocutors regarding the evolving role of advocacy within their organizations. As in the cases of other chapters, we acknowledge that our data on advocacy does not cover all of the details of the advocacy programs in each NGO, and much information on specific campaigns was in fact left out of the chapter. Our intent was to capture the main characteristics of advocacy programs and compare general approaches across the organizations, rather than provide a comprehensive review of the advocacy program in each NGO.

Motivations Not Discussed

Our discussants spoke openly about both motivators and barriers to advocacy work. The motivators behind NGO work in advocacy that might not have been discussed include the interest and passion on the part of senior managers for advocacy work. This work can be exciting and high-profile for NGO presidents and thus a very compelling addition to their work as managers. In addition, discussions might not have captured the extent to which Northern-based NGOs are motivated by concern for developing a new niche, given the increase in Southern NGO activity in their traditional operational work. Furthermore, the full extent to which donors influence advocacy decisions may well have been understated in our discussions.

Details and Nuances

Effective advocacy entails complex layers of work to influence policy decisions. Many of the nuances in the work such as "corridor lobbying" and the role of relationships between advocacy staff and policymakers were not discussed in detail. While the complexity of reaching consensus and coordinating between different NGOs was discussed, the details of how this works did not fully emerge, particularly in terms of the frustrations that NGOs certainly experience when working closely with other groups that have a different culture and approach.

While our interlocutors spoke very frankly with us regarding the resistance of certain stakeholders to advocacy work, it is not likely that all of the details on the hurdles they face in this area were revealed. This is to be expected, considering the sensitivity of these issues and the fact that many NGOs are still in the process of working through some resistance to advocacy from their constituents.

Emerging Trends in Need of Exploration

This chapter suggests that there are several important trends to be explored in the future. It is apparent that global campaigns and more sophisticated advocacy work will become a norm among Northern development and relief organizations. The increase has been dramatic over the last five years and shows every sign of continuing. The changing dynamics in global structures is increasingly moving the role of Northern NGOs to be one of coordinator, marketer, and advocate while Southern NGOs take on increasing responsibility for operations in the field.

At the same time, Southern NGOs are also increasing their capacity to carry out advocacy work not only in their own countries but also at an international level. The pace of this progress is uncertain, but it is likely to occur more rapidly than some expect (as was the case with the emergence of strong operational NGOs in the South). The dynamics of partnerships and the comparative roles of Northern- and Southern-based organizations will need to evolve.

While many of the NGOs in this study are still in the process of fully establishing themselves as "third generation" NGOs that focus on lobbying to change specific policies (using David Korten's classifications), the future may well involve their further evolution to the "fourth generation." This next step would entail coordinating and participating in global, people-centered social movements.[38]

Notes

1. Thomas W. Dichter, "Globalization and Its Effects on NGOs: Efflorescence or a Blurring of Roles and Relevance?" in *Nonprofit and Voluntary Sector Quarterly* 28, no. 4 (Supplement 1999).

2. Michael Edwards, "International Development NGOs: Agents of Foreign Aid or Vehicles for International Cooperation?" *Nonprofit and Voluntary Sector Quarterly* 28, no. 4 (Supplement 1999).

3. Stephen Commins, "Non-Governmental Organizations: Ladles in the Global Soup Kitchen?" (paper prepared for Conference on the Challenges of Globalization of International Relief and Development NGOs, Bellagio, Italy, September 1998).

4. Peter Uvin, *Aiding Violence: The Development Enterprise in Rwanda* (West Hartford, Conn.: Kumarian Press, 1998).

5. Alan Fowler and K. Biekart, "Do Private Agencies Really Make a Difference? in *Compassion and Calculation: The Business of Private Foreign Aid* (London: Pluto Press, 1996), 132.

6. RealImpact Web site, December 2000, www.realimpact.net.

7. David Bryer and John Magrath, "New Dimensions of Global Advocacy," *Nonprofit and Voluntary Sector Quarterly* 28, no. 4 (Supplement 1999).

8. Lisa Jordan and Peter Van Tujil, "Political Responsibility in Transnational NGO Advocacy," *World Development* 28, no. 12 (December 2000): 2051–65.

9. Pat Carey, "A Rights-Based Approach to Achieving HLS" (Internal letter to all CARE USA staff, November 10, 2000).

10. Oxfam America Web site 1999, www.oxfamamerica.org.

11. David Nussbaum, finance director of Oxfam GB, interviewed by Coralie Bryant and Christina Kappaz, Oxford, March 2000.

12. Médecins Sans Frontières (MSF) Web site, 1999, www.msf.org/intweb99/going/witnes.htm.

13. MSF Web site 1999, www.msf.org/intweb99/going/witnes.htm.

14. MSF (paper prepared for Conference on the Challenges of Globalization of International Relief and Development NGOs, Bellagio, Italy, September 1998).

15. MSF Annual Report 1999.

16. MSF 1999 International Activity Report. Available online, www.msf.org/publications/activ_rep/1999/europe/france.htm.

17. Andy Pugh, director of policy and advocacy, CARE USA, interview by Christina Kappaz, January 9, 2001.

18. Kevin Watkins, *Education Now: Break the Cycle of Poverty* (London: Oxfam International, 1999).

19. The legal context for advocacy work may soon be changing in the United States. New legislation may be enacted that includes lobbying of legislatures in other countries within the 25 percent limit. Even for NGOs that are well below expenditure limits, such policies would significantly increase the amount of paperwork and accounting of advocacy work (from interview with Andy Pugh, CARE USA, January 9, 2001).

20. Don Mahin, "Leader Works to Expand CARE's Outreach: Fighting for Global Justice Among Goals" *The Atlanta Journal-Constitution*, October 8, 2000, B1.

21. Ray Offenheiser and Susan Holcombe, Oxfam America (paper prepared for Conference on the Challenges of Globalization of International Relief and Development NGOs, Bellagio, Italy, September 1998).

22. Chris Roche, Oxfam Great Britain, interview by Coralie Bryant and Christina Kappaz, Oxford, March 30, 2000.

23. Sam Moyo, *NGO Advocacy in Zimbabwe: Systematising an Old Function, Inventing a New Role?* (Harare, Zimbabwe: Environmental Research Organization, 1992), 11.

24. Offenheiser and Holcombe, paper prepared for Bellagio Conference.

25. Charles MacCormack and Burkhard Gnaerig, Save the Children (paper prepared for Conference on the Challenges of Globalization of International Relief and Development NGOs, Bellagio, Italy, September 1998).

26. Ernst Ligteringen, executive director of Oxfam International, interview by Coralie Bryant and Christina Kappaz, Oxford, March 30, 2000.

27. Jordan and Van Tujil, "Political Responsibility in Transnational NGO Advocacy," 2053.

28. Manuel Chiriboga, "Constructing a Southern Constituency for Global Advocacy: The Experience of Latin American NGOs and the World Bank" (paper presented at the NGOs in the Global Future Conference, University of Birmingham, U.K., January 11–13, 1999).

29. Global Policy Forum, *Security Council Consultation with Humanitarian NGOs*, 1997. Web site: www.igc.apc.org/globalpolicy/security/mtgsetc/somavint .htm.

30. MSF Web site 1999, www.msf.org.

31. International Campaign to Ban Landmines Web site, December 2000, www.icbl.org

32. Landmine Monitor, *Landmine Monitor Report 2000: Toward a Mine-Free World* (Washington, D.C.: Human Rights Watch, 2000).

33. Jubilee 2000 Web site and press releases, www.jubilee2000uk.org.

34. Oxfam Great Britain Web site, 2000, oxfam.org.uk/educationnow/allover .htm.

35. Julie Fisher, *The Road from Rio: Sustainable Development and the Nongovernmental Movement in the Third World* (Westport, Conn.: Praeger Publishers, 1993), 109.

36. MSF Web page, 1999, www.msf.org.

37. Bryer and Magrath, "New Dimensions of Global Advocacy."

38. David Korten, "From Relief to People's Movement," in *Getting to the Twenty-First Century: Voluntary Action and the Global Agenda* (West Hartford, Conn.: Kumarian Press, 1989).

– 8 –

Accountability, Evaluation, and Organizational Learning

TODAY, contributors, donor agencies, scholars, and relief and development practitioners are all asking: Do NGOs practice what they preach? How do we know? Are claims of closeness to the grassroots a reality? Have NGOs become too dependent on public money? How effective are their programs and projects? How credible is the evidence? Would donors reach the grassroots better by connecting with local NGOs in developing and transitional countries? If donors must be transparent about evaluation results, why not NGOs?

In short, in this field and many others, accountability is the central issue of our time. We turn to this issue as this book winds toward its close. In fact, however, elements of the accountability challenge are present implicitly in all of the preceding chapters: coping with globalization, transformation, new challenges in relief work, poverty reduction, partnerships, advocacy work—each of these has an accountability component. As that is the case, what remains to be discussed here are the components within the accountability equation that have not yet received close attention: accountability's contingent character and complexity, the role of evaluation systems, and the learning process that should emerge through collective reflection on past performance. Before turning to these three major themes, we will prepare the way with some background discussion and address why this issue emerged as salient in the 1990s.

Introduction: The Challenge

NGOs are at present challenged as never before to demonstrate *results*. Internet users can, within minutes, compare and contrast who is doing what and with what outcomes. Current and prospective donors ask questions about impacts. Nor is there any indication that these pressures will abate. Calls for stronger accountability grew steadily throughout the late 1990s. In Europe, Roger Riddell and Mark Robinson detailed the weak evaluation capacity in European-based NGOs.[1] Michael Edwards and David Hulme made accountability the major theme of *Beyond the Magic Bullet*.[2] Jonathan Fox and David Brown examined at length the conceptual thinking in the NGO demands for World Bank accountability.[3] Now NGOs are hearing comparable calls for their own accountability.

In the early 1990s, NGOs pressured the World Bank and the IMF to be more "transparent" and accountable. By the end of the 1990s, the World Bank enacted and implemented new regulations on public access to project evaluations. Sometimes the NGOs were asking the Bank to provide more public access to their project information, including evaluations, than NGOs themselves were prepared to allow. Of course, they were not alone—few official bilateral development agencies were disclosing project documentation in the early 1990s. Yet inexorable pressures in the information revolution, coupled with calls for performance-based management, are now pushing NGOs for more accountability.

Accountability and Public Funding

One reason often given for needing more NGO accountability is growing dependence on public money. Ian Smillie's reckoning, for example, is that "by the early 1990s, 75 percent of British food aid was being channeled through NGOs, and 40 percent of Swedish spending on emergencies and refugees was going through Swedish NGOs. By 1996, 46 percent of French emergency funding was being spent through NGOs, and half of all the EU's European Community Humanitarian Office (ECHO) funding was being spent the same way. Between 1992 and 1997 the United States Agency for International Development (USAID)—with the largest emergency budget in the world—spent over 60 percent of it, not counting food aid, through NGOs."[4]

International organizations are also increasingly working through NGOs: "The World Food Program channeled an estimated $580 million through NGOs in 1997, UNHCR, about $300 million. Twelve percent of UNICEF's country level programming is directed towards NGOs. Further NGO grants, co-financing and contracts are made by UNDP, the United Nations Fund for Women (UNIFEM), the International Fund for Agricultural Development (IFAD) and other UN agencies."[5]

Yet some of the NGOs with the strongest accountability cultures are the same ones that are taking the lowest amounts of public money. Thus the motivations or "drivers" for accountability within NGOs are more nuanced and complex than the role of public money; financial drivers are not determinative.

Accountability and Advocacy

The previous chapter detailed the increase in advocacy work. As the visibility of that work increases, it underscores and provokes demands for accountability and its correlate, responsibility. If NGOs are to be advocates in public policy, to whom are they accountable for that role? They are not membership organizations; hence they cannot readily claim to represent distinct membership needs.[6] While their claims to credibility on policy issues derive from their claims to "field"-informed knowledge, they are expected to answer for these claims as much as for their programs and projects.

Policy advocacy also raises legal issues of standing which requires that any claimant for a legal action must have some immediate interest at stake providing that agency, or person, with a right to public recourse. In the case of the NGOs' meetings with the UN Security Council, the NGOs had standing for seeking recourse, given the risks to their own staff in civil wars. But in their advocacy work on issues around a broadly shared common good—education for all, or debt relief—they are interpreting and advocating on behalf of others. They are taking up a cause on behalf of the poor, but cannot claim to be elected representatives of the poor. Norman Uphoff argues in light of this point that NGOs cannot be referred to as a "third sector," as that should be reserved for membership organizations and community groups grounded within localized systems of accountability.[7]

Most national governments have regulatory standards in regard to NGOs, usually insisting upon fiduciary responsibility, accounting, and auditing reports. From time to time, various national regulatory bodies for monitoring nonprofit work will look in more detail at the advocacy work of an NGO as well. The Charities Commission in Britain, for example, has from time to time examined Oxfam GB's advocacy work. In France, the Cours des Comptes selectively undertakes intensive financial audits of NGO accounts. A critical review from the Cours des Comptes can spell real trouble for an NGO—affecting its fundraising appeal if public credibility is tarnished. As the work, size, numbers, and financial scale of NGO activity increases, we can expect that the legal and regulatory environment of NGO work will be impacted by national accountability standards.

Definitional Problems

Accountability, an elusive concept, is more discussed than clarified. For example, Jonathan Fox and David Brown say that "accountability refers to the process of holding actors responsible for actions," but without clarifying who holds whom accountable, or how. Mark Moore argues it has to do with responsibility. For some, the term means "giving an account" for decisions, with particular attention to decisions that entail expenditures. For others, it means responsibility to, above all, the people affected directly by projects and also to donors as well as the NGO board and other stakeholders. For the purposes of this discussion, accountability means answering to stakeholders, including beneficiaries, boards, donors, staff, partners, and peers for the results and impacts of performance and the use of resources to achieve that performance. In short, these agencies must respond to demands that emanate from multiple sources. There are inevitably both normative and legal drivers in the accountability equation.

While accountability is used frequently as synonymous with transparency, there are distinctions between the two. Accountability is providing an account for decisions, actions, and their consequences. Transparency is about providing information—not necessarily an explanation. Although they are interrelated, these concepts are nonetheless separable. Quantities of information may be provided in ways that do not directly address or reveal the connections between decision-makers, decisions taken, and their consequences. Moreover, techniques, or recourse for holding decision-makers accountable, vary—from lawsuits to elections. The forum and processes for accountability vary. Information is essential, but not determinative for achieving accountability.[8]

Commitment and Complexity in Accountability Processes

Throughout our sessions with them, our interlocutors frequently discussed their abiding commitment to strengthen accountability. In a discussion on what was involved in doing so, there was broad agreement when Reynold Levy, CEO, International Rescue Committee, said that accountability to beneficiaries had to be the highest priority. James Orbinski, president, Médecins Sans Frontières International, added that it was hard, however, to prioritize as answering to volunteers, beneficiaries, and donors were all equally important—creating a circle of accountability. Charles MacCormack, president of Save the Children US, added that one .part of the problem is how broadly or narrowly to set aspirations, as it is easier to measure and be accountable for narrower ones.[9]

For all of them accountability means adhering to organizational core values, their mission, and performing up to their own standards. The ways to "render an account" range from answering to the collective wisdom of shared values across the NGO family; to using public speeches and public education campaigns to exercise responsible leadership; to providing financial and programmatic data via Web sites, annual reports, press releases, and documentation. It also means telling people what their operational work is achieving and answering to boards, contributors, beneficiaries, and other stakeholders for their decisions.

The several tiers of groups and agencies these NGO families operate with requires a multi-directional flow of information that reaches from headquarters to the field and to the people directly affected by programs and projects and back again to the NGO. Robert Chambers asks: *Whose Reality Counts?*[10] One must ask in turn, Who decides? Boards, stakeholders, donors, partners, project participants? Those in NGOs work with these uncertainties every day, while fielding operations or executing advocacy campaigns. Unfortunately, all too often work pressures preclude reflection on critical questions.

Whose reality *does* count? And therefore, to whom, when, and how does one give an account? This chapter looks at these questions and conveys what various NGOs are doing now about accountability. We will also consider how much progress there is with "becoming learning organizations." As in all chapters, we will then turn again to the four ethnology questions addressed at the end of every chapter. But first we turn to ask why this issue is now being raised everywhere—and with such virulence.

Why Now? What Has Changed?

What has put NGO accountability on the public agenda? After all, for the first decades of their lives, most NGOs enjoyed widespread public approval without many probing questions. Why has that changed?

As we saw in the earlier chapters, *the whole context has changed.* Only in part are the changes in roles being assumed by NGOs responsible for the changed demands for accountability. The fact that many NGOs are receiving greater amounts of public money drives some of the demand, but it, too, is only part of the story.

The second part of the explanation is embedded in the changed ideological climate of the new era. The politically charged and ideological climate of the Cold War era dampened the development debate generally and the role of NGOs as well. Especially in the United States, during the Cold War, there was little tolerance for anything that could be interpreted as left of the political center. As the Berlin Wall came down development theory and practice shook loose as well. Amartya Sen's book, *Development as Freedom*, exemplifies this new climate; his role as honorary president of Oxfam epitomizes new roles and orientations in this millennium.[11]

Discussions of poverty today that call immediate attention to vulnerability, to powerlessness, were not well received when they were articulated during the Cold War. Liberation theology, which did make those points, was labeled dangerous and subversive. But now even the World Bank argues that poverty is about powerlessness, and the European Union has a policy on social exclusion. The drafters of the World

Bank's 1980 World Development Report on poverty would have found themselves in serious trouble had they tried to incorporate "vulnerability" and "powerlessness" into their analysis. But NGOs were making that point during the 1980s—and even earlier. Oxfam and Save the Children have long records of working on "empowerment" as central to development, and they have trained trainers to carry that message. NGOs are often concerned to help empower the poor—to give them voice, to facilitate their becoming more powerful.

Coming with this new freer climate, however, is a call for accountability, for demonstrating results, for giving an answer to constituents about what works. Is accountability the current price for the current, more open environment? Maybe. But maybe not. Maybe accountability is the current price, and responding openly may help keep the open environment—open. In general, that is what we implicitly argue in this chapter. But we also want to make the risks of some of the current pressures for demonstrating results more apparent. Demonstrating results is a popular idea. Interpreted too narrowly, it has unintended negative consequences.

Michael Edwards and David Hulme point out that the new emphasis on empowerment adds a political dilemma for those charged with providing accountability: "If the organization's overt or covert goal is empowerment (making those who have little power more powerful), then transparency on this issue will, at best, make it easier for vested interests to identify what is happening and thus more effectively oppose it, or, at worst, lead to the deregistration and closure of the organization for being subversive."[12]

It is not clear that they are right. In the 1970s, many NGOs, including Oxfam GB, were active in Latin America and Central America during the struggles in those countries—doing just what one would have thought not possible: working with opposition groups struggling for more democracy. They were not deregistered, or closed. Moreover, contrary to Michael Edwards's and David Hulme's claim that no NGOs have been successful at democratization, the carefully researched work of Brian Smith in *More Than Altruism* documents that several NGOs were successful in reaching and facilitating alternative paths to influence, and that many of the democratic leaders who emerged later in Central America came out of the NGO movement seeded by this work.[13]

Yet in some ways they are right—and their point should be heeded. Empowerment comes through long-term, incremental steps—it is a fragile process, easily uprooted. Demanding "results" can mean either pushing for quick fixes, or insisting upon digging up the seedling to examine its roots before it can bear fruit. Domestic poverty work often is abandoned when narrowly measured results are demanded—and not found. Empowerment is sometimes more tolerated at a distance than it is at home; it seems easier to deal with powerlessness in small countries than with the powerlessness of poor people within Northern post-industrial countries. John Gaventa writes about the speed with which the War on Poverty in the United States in the 1960s was dismantled when it began to be effective. It is a powerful case in point.[14]

The "indicator movement" irrevocably changed the way that development theorists and practitioners think about "results." Techniques and skills for the measurement of results have changed in the last three decades. As early as the 1960s, the Yale University Political and Social Data Center was developing social and political indicators to parallel the indicators in use by economists. Knowledge spread that something akin to social accounting (measuring results) was possible. By the 1980s, the multilateral development banks had picked up on performance indicators—and so had managers coming out of business schools. This led in turn to more calls for improved accountability in the public sector. It was only a matter of time until this would be echoed in development work, even though national statistics and census politics in developing countries meant weak databases for measurement.

Multi-Directional Accountability

Those who write about domestic nonprofit organizations point out that nonprofit evaluation is complicated by the organization's multiple goals, multiple constituencies, and market insulation. If this is true of a domestic NGO working where the contributors see the results of their donations, consider how it works for international NGOs. Alan Fowler provides a thoughtful example of the long chain through which resources must flow winding through geographic, sectoral, and institutional spaces to affect objectives, goals, and performance.[15] These interactions determine outcomes. The nature of these layered tiers of agencies affects several dimensions of accountability.

Accountability must be *multi-directional* as a result of these tiers—not only from bottom to top, or from top to bottom. In reality, different parts of any NGO family have to respond to different stakeholders, partners, and people—immediate beneficiaries and others—in order to meet the accountability challenge. Figure 8.1 on the following page depicts the multi-directional nature of the accountability process.

Accountability for emergency relief work is different from that of poverty-reducing work, or longer-term development work. As there are weaker links in emergency situations, and different constraints, it is extremely difficult to measure effectiveness. Both public opinion and the donors funding relief work (for example, UNHCR, or the Office of Disaster Assistance) have reporting and auditing requirements that differ from those of ongoing development assistance with a longer timeline.

Figure 8.1. Multi-Directional Accountability

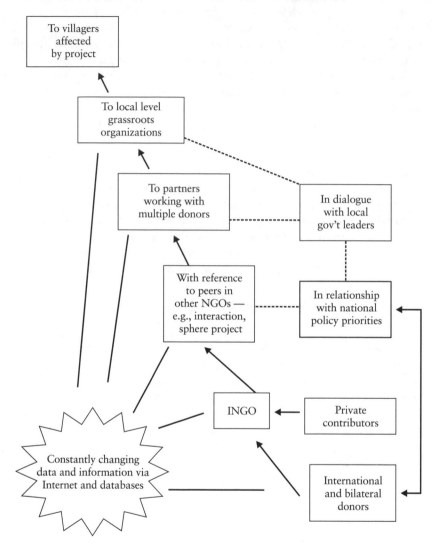

Given the changing context for humanitarian work, however, changed accountability standards will emerge, especially as the borders between relief and development blur. But to date, differences in approach and techniques have meant different reporting and evaluation guidelines as well. In the case of development work, there is longer-term engagement with people and Southern NGOs over a period of time, making possible more participatory and thorough evaluation.

The very volatility of work with internally displaced people and refugees adds dimensions of difficulty to evaluation processes. That said, the Sphere Project has as its aim to improve the quality of assistance provided to people affected by disasters, and to enhance the accountability of the humanitarian system in disaster response. This project was worked out by the NGOs together with the UN to develop minimum universal standards and codes of conduct for disaster response.

While public opinion in general has been sympathetic to the added demands of relief work, and thus has lowered expectations for accountability, in the case of Rwanda, as we saw in Chapter 3, there was in fact more criticism of NGO work. Peter Uvin has suggested that NGOs should be held accountable, as should the international community, for the structural violence in Rwanda.[16] His argument is that NGOs working directly with people at the grassroots had before them all the signals of impending major violence, but that they remained too silent for too long. Enmeshed in their own worlds, they did not blow the whistle. When the violence escalated, and they undertook emergency work, they were often manipulated by terrorists, who outmaneuvered them—for example, by using food programs in refugee camps as foraging places to "refuel" before their next rampage. While some NGOs did decide to withdraw when they became convinced that they were being used by those committed to violence and further bloodshed, others did not decide to withdraw—on equally compelling grounds that the people with whom they were working would be even more immiserated if they abandoned them than if they remained and kept working. The debates about those choices—each of which was very context-specific—will continue for years to come.

NGO emergency relief work is not likely to be the same in the post-Rwanda world. While the Group of Seven industrial powers was largely focused on the wars in Bosnia and Croatia and later on in Kosovo, the numbers killed in those wars, grim as they were, were nowhere near the nearly million lives lost in Rwanda. Nor were NGO staff as deeply at risk.

The sum total of the multi-directionality entailed in these various calls for increased, and differently conceived, accountability and responsibility systems has changed the context for NGO senior managers and staff. Since the accountability process is both multi-faceted and diverse, conceiving of it in terms of a contingency approach may be helpful. Below we turn to this contingency model for accountability—an approach pointed out to us by, among others, David Brown and Julie Fisher, while discussing NGO accountability with them.[17]

A Contingency Model for Accountability

In all our discussions with them, NGO leaders confirmed that their accountability is both multi-dimensional and multi-directional. While most perceived their primary responsibility to be toward those directly affected by programs and projects, they added that they must also answer for performance to contributors and donors. One of the implications of multiple and competing audience pulls is that different kinds of information and feedback are needed for different audiences. Therefore accountability is necessarily contingent upon both the demander and the context of the demand. For example, donors often require formal evaluation reports, while other contributors expect some summary financial reports and annual mailings; beneficiaries, on the other hand, need results—though their own interpretation of favorable results can differ from the interpretations imposed by donors. Thus the contingency model of accountability presented below reflects these differing demands.

The way in which NGO family networks differ within themselves is also part of this contingency model. Moreover, often national members work collaboratively within particular countries when working in, for example, Africa or Latin America. Thus, Save the Children UK could be working in Guatemala with Save the Children Sweden in Guatemala—and there is also a Save the Children Guatemala national member. Each of these SAVEs has different Guatemalan partners and somewhat different objectives in their work (they are, after all, working collaboratively because of their special expertise on a part of the problem at hand). The modalities for holding them accountable within the United Kingdom, or Sweden, or Guatemala are in each case different, as are the kinds of requests made by contributors, donors, or boards to which they need to respond.

The kinds of processes and "products" that NGOs generate inevitably add to the complexity of their accountability systems. Unlike the private sector with its sharp focus on a single bottom line, NGOs, as Mark Moore has said, have two major bottom lines: their mission's effectiveness and their financial sustainability. He points out that for nonprofits, "Mission attainment is calculated in terms that are different from revenue assurance. In this important sense, there are two bottom lines: mission effectiveness and financial sustainability."[18] He adds, rightfully, that this makes for greater managerial complexity than a single bottom line.

The Internet has both eased and complicated the kinds of reports and data that can be presented. Annual reports are often made available via the Internet, easing the mailing costs of getting these to donors. Some contributors can, and do, check Web sites to find out how projects and programs are progressing. For other contributors, mailings that are less formal than evaluation reports are needed. Because of changes in technology, the total amount of data produced and distributed has increased. The new modalities of communication are of course additional to all of those which senior decision-makers have traditionally used to meet accountability expectations, including meetings and consultations, discussions with key stakeholders, taskforces, and committees. Having an evaluation system, a staff tasked to perform that function, and budget resources allocated for evaluation are critical components—but they do not add up to the full range of accountability functions, and may even be a relatively small part of the whole.

In short, it is not easy to account to a diverse set of stakeholders who have different and sometimes conflicting demands. While Chambers is right to insist on pride of place in the accountability equation for the views of those on the ground who are directly affected by development projects and programs, they are in practice only *one* of the audiences. Figure 8.2 on the following page is one way to depict this contingency model.

As we have noted before, our key informants consistently cite responsibility to the people their organizations serve as a major priority. The input of those served—preferably obtained through a participatory evaluative process assessing whatever improvements have resulted in their livelihood or well-being—is the critical factor. While putting people first is normatively right, Uphoff reminds us that the fiduciary responsibility to donors cannot be slighted. Donors, on the other hand, tend to focus on individual project results, on their sectoral focus, and on their own policy programming priorities. What can get lost in the fray is the complexity of the needs of the communities in which the NGOs are working.

The contingent model of accountability responds to the fact of widely diverse and equally deserving constituencies and multiple modalities for responding to those constituencies. The managerial questions include the who, what, when, and how of giving an account to these dispersed and sometimes competing constituents. To the people in far-flung villages and communities—or refugee camps or settlements—for which they are working? To the foundations or corporations that contribute to their programs? To peer NGOs? To the bilateral aid agencies whose programs they are administering? To the international donors for whom they perform services? And, in the worse case, if it is all of the above, how is this accounting to be sequenced? Since the NGOs most often work through locally based partner agencies, dividing this challenge with those partners is another part of the equation.

Alan Fowler argues that the linear thinking—as exemplified by the logical framework for project design—imposes a presumed certainty that is not the reality at the village level. Like others, Fowler is concerned

Figure 8.2. Contingent Model of NGO Accountability

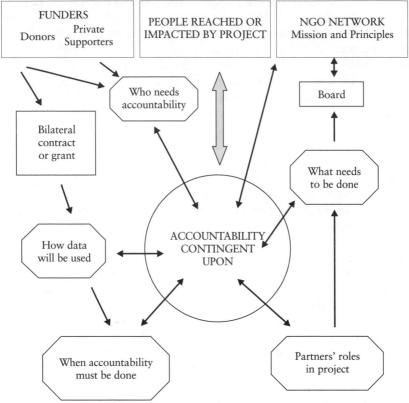

that the donor agency may force upon an NGO a narrow window through which to view its work. (Of course, lurking in the background for a donor like USAID is the U.S. Congress, which also will want quantifiable evidence of real results for monies disbursed—and Congress's timetable is governed by a short-term election cycle.) Suffice it to say that the emphasis on accountability to donors can lead NGOs to focus on their immediate projects without examining the broader economic, social, and political realities having an impact on communities. In relief work—where little is understood, and less is appreciated, about the relationships between relief and longer-term development—this problem is exacerbated. What will matter over time is not just how many blankets or food rations were distributed, but how community-level problem solving, for example, began to be reinstated.

All of these questions and criticisms have led to greater insistence on accountability without much clarity about what it is that should be assessed and which of the stakeholders need what information. The need for accountability has been accompanied by calls for demonstrated evidence of effectiveness, or results. But ironically, an over-emphasis on quickly apparent "results" can and does undermine long-term sustainable development. In fact, it puts a premium on quick technical fixes, not on well-grounded, lasting, long-term consequences. To further unpack all the issues around impact and results means more focus on evaluation, and on organizational learning as processes to strengthen long-term effectiveness as well as accountability.

NGO leaders have always had to respond—account to—different constituencies. Donors, however, were always more than just another constituency—they were increasingly implementing programs through NGOs. Each donor has some kind of specific evaluation requirements and generally specified in the contract with the NGO how those requirements were to be met. Recall also that each of these NGO families include numerous national members and each member has in turn hundreds of operational partners in widely dispersed country settings. (Table 2.1 in Chapter 2 above reflects this pattern.) Moreover, projects are often multidonor-funded, and donors generally have different evaluation and accountability demands.

While much has been written about the possible threats to the long-term mission of NGOs when or if they become more dependent on donor funding, in general the assumption has been that increased donor funding would require more attention to evaluation than had been the case to date in many NGOs. One of the preliminary surprises our interviews surfaced, however, was that the NGOs that are the least dependent on donor funding are in fact the NGOs doing the most about evaluation. It is not yet clear how to explain this counter-intuitive finding. A part of the answer, however, may be that donors specify a final evaluation, sometimes hiring their own outside team to conduct it. That evaluation then is to meet donor needs, not the learning needs for the NGO. Often, for example, the NGO simply ensures that the evaluation is done, and does little more than treat evaluation as a part of contract compliance, rather than as part of their own ongoing reflection. While it is true that increased donor funding has called into question the role, function, and cost of evaluation, it has not yet become as robust in the process as might have been expected.

Evaluation Systems

While accountability is broader than evaluation, accountability drives NGOs to focus more attention on performance, and hence on strengthening their evaluation systems. Monitoring and evaluation processes are, after all, the ways that data are generated on program and project performance. Improving them depends on staffing and operational budgets, so that strengthening either of these drives up overhead costs. Ironies abound: Donors want to work with NGOs because NGOs' voluntary character means they are less costly than consulting firms. Yet the earlier NGO tradition of voluntarism can be steadily eroded by the same set of actors and factors that led to its initial growth. Now NGOs are often implored to become more "professional." Most donors, however, show little willingness to pay for increased professionalism as it means staff and equipment costs, hence overhead. Support for overhead costs is not available. Professionalism in accountability is not as readily financed as it is demanded.

Monitoring and evaluation systems for large organizations take several different forms, and within the NGO families with which we are concerned, they vary within and among national members. Some are quasi-independent of line operations and report directly to boards. They may be so constituted in order to act as a check, or countervailing power to operations, or because a strong executive board wants the evaluation office to have a "watchdog" function.[19] Other organizations—especially smaller ones on lean budgets—integrate monitoring and evaluation so that the two processes can be iterative, with mutual learning of "best practice" through workshops, seminars, conferences, or a wide variety of other means. The variables within monitoring and evaluation systems are depicted in Figure 8.3.

Evaluation, like any other function, requires organizational commitment of budget and staff to make it happen. Its advocates are invariably quick to note that making use of lessons learned will save costly error, and that investing in evaluation is therefore a sound investment. That may be, but the question remains of how to undertake evaluation of programs over time most efficiently as well as effectively. Portfolio reviews by regions, as CARE has done, make sense. But there are no easy answers to the questions of how much to invest in undertaking these works, at what intervals, or how often. Coupled with that, when or whether to share the findings from evaluations, and how to do so, is a troubled terrain. Predictably, there will be increased pressure from stakeholders for greater transparency. Transparency taken as a rule can put in place pressures to avoid sensitive areas, and some candor can be lost. Privacy rules and practices are culturally contextual, so that transparency practices in one place put burdens on partners in a different context. There are no right answers to these difficult trade-offs.

The evaluation offices in most Northern NGOs are small, spare in resources, and usually focused on setting guidelines and large parameters for the work that is to be done either by partners, or consultants, or both. Oxfam America and Save the Children US have one or two people fully committed to evaluation in their headquarters offices. These staff members are charged with evaluation responsibility where this means

Figure 8.3. Variables in Monitoring and Evaluation

Stakeholder reviews and assessments		Program review Sector evaluations Lessons learned
Partners' roles and capacities for participatory approaches	System-wide standard setting and strategies	Donor requirements
Partners with different donor requirements		Donors' roles and relationships

Monitoring and evaluation assessing impacts

GOAL:
Widely enhance performance accountability and learning across family network

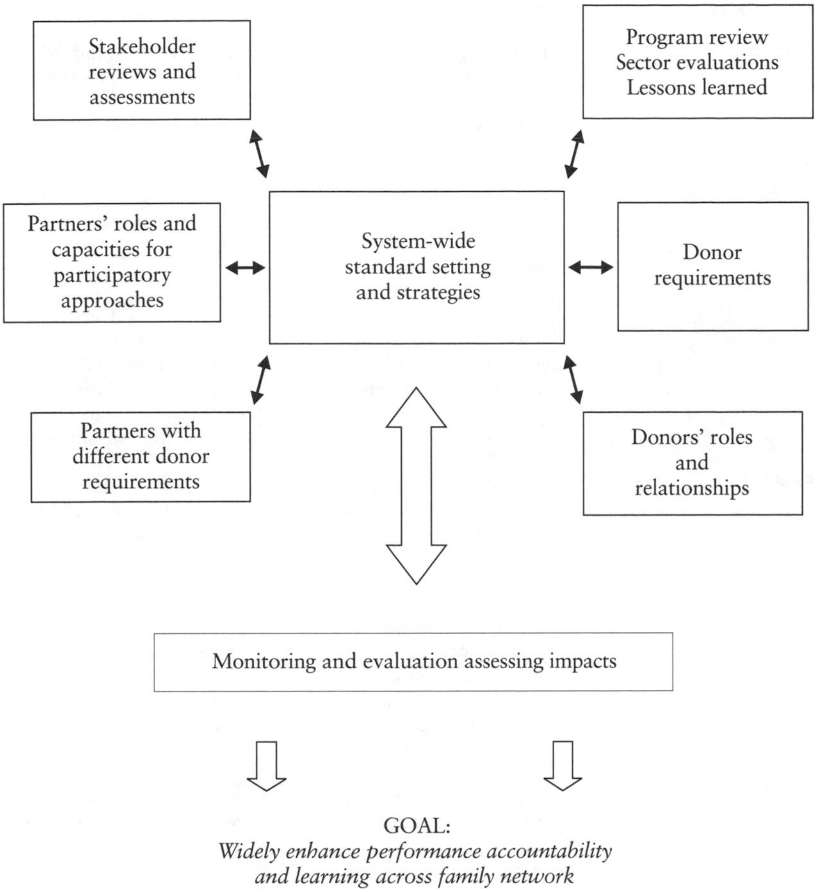

setting guidelines, establishing policy frameworks, assisting with some training for regional offices, and supporting partners. While others may be tasked with aspects of this work, often there is no internal staff to do the work itself. Moreover, since most of these NGOs work with partners, they may ask a Southern partner to manage evaluation research, yet the partner may have even fewer trained staff to do so than the Northern partner. The large bulk of evaluation work that is done for NGOs is done by consultants contracted to undertake various assessments, studies, and impact evaluations. The costs—real and opportunity costs—for undertaking evaluations make them unwelcome demands on the organizational budget. Table 8.1 on the following page provides in the matrix an overview of the current state of these NGOs' evaluation systems.

Table 8.1. NGO Evaluation Systems

Organization	Past Practice	Current Practice
CARE	Largely qualitative and descriptive evaluations done in field for individual projects.	Last five years standard setting for best practice as well as performance developed—now is system-wide.
Médecins Sans Frontières	Largely qualitative and descriptive except for quantitative health and medical information.	Done on an as-needed basis to drive internal program needs.
Oxfam (UK)	Combinations of approaches using participatory data collection. Careful attention to impact assessments.	Learning around impact assessments. Linked to Strategic Change Objectives at global level. Individual projects continue to respond to donor evaluation needs.
PLAN International	System-wide standards reflected in benchmark indicators.	Strong system-wide standards with agreed-upon benchmarks for PLAN priorities.
Save the Children (UK)	Variety of approaches. Ad-hoc, often driven by donor requirements. Reliance on initiative of project managers.	Serious attention to new indicators for each program area. Systematic, global approach linked to strategic planning.
Save the Children (US)	Donor-required evaluations routinely performed.	Donor-required evaluations done in field with different kinds of teams.
World Vision	Some evaluations done on an as-needed basis.	Increased interest in stronger, more systematic evaluations.

When NGOs work on government contracts, evaluation is generally pre-specified in the contract negotiations—often for a mid-course as well as a final evaluation. Consultants are contracted—either by the NGO, or by the donor to meet the contract compliance needs. Most often in contract work, the donor agency's field mission will supervise the evaluation work and be the recipient of the final report (along with the partner field organization, or the field office of the NGO). The evaluation staff in the Northern NGO's central office often do not see these

Table 8.1 (continued). NGO Evaluation Systems

Drivers for Change	Evaluation Unit	Learning Process
Largely internal; donor requirements had been met in previous system.	Yes. Director of monitoring and evaluation position created 1995.	Working towards having a learning system but not in place as an organizational process and system yet.
Largely internal; some external (e.g. UNHCR or ECHO requirements).	No. Staff across family network do evaluation based on knowledge and past experience.	Learning for those who most need the operationally relevant findings.
Internal and external (partners, stakeholders and donors).	Yes. Under Policy Department. Serves advisory and support role to regions where evaluations are done.	Evaluation results and indicators worked into strategic planning process.
Largely internal—strong corporate culture of accountability.	Yes. Evaluation unit with emphasis on system wide indicators. Also strong Auditing unit.	No. Process underway to get all members in PLAN into corporate-wide standards and measuring performance first.
Internal drive to improve on previous ad hoc system to facilitate organizational learning.	Yes. Under Policy and Research Department. Responsible for designing core indicators and supporting project managers in evaluation.	Indicators and change objectives are integral part of programming around core areas. Goal is to use evaluation for learning.
External-donor requirements.	No. A Director of Evaluation sets policy guidance on evaluation.	No. While interested in moving in this direction currently workloads preclude much time available for reflection.
Want donor pressure for more systematic data collection.	No. Evaluations done as driven by regional needs.	No. Other internal organizational restructuring kept this from being possible.

evaluations, precisely because they go to those most directly involved with having implemented the project at hand.

The constant search for improved ways of doing business, gathering and reflecting upon lessons learned, and measuring impact and consequences requires having people tasked to do that work. That in turn costs money and comes out of overhead. The challenge for NGOs, who often have to argue that as large a percentage of the funds contributed to them reach the grassroots as possible, have real difficulty financing evaluation. Those who want greatest accountability—meaning narrowly that results are quantified and measurable—are not necessarily those private contributors writing their Christmas checks. Pointing to a stronger evaluation system is, however, not a widely favored way to increase an NGO's popular appeal. It increases the overhead, and annual appeals have to point to low, not rising, overheads.

Interestingly, in spite of all these hurdles, there is a great deal of work underway within most of these NGOs on strengthening their evaluation systems. Let us turn to some of the examples of the changes under way.

Program and Project Evaluation

While much is written about the shortcomings and the critical reviews of NGO projects, there is equally compelling evidence of many successes. Roger Riddell and Mark Robinson report on, among other things, a major review by the Overseas Development Institute in London of sixteen poverty-alleviating projects in Bangladesh, India, Uganda, and Zimbabwe, several of which were projects supported by Oxfam, Save the Children, and CARE. The aim of the study was "to formulate an approach for assessing not all projects and programs but, more narrowly, those whose purpose was to alleviate poverty and/or improve the living conditions of the beneficiaries, principally people living in rural areas."[20] Almost all of the projects and programs reviewed were found to have improved living conditions, or to have raised the incomes of those living in poverty. Riddell and Robinson report on these projects in detail, including their immediate context, country context, and what was learned.

The study is especially noteworthy because it appears to be far less known in the United States than in Great Britain, while in the United States there has been more criticism of NGOs without in-depth empirical research on project and program impacts. But it is also true that evaluation techniques and interest in them spread more rapidly in the United States than in Europe. As Roger Riddell and Mark Robinson pointed out in 1995,

> For most European NGOs working in the development field, evaluation is still very new and if used at all tends to be more of a one-off affair, most often embarked upon either because things have gone very wrong—the fire brigade approach—or when a particular project is completed but there is a request for future funding, or when a second or third phase of a particular project is to be launched. Indeed, the vast majority of projects and programs funded by British NGOs in developing countries are not subject to any sort of formal evaluation nor bound to specified cycles of

expenditure for committed support, as is common with official aid projects.[21]

Yet even as they wrote this in 1995, Oxfam GB, the largest NGO in Britain, had a separate unit for research and evaluation, though Riddell and Robinson added "but even here, no common framework, guidelines, or procedures have yet been adopted. The same is broadly true of current practice among even the largest NGOs in the Netherlands and Germany and among other Northern European NGOs, such as those in Finland and Sweden."[22]

While the absence of common guidelines might have been true in 1995, it was no longer true in 2000—either for Oxfam GB, or for Save the Children UK. Both of these NGOs, and others, have been rapidly building evaluation capacity and systems appropriate to their needs in the past several years.

Save the Children UK improved what it was getting from field-level evaluation by producing its own guide on how monitoring and evaluation might be done—a guide that was publicly available and entitled *Toolkits—A Practical Guide to Assessment, Monitoring, Review, and Evaluation*. Their point in this publication was to lay out to field staff and partners the tools for improving how they went about doing monitoring and evaluation.

Subsequently, in 1996–97, Save the Children UK collected 245 reports of SAVE reviews and evaluations, and, using a sample drawn from that database, summarized the recommendations looking at how institutional and conceptual approaches could be improved. Among the conclusions was that evaluations too often emphasized the achievement of outputs—numbers of children immunized, or wells put in place—but did not address the larger concern: how lives were improved and whether children were healthier. The report pointed out that: "Evaluation should be seen as part of a wider framework of lesson learning aimed at selecting, targeting, and implementing aid activities that will be most effective. This issue of going beyond counting outputs to address impacts, on how lives are improved is not a narrow issue but one that goes to the heart of institutional change."[23] The author goes on to say, "Save the Children is already part of this process, developing methodologies for impact monitoring in the field. However this work is currently disparate and great attention needs to be given to integrating evaluation, and its component parts (assessment, planning, monitoring, review, formal evaluation) into program management, providing a strategy for continuous checking, learning, and adjusting within a wider institutional culture of reflective self-criticism."

CARE USA has also made great strides in strengthening its monitoring and evaluation system since 1995. They too are fully seized of the problem of assessing impacts—not just fulfillment of project activities. In their case, as there had also been a change internally to a different programming model—the Household Livelihood Security (HLS) system—they could then devise a monitoring and evaluation process keyed to HLS. By the end of 1999, they had developed CARE Impact Guidelines, with a menu of impact indicators for use in light of their goal of strengthening Household Livelihood Security. They are in the midst now of securing across all the CARE national members greater commitment to monitoring and evaluation work in light of these new standards.

Oxfam GB's Chris Roche has recently produced a new book, *Impact Assessment for Development Agencies,* that details with clarity how impact assessment might be done.[24] Oxfam has also published a guide, *Monitoring and Assessing Impacts,* that reflects Oxfam's internal change process around these same themes. Oxfam GB has housed its evaluation work in different units over time, but it consistently has made evaluation a core function. Currently it is putting into place a new department on policy planning and evaluation. The earlier, three-volume handbook, *Oxfam Handbook on Development and Relief,* includes several sections on evaluation. Noteworthy throughout these handbooks is their emphasis on participatory evaluation—ways in which those directly reached by a program are engaged in evaluating the program's effectiveness.

Participatory Evaluation

Where a Northern NGO has been working through and with a Southern NGO partner, or is working directly through their own local field office, it is likely that participants in a project can be identified to engage in a participatory evaluation process. This depends on the local partnering NGO's perspectives on evaluation, its evaluation capacity, and its willingness to comply readily with an externally hired evaluation consultant. The kinds of data that can emerge from careful participatory evaluations are particularly valuable. If the line of inquiry to be used is planned ahead of time, the kind of data gathered can help both the partner and the funding Northern NGO to learn in ways that may improve future effectiveness. Learning about what happened, how, why, and with what results provides information and insight that can help inform the next generation of projects or programs.

Participatory evaluation is logical and appropriate. The people who experience the impact of relief programs, or of development projects and programs, by definition have firsthand experience with the impact of those projects, and they should have much to say about effectiveness or impact. And, in general, development professionals undertaking evaluation research endeavor to reach and listen to those directly reached at the grassroots. There is a large and growing literature on how and why evaluation research must include this kind of qualitative empirical work.[25] But there are severe constraints on ensuring that such work is carried out. It is costly, labor-intensive, and requires skill; it takes time—in several different locations. If it is not well done, the findings are not useful.

The larger the project, the more costly it is to sample and reach those directly affected. Project participants are difficult to track down, and baseline data is often missing: refugees often relocate. It is also true that participants directly impacted will not necessarily be able to provide data on aspects of their situation that are needed in order to put into context the data they do have. For example, they know their income level, but know little about the average income level when the project began and even less about the average for the region. The real strength of qualitative data comes in the insights into *why* something did or did not work. Its weakness comes in its not providing generalizable data. Respondents also may not identify long-term consequences (even for themselves) that the program has had. For example, in evaluating a food distribution program in a refugee camp, the refugees themselves will not have access to data on nutritional levels, food availability in different locations to appraise the areas of greatest need, or whether and when the percentage of those being fed are in reality terrorists who are "foraging" until the next battle call is sounded.

Evaluation of Emergency Relief Work

It is no surprise that we are most short of evaluation data on emergency relief work. The UNHCR, one of the main international agencies funding NGO work in relief, most generally requests a final financial audit but not an evaluation—in part because of the inherent difficulty of tracking those who benefited from emergency services. The spate of books criticizing NGOs for their roles in Rwanda grew out of non-sampled interviews, anecdotes, and observation drawn not from interviews with large numbers of refugees, but from interviews and recollections from external observers, agency staff, or journalists hazarding guesses about what happened. The more severe the emergency, the less likely it is that the internally displaced people reached through a relief effort are able to help document their perceptions of NGO effectiveness. Refugees or internally displaced people voice their issues, the media picks up anecdotes and rumor, and these are beamed rapidly to audiences in distant countries. Systematic evaluation from which cumulative learning can take place is not readily available and is expensive—and, by the time it is available, it is much less newsworthy.

The importance of strengthening evaluation systems has gained in salience as a result of the increasing pressure for demonstrated effectiveness. Evaluation in development projects and programming has become increasingly skillful in the past decade, but widespread adoption of the cutting-edge techniques is still hindered by logistical and financial barriers as well as barriers stemming from the organizational culture and norms within the nonprofit community. There are significant overhead costs and organizational and staffing implications since evaluation research has grown in sophistication and technique in the past decade. Adoption of evaluation systems has also been affected by the fact that many of the techniques for measuring program effectiveness tend to contradict the inherent organizational culture within most NGOs.

Indicators and Benchmarking

Data is central to an evaluation system that allows for comparisons across similar kinds of programs or projects. NGOs, and other organizations, have found that the use of indicators, when these are carefully constructed, can be helpful. But getting those indicators, creating a culture of evaluation and learning, and then bringing staff fully on board across a system of national affiliates is an ongoing process—and not a short-term goal that, once achieved, stays in place. Nonetheless, PLAN International has been working on doing just that, and appears to be one of the leaders among Northern NGOs for its work on evaluation. It is now beginning to implement an evaluation system for their core areas of work: livelihood, habitat, and health. PLAN International went outside to get professional help to come up with indicators for each of the components of these core areas. Wherever it works, it gets baseline data. Of course its operations are long-term and integrated, and it largely operates through programs. Because PLAN works in communities for fifteen to twenty years, it can monitor those programs as well.

Performance indicators can be developed to distinguish between measuring inputs, outputs, results, and impacts. Indicator data collected over time provides information critical to learning where attention needs to go to further improvement. PLAN International's work in this area has attracted attention from other peer organizations; for example, NOVIB (the Dutch Oxfam affiliate) turned to PLAN in order to strengthen its own system. What is especially noteworthy about PLAN's approach is that it is a system-wide approach being used by all of PLAN's operational offices. PLAN's operational work is undertaken by Southern PLAN offices, with much more central coordination and quality control by PLAN International in support of those country offices. PLAN is, after all, more fully multinational than other Northern NGOs. It is globally structured and staffed with strong coordination across national boundaries. The PLAN UK office and PLAN US office exist for the purposes of fundraising only; when people within those offices refer to "operations," they mean not field-level operations themselves, but quality control, standard setting, and policymaking vis-à-vis field-level operations. Actual field-level operations in livelihood, habitat, and health are wholly undertaken by Southern PLAN International offices and generally wholly by locally hired staff.

Save the Children UK is also in the process of developing a more systematic approach to monitoring and evaluation that will be consistent across its projects. This process builds upon their 1999 Strategic review, which prioritized Save's work into six core areas (health, education, social policy, food and nutrition, child labor, HIV/AIDS) and four cross-cutting themes (gender, emergencies, disabilities, advocacy). Preliminary indicators (mainly process-oriented) have been identified but much work remains to be done in obtaining baseline data, developing more impact indicators, and in integrating the new approach within country offices.

At CARE, the experience of introducing benchmarking and portfolio analysis approaches found resistance stemming from the strongly individualistic and independent style of staff and the service culture, which sometimes places a higher value on helping people than on doing things efficiently. Relief situations again accentuate the problem, since the urgent need for action takes precedence over detailed analysis and data collection. Furthermore, the very nature of the work that is being measured is much more ambiguous in relief and development organizations than in the for-profit world. The long-term contribution of any one development or relief effort to the long-term goal of improving people's livelihood is difficult to measure.

John Greensmith, international executive director of PLAN International, adds that the independence of staff impacts on an evaluation system. When he arrived at PLAN, he found the commitment of staff to their work far stronger than in the private sector. He noted, however, that the other side of that great commitment relates to the biggest challenge as well:

> These people are very independent—they have to be to do what they are doing—taking more risks, and not your everyday conforming to expectations—and yet that independence means resistance to doing things with consistency across the organization, or being concerned with efficiency. Everyone wants to do their work their own way—and they find it very very hard to work on teams. We are still working on getting the incentives right—and unlike commercial life—pay incentives are not the answer—in fact sometimes people are insulted when that is offered. They demand inclusion, but then including them is not enough either, for that independence factor means that even after the decision is made, they will go off and do what they want to do anyway. The demand for transparency, efficiency, and accountability in our sector is steadily growing, but getting it to happen is challenging.[26]

An in-depth study of CARE echoes Greensmith's observation on staff commitment and independence, and adds that "in spite of natural barriers, CARE staff were initially receptive to a program impact initiative because there was virtually no CARE-wide data on numbers of projects, beneficiary numbers, costs per participant, and there were few project baselines to compare project performance. CARE staff had a strong personal interest as highly driven professionals in knowing whether their projects were having an impact."[27]

The strategic management process in short led to several things—attention to their mission, incentives, and attention to benchmarking and looking at impacts. It led initially to training—regional impact evaluation training. In addition the headquarters technical division was asked to create project data baselines by sector (water, agriculture, health, family planning, microenterprise development). The data were even to be collected on a form called the project implementation report. CARE headquarters asked all country offices to approve no new projects without baselines. In an effort to provide different approaches to best practice, three technical approaches were suggested—all of them shared the objective of comparing projects to some performance standard. Staff who believed they had unique projects could do self-comparison, in which staff set performance standards and then monitored for them. For others using a portfolio approach, it was possible to use indicators against national standards.

But CARE's extensive work on benchmarking methodologies had mixed results.

> While top-down external rankings, which included good global best practice, were technically strong, they frequently backfired when angry project managers felt they were being ambushed. NGO participative culture made it hard to use external information in a non-threatening way. In a regional management conference in Asia, project staff rejected the top down approach . . . even when participative methods are used, it continues to be a challenge to get field staff to accept data from global empirical studies and broader evaluations. . . . What is more effective is an overall strategy which includes training in program design and evaluation, standards about project design baseline data, benchmarking, and participative evaluation.[28]

CARE staff went on to develop its learning around the development of the household analysis tool as an example of reconfiguring internal programming approaches in order to improve effectiveness. The household analysis tool also helped reposition CARE's comparative advantage.

World Vision has recognized the need to place greater emphasis on program quality and impact and has begun this process by sharpening the organization's core focus and priorities, developing clearer impact goals and indicators, and establishing new mechanisms for mutual accountability between national offices in its partners.

Oxfam GB has also undergone a process of internal review that has resulted in the definition of specific challenges and steps related to a range of issues. To address accountability issues, it will establish a quality assurance system involving the establishment of quality standards and a system of auditing, and it will develop a new approach to the ways in which it listens to and assimilates the views of its diverse stakeholders.

Given the difficulty of putting in place a system across all national members of an NGO family integrated evaluation process, there will always be questions whether this is the best investment in light of the relief and development NGOs' scarce resources and high opportunity costs. While the answer is contingent upon the context and situation of any particular NGO, there is a case for considering how staff are to learn over time, and how organizational learning is to be fostered. An old aphorism teaches us that "While the unexamined life is not worth leading, the overexamined life is not worth writing home about either." That is true of evaluation. While an evaluation system that feeds into and encourages organizational learning is eminently worthwhile, over-investing in it given the opportunity costs in a world where more work on poverty reduction and refugee relief cries for attention is not wise.

That said, most of the NGOs we have looked at have a way to go to improve the quality of their evaluation work. They need to do so in order to understand their own effectiveness. Linking that learning into organizational learning more generally would be meaningful for staff—and helpful in maintaining morale and averting "burnout" as well as increasing productivity. While almost all authors commenting on evaluation start from the assumption that with increased official assistance, organizations will perforce move toward strengthening evaluation, we found in our interviews that two organizations with strong evaluation systems, Oxfam and PLAN International, are not accepting significant amounts of official donor assistance. Oxfam America accepts no official development assistance. These agencies therefore moved in this direction in response to internal, rather than external, demands or needs. Further empirical research on the relationships between percentages of budget derived from official development assistance, concern with program impact, and organizational learning would be useful. The implications of organizational learning for staff productivity and morale are significant, and evaluation has a large role to play in a great learning system.

In short, there is a larger case to be made for creating more of an evaluation culture coupled with, and integral to, increased staff learning about effectiveness. An organizational learning process moves toward re-establishing meaning for staff. Learning—especially when self-directed—is intrinsically invigorating. It is worth considering how this process works.

Organizational Learning

Organizational learning is one of the intriguing concepts currently receiving significant attention as well as scholarship. Peter Senge, director of the Center for Organizational Learning at MIT's Sloan School of Management, works with a large group of professionals on what has become the leading concept in much of the organizational theory and practice field.[29] The core concepts are focused on reinventing relationships, being loyal to the truth, developing strategies for personal mastery, building a shared vision, strategies for team learning and systems thinking, designing governing ideas, and treating organizations as communities. In brief, several schools of thought are at work—mixing and drawing upon the classical work of, for example, Chris Argyris, Russell Ackoff, and Jay Forrester, and incorporating material from, for example, strategic planning, quality management, and the emphasis on excellence. Thus in many ways this current model (and its practice) has long, strong roots and is not dismissable as another management "fad." It is particularly appealing in the context of the development and relief NGOs, since it puts people at the center—thereby building upon the international development management tradition of people-centered development as fostered by David Korten, Louise White, and Robert Chambers.[30]

The core elements of the organizational learning process are rooted in the field of organizational development. By engaging staff working in groups through queries that evoke reflection and analysis on their work, the participants begin to drive the agenda. Oxfam America has gone furthest with organizational learning. Their president, Ray Offenheiser, says that "organizational learning is driving the strategic management of our transformation process. We had to rethink our organizational model...the older traditional organization models are gone in light of global changes. Now our core currency is information and organizational learning is our over-arching principle."[31] Oxfam America began by working in groups to develop a strategic plan, and then turned to implementing that plan. To lead off the implementation, they had a week-long workshop at the Goree Institute in Senegal bringing together partners, regional representatives, regional managers, and senior managers (including Ray Offenheiser) to discuss implementation of the theme, "Participation for Equity." It was one of the first times that a large number of managers, staff, and partners had talked with one another systematically about their work. Those who participated conveyed their excitement and commitment to building upon and deepening the process. The Goree week produced a series of guidelines that were then used to guide the management of their strategic planning process. These are still being used: speak with authority and substance on key development issues; invest in knowledge for action; link the local with the global; program outcomes lead to social change; and serve partners and work toward their empowerment.

The core elements in this process are that it focuses on being a learning organization in practice—by breaking down the boundaries between departments, and between center and field and partners; puts people at the center of the organization; and flattens organizational structure. It also—and predominantly from the perspective of operations—creates permeability between planning and taking action. No longer is there a separation between those who plan and those who implement; these are seen to be, and they become, interchangeable.

Flattening the organizational structure, however, proved to be one of the difficult parts of the process. All the Oxfams are unionized and Oxfam America is no exception. The union (Service Employees International Union) has detailed rules about structure and these precluded giving staff supervisory responsibility. How then could they get to more movement between those who plan and those who implement—a more horizontal organization? Again, this was worked through bit and piece by managers and staff working in groups, devising ways to proceed and yet be in conformance with the union rules. As many union leaders and members experienced organizational learning as empowering, they basically worked their way through a thicket of problems. Some of the old school union leaders—more accustomed to the fist fight model of adversarial relationships—had trouble making the change; eventually they lost out in union elections.

Oxfam America drew heavily upon training in what has come to be called interspace bargaining—an approach in which small groups work through competing interests rather than posturing for positions in an argument. This training proved invaluable; staff now knew how to do interest-based negotiating. As the time was approaching for a renewal of the union's contract, this proved important. Instead of drawing upon the older adversarial approaches to union contract issues, groups of staff worked through what needed to be done and drafted side letters that reflected the agreements reached. Then during the contract negotiations, these side letter agreements were incorporated into the contract. Now Oxfam America has moved on yet again, moving away from the big bang approach to five-year planning to a more flexible and responsive planning. Organizational learning is firmly driving their planning process, and bringing transformation with it.

There is no doubt that, from the point of view of achieving results,

NGOs need an iterative process of engaging staff from top to bottom in identifying and illuminating what is and is not working. It is very easy to be caught up in processes and meeting deadlines, fundraising, disseminating information, and measuring those "inputs" without getting time to reflect and think about the impact or results of this work. Laura Roper, Oxfam America's director of program planning and learning—the office where setting guidelines and policy on evaluation takes place—told us that there is a real need "to create space and opportunity for staff to reflect." Reflection, especially when informed by data on results or consequences of actions taken to date, leads naturally to learning, or at least identifying what remains to be done. Roper has also recently contracted for assistance to get more quantitative data on program results because she knows that Oxfam's qualitative data from these various processes would be better informed with more quantitative measurement of impact and results.

Ethnology and Beyond

Throughout this book, we have ended each chapter with a step back and a look at the same more probing questions: Can the views of our interlocutors be supported by empirical data? What motivations, as well as nuances and details, may our respondents not have explicitly discussed? And what emerging issues or trends need further exploration?

Empirical Data

The leaders with whom we met are committed to accountability and in many instances also have worked to strengthen monitoring and evaluation systems. Few, however, consider these functions their highest priority. For all, achieving their organization's mission is the uppermost goal; this is what drives them to work on advocacy, on fundraising, and, above all, on programs. Yet they are fully aware that improving performance requires knowing more about that performance—and hence accountability, and its components, monitoring and evaluation systems are strong intermediate goals.

We must acknowledge that our data on accountability systems is incomplete. The variations in accountability systems among national members of all the six NGO families in our core group of interlocutors militate against our having a complete data set on accountability. What we were able to learn is that these variations are real and pervasive. Our timetable did not permit collecting everything that needed to be known within any given family—let alone account for the differences across the different networks. But what we did learn is that there have been significant and serious efforts to improve evaluation systems in the past five to eight years, and that new approaches and learning from them are readily shared across NGO family borders.

Motivations Not Discussed

The motivations most likely to be left undisclosed in regard to accountability are those that are rooted in serious differences of perspective within any given NGO family on how to manage the contingencies in accountability. These NGOs' separate country political contexts vary too much for there to be ease with a system-wide approach. For example, Oxfam GB is large enough within the political system of Great Britain that the head of Oxfam GB has ready access to the Prime Minister. Moreover, since a significant percentage of the British electorate uses a payroll deduction system to contribute to Oxfam, most parliamentarians will listen when Oxfam speaks. That is in marked contrast with the situation of Oxfam America—or of any other NGO based in the United States.

As different national members have different constituencies to whom they respond, as well as an array of domestic political and legal forces within the country where they are headquartered, their accountability systems differ more than any other function. While we could, and did, learn about such differences within NGO families, there was no opportunity to explore the myriad implications of those differences for internal management of the accountability process. There are also competitive pressures among all the NGO families. The Internet, for example, makes it far simpler for prospective donors to compare and contrast the information on Web sites when trying to decide about an annual gift. Hence the Internet has inevitably brought some competitive forces to the fore among these NGO groupings. For example, an innovation on one Web site that, for example, highlights significant results achieved puts pressure on others to demonstrate comparable success as well. Leaders were not eager to talk about tensions they are experiencing either within their own NGO families, or across the spectrum with others. Moreover, the very ethos of their missions puts a premium on social service and outreach—which carries over a values-centered premium for being, or at least appearing to be, cooperative rather than competitive like the private sector.

Further Nuances and Details

In researching the NGOs on the topics covered in this chapter—more than on any other—it was striking to see how little is actually known about monitoring and evaluation systems in NGOs. Most of the literature takes a very broad-brush treatment of the accountability factors. One of the results of that is a paucity of hard data on exactly what the evaluation systems are within these NGOs. One aspect of that is that the

NGOs' leaders also are not very likely to go into details. When probing for this information, one is sent on to others—even when it is said that accountability is a senior management goal.

Underexplored Trends and Issues

Of the several trends on the theme of this chapter that warrant further exploration, the one that commands the most attention is the growing interest in understanding the longer-term impact, not just the outcomes and outputs, of projects and programs. In our interviews, staff expressed a keen interest in that, and in having more time for reflection on lessons learned. At the center of this issue is a conundrum: both outsiders and staff would like to know more about when and why NGOs are effective (as many staff believe they are). Replicating that success becomes more possible with such knowledge. Development projects come with hidden surprises and unexpected outcomes, and sometimes beneficiaries most value outcomes that were not planned but just happened. Still, more learning is both possible and wanted. Given the scale of the human needs with which these NGOs are struggling, this search for explanations of effectiveness needs further exploration.

It is also worth examining why the pressure for such learning sometimes comes more from the field or the staff than from headquarters. It may be that those most immediately engaged in the work are most keen to discover, and document, when they have had an impact. Senior managers, however, whose workloads pull them in different directions, are inevitably focused on the big picture.

Notes

1. Roger Riddell and Mark Robinson, *Non-Governmental Organizations and Rural Poverty Alleviation* (London: Clarendon Press, 1995).

2. Michael Edwards and David Hulme, *Beyond the Magic Bullet: NGO Performance and Accountability in the Post–Cold War World* (West Hartford, Conn.: Kumarian Press, 1996).

3. Jonathan Fox and L. David Brown, *The Struggle for Accountability* (Cambridge, Mass.: MIT Press, 1998).

4. Ian Smillie and Henny Helmich in collaboration with Tony German and Judith Randell, *Stakeholders; Government-NGO Partnerships for Development* (OECD and Earthscan Publications, 1999), 9. With worries about these relationships, Edwards and Hulme followed up their first book with one entitled, *NGOs, State and Donors Too Close for Comfort?* (London: St. Martin's Press, 1997).

5. Smillie and Helmich, *Stakeholders*, 16.

6. Norman Uphoff has cogently argued that NGOs should not be considered a "Third Sector" because they are neither people's associations nor membership groups. He goes on to discuss the implications of this for accountability. See

Norman Uphoff, "Why NGOs Are Not a Third Sector," in Edwards and Hulme, *Beyond the Magic Bullet* (West Hartford, Conn.: Kumarian Press), 23–39.

7. Uphoff, "Why NGOs Are Not a Third Sector," in Edwards and Hulme, *Beyond the Magic Bullet.*

8. One of the first major official development sources on these issues was the World Bank's policy paper on governance, *Governance and Development* (Washington, D.C.: World Bank, 1992). This paper argued for three concepts as central to good governance: accountability, transparency, and predictability (rule of law). These were interrelated, but separable, as it is possible for an organization or government to perform one without the other. For example, they could share information, provide data, and release documents without there being a process by which that organization's leaders are held to account for their decisions.

9. These participants held this discussion in the Global Leaders' Meeting in Seattle, Wash., Session 1, May 7, 2000, meeting session notes.

10. Robert Chambers, *Whose Reality Counts?* (Brighton, England: University of Sussex, 1997).

11. Amartya K. Sen, *Development as Freedom* (New York: Alfred Knopf, 2000).

12. Edwards and Hulme, *Beyond the Magic Bullet,* 11.

13. Brian Smith, *More Than Altruism* (Princeton, N.J.: Princeton University Press, 1990).

14. John Gaventa, "Poverty, Participation and Social Exclusion in North and South," in *Poverty and Social Exclusion in North and South,* ed. Arjan de Haan and Simon Maxwell (*IDS Bulletin* 29, no. 1, January 1998), 50–57.

15. Alan Fowler, "Assessing NGO Performance, Difficulties, Dilemmas, and a Way Ahead," in Michael Edwards and David Hulme, *Beyond the Magic Bullet,* 169–86.

16. Peter Uvin, *Aiding Violence: The Development Enterprise in Rwanda* (West Hartford, Conn.: Kumarian Press, 1998). It is worth noting, however, that the large four-volume study by John Eriksson with contributions from Howard Adelman, John Borton, Hanne Christensen, Krishna Kumar, Astri Suhrke, David Tardif-Douglin, Stein Villumstad, and Lennart Wohlgemuth was one the first places to discuss the problem of structural violence. See Chapter 2, *Early Warning and Conflict Management,* in *The International Response to Conflict and Genocide: Lessons from the Rwanda Experience,* ed. John Eriksson (New York: Steering Committee of the Joint Evaluation on Emergency Assistance to Rwanda, 1996), vol. 1, 17–24.

17. At a meeting at the Brookings Institution, October 29, 1999, with L. David Brown, Julie Fisher, Peter Hall, Virginia Hogkinson, Ray Horten, Steve Smith, Christina Kappaz, and Crispin Gregoire, we discussed, among other issues, the accountability dilemmas, and this model was suggested. It should also be noted that Alan Fowler uses the same term in his outstanding article, "Assessing NGO Performance, Difficulties, Dilemmas, and a Way Ahead," in *Beyond the Magic Bullet,* 169–86.

18. Mark Moore, "Managing for Value: Organizational Strategy in For-

Profit, Nonprofit, and Governmental Organizations," in *Nonprofit and Voluntary Sector Quarterly* 29, no. 1 (Supplement 2000): 194.

19. The World Bank, for example, has the evaluation function housed in the Operations Evaluation Department (OED) for this reason. OED reports directly to the Board of the Bank and as such has complete independence from control by the senior managers within Bank operational departments. Task managers of projects, however, may also build project evaluation into their project budget and then design the manner in which that is to happen. That would not, however, preempt any independent evaluation by OED. The United States Agency for International Development (USAID), on the other hand, generally houses monitoring and evaluation within a center or separate department, sometimes adding the task of learning as part of that function. USAID generally builds linkages between operational work and the monitoring and evaluation work. There are a wide variety of ways that this function can be organized, each with advantages and disadvantages.

20. Riddell and Robinson, *Non-Governmental Organizations and Rural Poverty Alleviation*, 45.

21. Riddell and Robinson, *Non-Governmental Organizations and Rural Poverty Alleviation*, 44.

22. Riddell and Robinson, *Non-Governmental Organizations and Rural Poverty Alleviation*, 45

23. David Mansfield, "Evaluation: Tried and Tested? A Review of Save the Children Evaluation Reports," Working Paper No. 17 (London: Save the Children UK, 1997), 9.

24. Chris Roche, *Impact Assessment for Development Agencies* (Oxford: Oxfam and NOVIB Publications, 1999).

25. Participatory evaluation was first promoted in Asia and Africa where it was also often linked with giving people a voice in influencing future policy choices. There was also a Society for Participatory Research in Asia that worked in conjunction with the African Adult Education Association. See Yusuf Kassam and Kemal Mustafa, *Participatory Research: An Emerging Alternative Methodology in Social Science Research* (Nairobi: African Adult Education Society Publication, 1982). That approach spread rapidly to Northern industrial countries, and is reflected in much current material on evaluation. See, for example, Edward T. Jackson and Yusuf Kassam, *Knowledge Shared: Participatory Evaluation in Development Cooperation* (West Hartford, Conn.: Kumarian Press, 1998).

26. John Greensmith, international executive director of PLAN International, telephone interview by Coralie Bryant, June 24, 1999.

27. Marc Lindenberg, "Are We at the Cutting Edge, the Blunt Edge, or the Wrong Edge?" *Nonprofit Leadership and Management* 11, no. 3 (March 2001). See also Christine Letts, William P. Ryan, and Allen Grossman, *High Performance Nonprofit Organizations* (New York: Wiley, 1999), see chapters 1 and 5.

28. Lindenberg, "Are We at the Cutting Edge?" 16.

29. Peter M. Senge, *The Fifth Discipline: The Art and Practice of the Learning Organization* (New York: Doubleday, 1990). This was followed up by Peter

Senge et al., *The Fifth Discipline Fieldbook: Strategies and Tools for Building a Learning Organization* (New York: Doubleday, 1994).

30. See for example David Korten, "Community Organization and Rural Development: A Learning Process Approach," *Public Administration Review,* September/October 1980: 480–511. *People Centered Development,* ed. David Korten and Rudi Klauss (West Hartford, Conn.: Kumarian Press, 1984); and Coralie Bryant and Louise G. White, *Managing Development in the Third World* (Boulder, Colo.: Lynne Rienner Publishers, 1982), and Louise G. White, *Creating Opportunities for Change* (Boulder, Colo.: Lynne Rienner Publishers, 1987).

31. Raymond Offenheiser, president, Oxfam America, telephone interview by Coralie Bryant, January 25, 2001.

– 9 –

Conclusions

W E OPENED THIS BOOK with a broad overview of the current roles of six organizational families from the nonprofit international relief and development sector, and their need to stay relevant in the context of globalization. That led in turn to looking at an array of their functions (transformation, structural change, partnership and accountability) as well as the content of their initiatives for poverty reduction, humanitarian action during internal wars, and policy advocacy. Throughout we tried to stay close to what we were hearing or observing from our interlocutors in interviews and meetings. Here we turn to speak more directly about our own conclusions on the key themes in this book.

Our conclusions are based on more than four years of active dialogue and action research with key members of the leadership teams and staff of these organizational families. We benefited from the use of questionnaire data, outside source materials, and interviews with stakeholders and critics. During the process we developed a healthy respect for the seriousness with which our colleagues have embarked on their transformation efforts. We also came away with a renewed sense of the commitment that motivates their staff and supporters and of the dangerous world in which they work. It is equally clear to us that these are fully human organizations with all of the strengths as well as limitations of the people who choose to participate in them. Thus, while identifying the strengths of the transformation efforts we observed, it is equally important to highlight problems and challenges and clarify where, in our opinion, their transformations are only just beginning.

We conclude that the senior teams of these organizations have a solid sense of the new dilemmas of globalization, the inequities created, and challenges for their own organizations and the world community. We believe that they have made a realistic appraisal of the inadequacy of current global institutions to respond effectively to these challenges. We recognize their effort to confront new problems of global poverty and conflict as a serious and responsible one.

Rather than falling into bankruptcy or irrelevance as some have predicted these organizations would, we see instead dynamic new efforts: to improve global humanitarian action, confront poverty in its new dimensions, help mobilize worldwide social action and advocate for the redesign of international institutions. While some may argue that the pace of change is glacial in these large and complicated organizational families, we were surprised that they were changing at all and even more surprised by the quick pace of change during the last decade.

These six families have achieved the greatest progress in their transformational journeys in the following areas. They have made a realistic diagnosis of the new problems of globalization and their impacts on poverty and conflict. They have effectively redefined their missions and have stretched them beyond outdated conceptions of charity. Some are stretching their aspirations beyond service delivery and into rights-based advocacy. Others are intent on learning how to become members of global networks. Most are taking off the blinders that came with old and more rigid conceptions of North-South relations. Instead they have started to think about the interrelated forms of poverty and misery which are multi-directional. This is leading to hard thinking about how to be a responsible participant in an emerging global civil society. A network of organizations from the industrial societies, the former Soviet Union and Eastern Europe, as well as Africa, Asia, and Latin America, will ultimately form such a society.

Some of the greatest innovation within these six families is taking place in the development programming that focuses on livelihood security for families and communities and on breaking the barriers of poverty due to social exclusion. Staff and senior managers are more aware than ever of the operational, ethical, and structural dilemmas of responding to war and natural disasters. Their coordination has improved. Their new efforts to work in post-conflict situations and to adapt "do no harm" programming is exciting. They are pressuring global institutions to deal with the issues of internally displaced people, and the inadequacies of global operational response. They are experimenting with their own roles in global advocacy and have participated in successful efforts like the campaign to ban landmines and the Jubilee 2000 debt forgiveness initiatives. They have begun to reshape their systems to incorporate new technology. While still the exception rather than the rule, some have embarked on experiments in partnership with the private sector and government. Others are testing the utility of both partnering with the private sector as well as advocating change in corporate behavior. This is evident in their involvement in discussions of fair trade coffee or in discussions of the relation between the diamond trade and conflict in Africa. Finally, they are redesigning their global family structures and relationships to stimulate greater cooperation, quality, and more effective resource utilization.

That being said, there are areas where transformation is going more slowly and where there is less insight and action than one might hope.

For example, there has been little real advance in the creation of genuine international governance boards with broad representation of stakeholders beyond the Northern industrial countries. This is evident when one compares who the global board members were a decade ago with who they are today. Although less true than a decade ago, family networks are still dominated by their largest members. Total resources are still not used as effectively as they could be within the family, particularly given the growing absolute numbers of the world's poverty population and the continued outbreaks of violence and conflict. These families continue to be plagued by repetitive cost structures, as well as competition and distrust within their own houses.

They have not made a great deal of progress in documenting impact and developing a deeper understanding of which programs best help to reduce poverty and conflict compared to others. While there has been recognition of the need for greater multi-directional accountability, this has not been accompanied by clear identification of practical steps to create greater transparency and accountability. Although they have been successful in streamlining many support systems and in incorporating new technology, ad hoc, customized financial, marketing, and general information systems are still in evidence. It has been extremely difficult to improve human resource, fundraising, and financial systems to keep pace with organizational growth. While much has been done to reduce the size of headquarters operations, cut fundraising costs, and decentralize decision-making, the full implications of new technology and the potential of virtual networks is only beginning to be explored. Even though many of the families we studied are incorporating organizational learning principles, the depth of diffusion of these ideas throughout these organizations is not as profound as it might be.

Furthermore, most of the transformation is taking place inside the six families rather than among these families and outside partners and global networks. Nor is there as much experimentation with creative public, private, and not-for-profit partnerships as we might have expected. This is understandable if one is sympathetic to the view that it is hard to find the time for outside experimentation when the daily operational challenges of large complex organizations must be managed. That said, it is undeniable that the senior teams of the six families have less understanding of the potential for alliances within the rich evolving network of new globalizing NGOs with roots in Eastern Europe, the former Soviet Union, Africa, Asia, or Latin America. However, the same could be said for the leaders of Southern, Eastern European, and other emerging global organizations. Perhaps none of the globalizing organizations from any part of the world have a fresh vision of how more genuine, multi-directional global networks for poverty alleviation and conflict reduction might be most realistically developed. All groups in emerging global civil society could benefit from listening to each other much more carefully.

Finally, rhetoric to the contrary, creative private, public, and NGO partnerships are still the exception rather than the rule. Relations between these families, corporations, and governments are still often grounded in suspicion. The discussions of effective partnerships and capacity building are sometimes murky. While some organizations have moved beyond the realm of naiveté and "political correctness" to develop a better understanding of the strengths and weaknesses of past attempts at partnership, others have not. Finally, only a few of the Northern families have begun dialogue about the future of global networks with colleagues from around the world. In addition, many have not come fully to grips with the new or changed roles they may play in such networks. New roles may lead them on a road away from service delivery and toward advocacy coordination, information generation and sharing, resource mobilization, and global system change.

So much has been done and much remains to do. But one thing is clear. In an age of increasing global cynicism and growing distrust in government and institutions, the international NGOs working on relief and development issues continue to inspire the young and old alike. Faith and hope are not "bad things." No other sector has won Nobel prizes several years running. We need only think back to the prize-winning campaign to ban landmines or fearless and principled efforts to provide assistance during war and conflict that resulted in the Nobel Prize for MSF International. Few other sectors have captured the spirit of collaboration that has led to creative alliances between the faith-based and secular communities and the passage of legislation for debt reduction as a result of the Jubilee 2000 campaign. There is much to be said for the importance of a growing global community of people who choose to live their lives as if the world can be better in the midst of a general climate of cynicism.

Yes, the people who choose to participate in these six families are human. Certainly they are not all-knowing. Of course they have complex motivations which reflect their self-interest, but they also have inspiring aspirations and optimism. They often willingly risk their lives to help others. They are not perfect and neither are any of the rest of us. The world is a far better place with them than without them.

People Interviewed

Core Organizations Studied

CARE

Peter Bell, President, CARE USA
Tom Alcedo, Country Director, CARE India
Damien Desjonquieres, Program Coordinator, CARE France
Paul Giannone, Emergency Group Assistant Director, CARE USA
Kevin Henry, Senior Assistant to the President, CARE USA
Ian Moncaster, Senior Director of Development, CARE NW Office
Andy Pugh, Director of Policy and Advocacy, CARE USA
Jim Rugh, Director of Evaluation, CARE USA
Anne Simon, EU Coordinator, CARE International
Guy Tousignant, Secretary General, CARE International
Marge Tsitouris, Emergency Group Director, CARE USA

Médecins Sans Frontières (MSF)

Jean Herve-Bradol, President (2000–present), MSF France
Philippe Biberson, President (1995–2000), MSF France
James Orbinski, President, MSF International Council
Antoine Gerard, Program Director, Doctors Without Borders USA
Odile Hardy, MSF France
François Jean, Research Director, Fondation, MSF, France
Karim Laouabdia, Director, MSF, France
Bruce Mahin, Director of Finance, MSF, France
Françoise Saulnier, Research Director, Fondation, MSF, France
Joelle Tanguy, Executive Director, Doctors Without Borders USA

Oxfam

David Bryer, Director, Oxfam Great Britain (GB)
Raymond Offenheiser, President, Oxfam America
Ernst Ligteringen, Executive Director, Oxfam International
Justin Forsyth, Policy Director, Oxfam Great Britain (GB)
Mike Delaney, Director of Humanitarian Assistance, Oxfam America
Susan Holcombe, Director of Global Programs, Oxfam America

Margaret Newens, Team Leader, Strategic Planning and Evaluation, Oxfam GB

David Nussbaum, Finance Director, Oxfam GB

Chris Roche, Team Leader—Gender and Policy Learning Team, Oxfam GB

Laura Roper, Director of Program Planning and Learning, Oxfam America

John Ruthrauff, Director, Washington Office, Oxfam America

PLAN International

John Greensmith, International Executive Director

Subhadra Belbase, Director, Eastern and Southern Africa Region

Martin McCann, Director of Programs

Sam McPherson, Development Officer, Corporate Planning, Monitoring, and Evaluation

Save the Children

Burkhard Gnaerig, CEO, International Save the Children Alliance

Charles MacCormack, President, Save the Children US

Bill Bell, Advocacy Director, Save the Children UK

Carolyn Miller, Director of Programs, Save the Children UK

Bob Neil, Associate Vice President, Save the Children US

Nancy Otterstrom, Office of Contract Compliance

Donald Palladino, Executive VP, Chief Operating Officer, Save the Children US

Angela Penrose, Policy Director, Programs, Save the Children UK

Gary Shaye, Vice President for International Programs, Save the Children US

Rudolph Von Bernuth, Vice President, Save the Children US

World Vision

Richard Stearns, President, World Vision US

Kenneth Casey, Senior Vice President, Strategy, Policy and Planning, World Vision US

Serge Duss, Director of Public Policy and Government Relations, World Vision US

Michelle Garred, Executive Officer, International Programs, World Vision US

John Reid, Senior Vice President of Strategic Support, World Vision US

David A. Robinson, Interim Peacebuilding Coordinator, World Vision International

Ellen Stewart, Program Reporting Analyst, Domestic Programs, World Vision US

Other Organizations Consulted

Action Against Hunger
Jean-François Vidal, Executive Director

Action Contre la Faim
Jean-Luc Bodin, Director-General

Agency for Co-operation and Research in Development (ACORD)
Judy El-Bushra, Acting Head

American Council for Voluntary International Action (InterAction)
James Bishop, Director of Humanitarian Response

Asociación Latinoamericano de Organizaciones de Promoción (ALOP)
Manuel Chiriboga, Executive Secretary, ALOP, Costa Rica

Carter Center
Larry Frankel, Chief Development Officer
John Hardman, Executive Director

Catholic Relief Services (CRS)
Amy Hillaboe, Director, Emergency

Center for Disease Control (CDC)
Brent Buckholder, Chief, International Emergency
Barbara Cardozo, Psychiatrist
Michael Gerber, Public Health Specialist

Centre for Humanitarian Dialogue
Martin Griffiths, Director

CIVICUS
Kumi Naidoo, Secretary General and CEO, CIVICUS, Washington, D.C.

Collaborative Action for Development Action
Mary Anderson, Director

Community Organizers Multiversity
Corazon "Dinky" Juliano-Soliman, Executive Director, Philippines

Conciliation Resources

Guus Meijer, Co-Director

Conflict Resolution, Education & Training

Judith Large, Executive Director

Department for International Development, United Kingdom (DFID)

Robert Walker, Conflict Prevention Specialist

Development Research Center, OECD, Paris

Henny Helmich, Senior Research Associate

Bill and Melinda Gates Foundation

Terry Meersman, Senior Program Officer
Jack Faris, Senior Program Officer

Hauser Center for Nonprofit Organizations

L. David Brown, Associate Director for International Programs
Mark Moore, Director

Institute for Development Studies, University of Sussex, Brighton (IDS)

Rosemary McGee, Fellow

Institute for Multi-Track Diplomacy

Ambassador John McDonald, Chairman and Co-founder

International Committee of the Red Cross (ICRC)

Peter Herby, Coordinator, Mines Unit
François Musy, Chef De Secteur

International Council of Voluntary Agencies (ICVA)

Ed Schenkenberg, Executive Director

International Federation of Red Cross & Red Crescent (IFRC)

Margareta Walstrom, Under-Secretary, Disaster Response
Peter Walker, Director, Political Relations

International Medical Corps (IMC)

Nancy A. Aossey, President and CEO
Stephen Tomlin, Vice President of International Operations

International NGO Research Center (INTRAC)

Jonathan Goodhand, Associate

International Rescue Committee (IRC)

Gerry Martone, Director, Emergency Response
Reynold Levy, President
Barbara Smith, Vice President Overseas Department

London School of Economics

Helmut Anheier, Director, Center for Civil Society
David Lewis, Senior Fellow, Center for Civil Society

Media Action International

Edward Giradet, Director

Mercy Corps International

Landrum Bolling, Director at Large
Neal Keny-Guyer, President
Nancy Lindborg, Executive Vice President

Microsoft Community Affairs Group

Joanna Demirian, International Program Manager
Melissa Pailthorp, Program Manager

NGO Voice

Giovanni Rufini, VOICE Coordinator

Norwegian Refugee Council

Brita Sydhoff, Representative
Marc Vincent, Coordinator

Overseas Development Institute, London

David Booth, Coordinator, Poverty and Public Policy Group
Lucia Hamner, Research Associate
John Healey, Research Associate
Tony Killick, Senior Research Associate

Oxford Brookes University, Center for Development and Emergency Practice

Hugo Slim, Director

Poverty Studies Program, University of Sussex

Michael Lipton, Professor

Quaker Peace & Services
Bob Neidhardt, Director

Steering Committee for Humanitarian Response (SCHR)
Joel McClellan, Director

Tufts University, Feinstein International Famine Center
John Hammock, Director

United Nations (UN)
Amjad Abbashar, Humanitarian Officer, Office for the Coordination for Humanitarian Affairs (OCHA)
Martin Barber, Director of the Policy, Advocacy and Information Division, OCHA
Michael Moller, Special Assistant to the Under-Secretary-General, Department of Political Affairs

United Nations Development Program (UNDP)
Larry Deboice, Director

United Nations High Commission for Refugees (UNHCR)
Tahir Ali, Special Advisor, International Protection
Frederick Barton, United Nations Deputy High Commissioner for Refugees
Erika Feller, Director, International Protection
Larry Fioretta, Private Sector Fund-Raising Officer
John Horekens, Director, Communication/Information Geneva
Scott Schirmer, Director of Development
Arnulv Torbjornsen, Head NGO Unit

United Nations Women's Commission on Refugee Women & Children
Mary Diaz, Executive Director
Sandra Krause, Director, Reproductive Health

United States Agency for International Development (USAID)
Antoinette Ferrara, Development Grants Director
Michael Mahdesian, Former Deputy of the Bureau for Humanitarian Response

University of Bradford, Center for Conflict Resolution
Nick Lewer, Lecturer/Research Fellow

World Bank

Nimrod Raphaeli, Consultant

World Concern

Paul Kennell, President

World Food Program

Manuel Da Silva, Director, Policy
Sara Langford, Senior Policy Analyst
Pablo Recalde, Head, VAM Unit
Debby Saidy, Senior Policy Analyst

Index

About the Authors

Marc Lindenberg is Dean and Professor at the Daniel J. Evans School of Public Affairs, University of Washington, Seattle, Washington. He has been a faculty member at Harvard University's Kennedy School, where he was awarded the Manuel Carballo Award for Excellence in Teaching. He also served as the Rector and Professor at INCAE, Central American Management Institute, in Nicaragua and Costa Rica, founded in conjunction with Harvard Business School. Most recently, he served as the Senior Vice President for Programs at CARE. Widely published, among his several books are *Democratic Transitions? Central America in the 1980s* (with Jorge Dominguez) and *The Human Development Race* and *Managing Adjustment in Developing Countries* (with Noel Ramirez). He has authored dozens of journal articles, and is a frequent organizer and facilitator of high-level consultative meetings. He assists in strategic planning efforts at the Bill and Melinda Gates Foundation, the Turner UN Foundation, and other public and not-for-profit organizations.

Coralie Bryant is Director and Professor of the Economic and Political Development Program at the School of Public and International Affairs, Columbia University. Prior to Columbia University, she was a Senior Policy Analyst and Senior Institutional Specialist at the World Bank. While at the Bank, she was one of the authors of the World Bank's Policy Paper on Governance. She was one of the founders, and subsequently Co-Director, of the International Development Program at American University. The author of other books, including *Managing Development in the Third World*, and *Poverty Policy and Food Security in Southern Africa*, she has also authored many journal articles. At Columbia University, she assembles the Applied International Development Workshop in which advanced graduate teams work on development and relief projects with clients such as UNDP, the World Bank, UNICEF, Technoserve, and the International Rescue Committee.

Also from Kumarian Press...

International Development

New Roles and Relevance: Development NGOs and the Challenge of Change
Edited by David Lewis and Tina Wallace

Patronage or Partnership: Local Capacity Building in Humanitarian Crises
Edited by Ian Smillie for the Humanitarianism and War Project

Street Level Democracy: Political Settings at the Margins of Global Power
Jonathan Barker

Transcending Neoliberalism: Community-Based Development in Latin America
Edited by Henry Veltmeyer and Anthony O'Malley

Environment, Conflict Resolution, Gender Studies, Global Issues, Globalization, Microfinance

Bound: Living in the Globalized World
Scott Sernau

Exploring the Gaps: Vital Links Between Trade, Environment and Culture
James R. Lee

Inequity in the Global Village: Recycled Rhetoric and Disposable People
Jan Knippers Black

Mainstreaming Microfinance:
How Lending to the Poor Began, Grew and Came of Age in Bolivia
Elisabeth Rhyne

Promises Not Kept: The Betrayal of Social Change in the Third World
FIFTH EDITION John Isbister

Reconcilable Differences: Turning Points in Ethnopolitical Conflict
Edited by Sean Byrne and Cynthia L. Irvin

War's Offensive on Women:
The Humanitarian Challenge in Bosnia, Kosovo and Afghanistan
Julie A. Mertus for the Humanitarianism and War Project

When Corporations Rule the World
SECOND EDITION David C. Korten

Visit Kumarian Press at **www.kpbooks.com** or
call **toll-free 800.289.2664** for a complete catalog.

Kumarian Press, located in Bloomfield, Connecticut, is dedicated to publishing and distributing books and other media that will have a positive social and economic impact on the lives of peoples living in "Third World" conditions no matter where they live.